Penguin Education

D. H. Lawrence on Education

Edited by Joy and Raymond Williams

D1458214

D. H. Lawrence on Education

Edited by Joy and Raymond Williams

Penguin Education

Penguin Education
A Division of Penguin Books Ltd,
Harmondsworth, Middlesex, England
Penguin Books Inc, 7110 Ambassador Road,
Baltimore, Md 21207, USA
Penguin Books Australia Ltd,
Ringwood, Victoria, Australia

First published 1973
This selection copyright © Joy and Raymond Williams, 1973
Introduction and notes copyright © Joy and Raymond Williams, 1973

Made and printed in Great Britain by
Hazell Watson & Viney Ltd, Aylesbury, Bucks
Set in Linotype Times

Contents

Introduction

1

The main reason for reading D. H. Lawrence on education is that he was one of the first English writers to have direct experience of ordinary teaching. Certainly he was one of the very first to have worked in our modern system of organized schooling for everyone.

In this, as in so much else, Lawrence was a forerunner. Since his time, many teachers have also been writers. The systems of qualification and training have changed since his day, but Lawrence is also a forerunner in that, born in a working-class family, he got his education on scholarships and went on to teach in an ordinary school. The meaning of this experience, which since his time has been so generally important, is a theme to which he often returns.

He taught at Davidson Road School, Croydon, for just over three years. By the autumn of 1911, when he was twenty-six, he was too ill to stay in regular work. For the rest of his life, until his death before his forty-fifth birthday, he made his living as a writer, often with great difficulty. But the teaching experience remained of great importance. It is a significant theme in his major novel, *The Rainbow*, and as this collection shows he wrote about teaching and education in every phase of his adult life.

Many writers have discussed education, in general ways. Lawrence, as we shall see, contributed consciously to a long tradition of educational argument, and some of his formal positions can be studied on their own. But first, in common with many writers in this tradition, his arguments about education are inseparable from his arguments about life and society. Education, for him, is not a separate or specialized subject. It is a set of active decisions about how we shall live. There can then be no dividing line, in Lawrence, between 'personal experience' and 'general argument'. Most of his arguments, as we shall see, are about what is meant and ought to be meant by 'personal experience', and then about its implications for education and society.

His particular experience is then centrally present. Nor is it only an experience of teaching; it is an experience of being taught and trained, and of each in relation to a close and particular life. There is not one piece in this book or anywhere which can be taken, definitively, as 'Lawrence on Education'. There is, rather, a long flow and ebb of experiences and interests and attitudes. The significance is as much in this movement as in any of the apparently separate points. And this is important to remember when we notice that Lawrence, often, sounds very dogmatic, absolutely sure of himself and his case. The hurried reader can then pick out one of these cases, for approval or disapproval, and think, mistakenly, that he has understood Lawrence. But as we read more widely, in this selection or, as we should, in the original books, we come to see that he went on questioning, arguing, altering an emphasis or a conclusion, restoring or admitting other feelings. We can then often say that he contradicts himself, and of course these contradictions need to be noted. But what he has mainly to offer is not so much a systematic position, on education or on anything else. It is a flow of observations, of feelings and of ideas; at times an overflow; at times dammed up and diverted; but in the main a changing record of a life's experience of education – its environment, its procedures and its consequences – which is in its way unique. Its value is not only that he was a very gifted man. It is also that through his particular educational history, as a pupil and as a teacher, he was one of the first to live through and give an account of situations and problems which are still, in our own day, very much alive.

2

The method of arrangement which has been used in this selection is only one of many that were possible. It would have been interesting, for example, to make the arrangement chronological, since his views developed and changed through time. The dates or probable dates of all the pieces included can be found in the source list, so that the chronological order can, if necessary, be followed through. But we decided, eventually, to make a different order, which might make some things clearer.

In the first section, Starting Points, we have included pieces which help to give bearings on the different kinds of writing that follow. The opening *Autobiographical Sketch* has an obvious interest. He wrote more than one of these sketches, and he often described his early life, but this piece is interesting because it was written very late, looking back and summing up, defending and explaining the position he had reached. He would not have put most of it like that if he had written it earlier, as we can see if we compare it with contemporary letters. But in the last years of his life Lawrence was in some ways changing his perspective, and this is really the best introduction to his own developed sense of his life as a whole. The three pieces which follow, in this first group, enable us to get to know, in a preliminary way, what Lawrence meant by 'knowing' and therefore by 'education': often, as will be seen, in sharp contrast with conventional ideas of both. 'We are hopelessly uneducated in ourselves': that stress is crucial, for it is an argument *against* most of the ordinary definitions of what children and adults should know or learn. *The Proper Study* makes this distinction clear, and the two following pieces, about the importance of the novel, extend the distinction and give it a positive emphasis. This is an emphasis about life which takes its particular form in relation to the kind of writing to which, in the end, he gave most of his energy. There is still enough prejudice against what is called 'fiction' to make Lawrence's claims for the novel essential reading. But we have also to realize, from the beginning, that Lawrence was challenging education as he knew it root and branch: 'Educated! We are not even *born* as far as our feelings are concerned.'

This emphasis leads naturally to the second group: Experiences. These are extracts from two of his novels, *The Rainbow* and *Women in Love*, and two very early short stories. As it happens they let us see different phases of educational experience: from a girl at school, through the assistant teaching which was then normal, through training college, and on to varied experiences as a teacher in the classroom. Most of what Lawrence has to say about education is expressed here in very particular ways.

Of course, after reading the extracts from the novels, we ought to look at them again in their places in the whole books. Some of the meanings can only be reached by that kind of following through. But there is some real use in looking at them, for once, as a particular experience of education. It is then not only the vivid detail, in the different situations. It is that in this kind of writing the personal presence of his characters makes immediate and actual what elsewhere can seem only a general point in an argument. Take the emphasis, for example, that whether as pupil, as trainee or as teacher, we are still all the time human beings, with other and often urgent interests and needs. A good deal of educational theory and discussion prefers to set that aside; it considers people, for the time being, only as 'pupils' or as 'teachers', divided into specialized stages or jobs in a life. But what Lawrence has to say is that the 'personal interests', the 'subjective dreaming', the 'mind wandering to things that are not on the syllabus', these standard complaints of so much educational argument, have to be seen differently: not as distractions but as the often unnoticed and unacknowledged yet in the end decisive realities. And this point is stronger, obviously, when we see it through the eyes of a particular character, whose whole life we know, rather than as an abstract point, where it can be quite quickly forgotten.

Essentially, then, the core of what Lawrence has to say about education is in the second section. But he wrote about the experience in several other ways, and the next section, Arguments, presents a selection of these. The most extended item is the long essay on *Education of the People*. This needs to be read, and as a whole, but it is by no means the most important thing he wrote on the subject. Indeed, it belongs, like other pieces in this section, to a period of great tension in Lawrence's thought, coming after the major novels and before the alteration of perspective of the final years. Yet the continuity of some of the ideas is obvious, and it is a matter of great critical importance to see what happens to them as Lawrence tries to build them into a general scheme. The other pieces in this section are in the same dimension of sharp argument. The essay on Benjamin Franklin, in particular, is too lively to be missed; a critical account of a life which is also a recommendation of how to live differently.

In the last section, Reflections, there are only three pieces, from the last years of his life. Again there is continuity, but the one thing they have in common, that they are all looking back at the life from which, by then, he had moved so far, is an important reason for an evident change of tone. Lawrence needs to be read in all his phases, but it would wrong him to take his view of education and society only from the period between the difficulties of the war and the early to middle 1920s. There is a breadth and humanity of vision, in these late essays, which is certainly as much part of him as the confused and intolerant and restrictive opinions of those earlier, transitional years.

3

Lawrence earned the right to having his own say. But this isn't only a right that has to be earned. If what he says means anything, it means, or ought to mean, that we can have our own say back. That is for readers, though, as well as editors. There is something about Lawrence's writing that in any case provokes response. Not only the vitality, the energy, that his admirers point to. Also the bossiness, the prejudices, that his detractors can point to. The fact is that these are all present. We can respond to them in detail, but in the kind of hurry that most studied response now is – and for admiration or detraction is then not so important – we can arrive at general judgements which are much too easy: 'Lawrence the most vital Englishman of the century'; 'Lawrence the liberator'; 'Lawrence the confused *petit bourgeois*'; 'Lawrence the fascist'.

None of it is clear enough to be simplified to that. Past the surface clarity, and the sense of entire conviction, there are problems and contradictions he never did work out, and that hardly anybody else has worked out either. The thing to do, I believe, when we have read what he has to say, in its different phases and forms, is to take one or two of his leading ideas and really follow them through. We can then postpone the adjectives and the formulas, and try to take some of the real weight.

Take as an example what he has to say about 'self-expression'. It is important to read his attacks on the idea of self-expression, in the second section of *Education of the People* and in *Education and Sex* (where as it happens he also argues against what is now called sex education). But we have then to look at the way in which he separated what usually passes for 'self-expression', which he said only made children self-conscious and falsely mental, and what real 'self-expression' might be, indeed has to be if his own ideal, described in the tenth section of *Education of the People* and often elsewhere, is to be realized:

Don't set up standards and regulation patterns for people. Don't have criteria. Let every individual be single and self-expressive.

That is to say, there is a difference between teaching self-expression and having schools in which children can really express themselves. Teaching self-expression may be not much more than projecting the teacher's sense of how children should express themselves. Yet teaching anything may be that, an imposition of regulation patterns. Lawrence wants people to be themselves, and at the same time, in his social system, in his prescriptions about what should and shouldn't be learned, he has got it all worked out for other people. Both feelings are real, and to follow them through is to arrive at a contradiction which is not only in Lawrence, but in a very wide area of our social and educational ideas.

Take again, in relation to this, Lawrence's notorious case (in *Education of the People*) for an unequal and hierarchical society and for what has to be seen as a segregated and class-divided educational system. This must be read in context, but it is even more important to read it alongside the closing pages of *Return to Bestwood*. Many readers will ask how a man who put such stress on people being left alone to become themselves could so confidently devise a rigid system of classes and functions and roles. Much of what he says is simply an angry reaction against the false ideal of classless education, for a society which in practice was not going to be anything of the kind, and the ideal would hide – perhaps was meant to hide – the reality. But then compare this with what he says, in *Return to Bestwood*, about the forcing of social roles which the existing system represents. This, in the end, becomes a demand for liberation, rather than the abstract construction of a 'noble' society.

Look again at what he says, convincingly, about the need to grow from one's self. But then, as between men and women, he takes over and even exaggerates a categorical division of 'functions' and 'roles'. His sharp insights into social and sexual tensions and failures sometimes lead him on to transcend the conventions and the system he has known and hated. But the insights sometimes get confused, even dangerously, with the very rigidities he is attacking. Men and women should be themselves, should flow from their own deepest centres; and Lawrence radically means it. But at the same time he thinks he knows what boys should learn in school and girls should learn in school; and these presumptions turn out to be reproductions of the social and sexual roles which the existing society has forced men and women into. There is a similar contradiction and tension in his idea of the 'pure individual' (in several essays in the third section) and the equally strongly felt critique of individualism, the argument for a new common consciousness transcending it, in *Nottingham and the Mining Countryside*.

And then you come to that sentence in *Education and Sex*: 'The top and bottom of it is, that it is a crime to teach a child anything at all, school-wise.' This has been quoted by all sorts of people. Reactionaries put it alongside his recommendations for teaching most children only useful crafts and physical education. Deschoolers put it with his more general arguments against the impositions of the system and of adult ideas. Yet, taking his whole work, neither group can use Lawrence. His demand for ending 'standards and regulation patterns' is the absolute enemy of the reactionary position. His proposal for a system in which the child shall *not* decide is the absolute enemy of the deschoolers.

Where, then, must he be placed? But first, he cannot be placed: the tensions, the changes, the contradictory impulses are too evident and too central. 'It is a crime to teach a child anything at all, *school-wise*.' Everything turns on that last word, but it is not only a matter of old or new school procedures. It is a matter of life interest, of living interest. It is the connection he makes between the deepest personal awareness and growth, and a more general awareness, including learning, about the natural world and its many forms of life. In this as in so much else no single precept or prohibition can be finally separated from his central emphasis and concerns. He wants to encourage growth from a different sense of being, in individuals and in societies. Education can hinder or can help with that, according to the way it is done and the way it is organized; but above all by what it is part of, what other kind of life.

This is an emphasis, not a doctrine, and even as an emphasis it has omissions and contradictions. But it has lived and living experience in it: that is why it is so often moving to read. If we can take this sense of Lawrence, finding in education – in his own experience of it – the brightest hopes, the deepest disappointments, the opening possibilities, the dreary and crushing frustrations, and all of these connecting with personal life, with the economy and the society, with what it is for men to live at all, we do more than learn a doctrine; we trace, as he would have wanted, a man alive. A man, too, in a time and place that still connect with us. For through all the subsequent changes, many of the problems, the contradictions, the illusions, the experiences seem still to be there. What he was trying to work through, for the most part on his own, can now be shared and taken up, taken further, by more than one generation.

Raymond Williams

Starting Points

Autobiographical Sketch

They ask me: 'Did you find it very hard to get on and to become a success?' And I have to admit that if I can be said to have got on, and if I can be called a success, then I *did not* find it hard.

I never starved in a garret, nor waited in anguish for the post to bring me an answer from editor or publisher, nor did I struggle in sweat and blood to bring forth mighty works, nor did I ever wake up and find myself famous.

I was a poor boy. I *ought* to have wrestled in the fell clutch of circumstance, and undergone the bludgeoning of chance before I became a writer with a very modest income and a very questionable reputation. But I didn't. It all happened by itself and without any groans from me.

It seems a pity. Because I was undoubtedly a poor boy of the working classes, with no apparent future in front of me. But after all, what am I now?

I was born among the working classes and brought up among them. My father was a collier, and only a collier, nothing praiseworthy about him. He wasn't even respectable, in so far as he got drunk rather frequently, never went near a chapel, and was usually rather rude to his little immediate bosses at the pit.

He practically never had a good stall all the time he was a butty, because he was always saying tiresome and foolish things about the men just above him in control at the mine. He offended them all, almost on purpose, so how could he expect them to favour him? Yet he grumbled when they didn't.

My mother was, I suppose, superior. She came from town, and belonged really to the lower bourgeoisie. She spoke King's English, without an accent, and never in her life could even imitate a sentence of the dialect which my father spoke, and which we children spoke out of doors.

She wrote a fine Italian hand, and a clever and amusing letter when she felt like it. And as she grew older she read novels again, and got terribly impatient with *Diana of the Crossways* and terribly thrilled by *East Lynne*.

But she was a working man's wife, and nothing else, in her shabby little black bonnet and her shrewd, clear, 'different' face. And she was very much respected, just as my father was not respected. Her nature was quick and sensitive, and perhaps really superior. But she was down, right down in the working class, among the mass of poorer colliers' wives.

I was a delicate pale brat with a snuffy nose, whom most people treated quite gently as just an ordinary delicate little lad. When I was twelve I got a county council scholarship, twelve pounds a year, and went to Nottingham High School.

After leaving school I was a clerk for three months, then had a very serious pneumonia illness, in my seventeenth year, that damaged my health for life.

A year later I became a school-teacher, and after three years' savage teaching of collier lads I went to take the 'normal' course in Nottingham University.

As I was glad to leave school, I was glad to leave college. It had meant mere disillusion, instead of the living contact of men. From college I went down to Croydon, near London, to teach in a new elementary school at a hundred pounds a year.

It was while I was at Croydon, when I was twenty-three, that the girl who had been the chief friend of my youth, and who was herself a school-teacher in a mining village at home, copied out some of my poems, and without telling me, sent them to the *English Review*, which had just had a glorious rebirth under Ford Madox Hueffer.

Hueffer was most kind. He printed the poems, and asked me to come and see him. The girl had launched me, so easily, on my literary career, like a princess cutting a thread, launching a ship.

I had been tussling away for four years, getting out *The White Peacock* in inchoate bits, from the underground of my consciousness. I must have written most of it five or six times, but only in intervals, never as a task or a divine labour, or in the groans of parturition.

I would dash at it, do a bit, show it to the girl; she always admired it; then realize afterwards it wasn't what I wanted, and have another dash. But at Croydon I had worked at it fairly steadily, in the evenings after school.

Anyhow, it was done, after four or five years' spasmodic effort. Hueffer asked at once to see the manuscript. He read it immediately, with the greatest cheery sort of kindness and bluff. And in his queer voice, when we were in an omnibus in London, he shouted in my ear: 'It's got every fault that the English novel can have.'

Just then the English novel was supposed to have so many faults, in comparison with the French, that it was hardly allowed to exist at all. 'But,' shouted Hueffer in the bus, 'you've got GENIUS.'

This made me want to laugh, it sounded so comical. In the early days they were always telling me I had got genius, as if to console me for not having their own incomparable advantages.

But Hueffer didn't mean that. I always thought he had a bit of genius himself. Anyhow, he sent the MS of *The White Peacock* to William Heinemann, who accepted it at once, and made me alter only four little lines whose omission would now make anybody smile. I was to have fifty pounds when the book was published.

Meanwhile Hueffer printed more poems and some stories of mine in the *English Review*, and people read them and told me so, to my embarrassment and anger. I hated being an author, in people's eyes. Especially as I was a teacher.

When I was twenty-five my mother died, and two months later *The White Peacock* was published, but it meant nothing to me. I went on teaching for another year, and then again a bad pneumonia illness intervened. When I got better I did not go back to school. I lived henceforward on my scanty literary earnings.

It is seventeen years since I gave up teaching and started to live an independent life of the pen. I have never starved, and never even felt poor, though my income for the first ten years was no better, and often worse, than it would have been if I had remained an elementary schoolteacher.

But when one has been born poor a very little money can be enough. Now my father would think I am rich, if nobody else does. And my mother would think I have risen in the world, even if I don't think so.

But something is wrong, either with me or with the world, or with both of us. I have gone far and met people, of all sorts and all conditions, and many whom I have genuinely liked and esteemed.

People, *personally*, have nearly always been friendly. Of critics we will not speak, they are different fauna from people. And I have *wanted* to feel truly friendly with some, at least, of my fellow men.

Yet I have never quite succeeded. Whether I get on *in* the world is a question; but I certainly don't get on very well *with* the world. And whether I am a worldly success or not I really don't know. But I feel, somehow, not much of a human success.

By which I mean that I don't feel there is any very cordial or fundamental contact between me and society, or me and other people. There is a breach. And my contact is with something that is non-human, non-vocal.

I used to think it had something to do with the oldness and the worn-outness of Europe. Having tried other places, I know that is not so.

Europe is, perhaps, the least worn-out of the continents, because it is most lived in. A place that is lived in lives.

It is since coming back from America that I ask myself seriously: why is there so little contact between myself and the people whom I know? Why has the contact no vital meaning?

And if I write the question down, and try to write the answer down, it is because I feel it is a question that troubles many men.

The answer, as far as I can see, has something to do with class. Class makes a gulf, across which all the best human flow is lost. It is not exactly the triumph of the middle classes that has made the deadness, but the triumph of the middle-class *thing*.

As a man from the working class, I feel that the middle class cut off some of my vital vibration when I am with them. I admit them charming and educated and good people often enough. *But they just stop some part of me from working.* Some part has to be left out.

Then why don't I live with my working people? Because their vibration is limited in another direction. They are narrow, but still fairly deep and passionate, whereas the middle class is broad and shallow and passionless. Quite passionless. At the best they substitute affection, which is the great middle-class positive emotion.

But the working class is narrow in outlook, in prejudice, and narrow in intelligence. This again makes a prison. One can belong absolutely to no class.

Yet I find, here in Italy, for example, that I live in a certain silent contact with the peasants who work the land of this villa. I am not intimate with them, hardly speak to them save to say good day. And they are not working for me; I am not their *padrone*.

Yet it is they, really, who form my *ambiente*, and it is from them that the human flow comes to me. I don't want to live with them in their cottages; that would be a sort of prison. But I want them to be there, about the place, their lives going on along with mine, and in relation to mine. I don't idealize them. Enough of that folly! It is worse than setting school-children to express themselves in self-conscious twaddle. I don't expect them to make any millennium here on earth, neither now nor in the future. But I want to live near them, because their life still flows.

And now I know, more or less, why I cannot follow in the footsteps even of Barrie or of Wells, who both came from the common people also and are both such a success. Now I know why I cannot rise in the world and become even a little popular and rich.

I cannot make the transfer from my own class into the middle class. I cannot, not for anything in the world, forfeit my passional consciousness and my old blood-affinity with my fellow men and the animals and the land, for that other thin, spurious mental conceit which is all that is left of the mental consciousness once it has made itself exclusive.

The Proper Study

If no man lives for ever, neither does any precept. And if even the weariest river winds somewhere safe to sea, so also does the weariest wisdom. And there it is lost. Also incorporated.

Know then thyself, presume not God to scan;
The proper study of mankind is man.

It was Alexander Pope who absolutely struck the note of our particular epoch: not Shakespeare or Luther or Milton. A man of first magnitude never fits his age perfectly.

Know then thyself, presume not God to scan;
The proper study of mankind is Man – *with a capital M*.

This stream of wisdom is very weary now: weary to death. It started such a gay little trickle, and is such a spent muddy ebb by now. It will take a big sea to swallow all its alluvia.

'Know then thyself.' All right! I'll do my best. Honestly I'll do my best, sincerely to know myself. Since it is the great commandment to consciousness of our long era, let us be men, and try to obey it. Jesus gave the emotional commandment, 'Love thy neighbour'. But the Greeks set the even more absolute motto, in its way, a more deeply religious motto: 'Know thyself'.

Very well! Being man, and the son of man, I find it only honourable to obey. To do my best. To do my best to know myself. And particularly that part, or those parts, of myself that have not yet been admitted into consciousness. Man is nothing, less than a tick stuck in a sheep's back, unless he adventures. Either into the unknown of the world, of his environment. Or into the unknown of himself.

Allons! the road is before us. Know thyself! Which means, *really*, know thine own *unknown self*. It's no good knowing something you know already. The thing is to discover the tracts as yet unknown. And as the only unknown now lies deep in the passional soul, *allons!* the road is before us. We write a novel or two, we are called erotic or depraved or idiotic or boring. What does it matter, we go the road just the same. If you see the point of the great old commandment, *Know thyself*, then you see the point of all art.

But knowing oneself, like knowing anything else, is not a process that can continue to infinity, in the same direction. The fact that I myself *am* only myself makes me very specifically finite. True, I may argue that my Self is a mystery that impinges on the infinite. Admitted. But the moment my Self impinges on the infinite, it ceases to be just myself.

The same is true of all knowing. You start to find out the chemical composition of a drop of water, and before you know where you are, your river of knowledge is winding very unsatisfactorily into a very vague sea, called the ether. You start to study electricity, you track the wretch down till you get some mysterious and misbehaving atom of energy or unit of force that goes pop under your nose and leaves you with the dead body of a mere word.

You sail down your stream of knowledge, and you find yourself absolutely at sea. Which may be safety for the weary river, but is a sad look-out for you, who are a land animal.

Now all science starts gaily from the inland source of *I Don't Know*. Gaily it says: 'I don't know, but I'm going to know.' It's like a little river bubbling up cheerfully in the determination to dissolve the whole world in its waves. And science, like the little river, winds wonderingly out again into the final *I Don't Know* of the ocean.

All this is platitudinous as regards science. Science has learned an uncanny lot, *by the way*.

Apply the same to the Know Thyself motto. We have learned something by the way. But as far as I'm concerned, I see land receding, and the great ocean of the last *I Don't Know* enveloping me.

But the human consciousness is never allowed finally to say: 'I Don't Know'. It has got to know, even if it must metamorphose to do so.

Know then thyself, presume not God to scan.

Now as soon as you come across a Thou Shalt Not commandment, you may be absolutely sure that sometime or other, you'll have to break this commandment. You needn't make a practice of breaking it. But the day will come when you'll have to break it. When you'll have to take the name of the Lord Your God in vain, and have other gods, and worship idols, and steal, and kill, and commit adultery, and all the rest. A day will come. Because, as Oscar Wilde says, what's a temptation for, except to be succumbed to!

There comes a time to every man when he has to break one or other of the Thou Shalt Not commandments. And then is the time to Know Yourself just a bit different from what you thought you were.

So that in the end, this Know Thyself commandment brings me up against the Presume-Not-God-to-Scan fence. Trespassers will be prosecuted. Know then thyself, presume not God to scan.

It's a dilemma. Because this business of knowing myself has led me slap up against the forbidden enclosure where, presumably, this God mystery is kept in corral. It isn't my fault. I followed the road. And it leads over the edge of a precipice on which stands up a signboard: Danger! Don't go over the edge!

But I've *got* to go over the edge. The way lies that way.

Flop! Over we go, and into the endless sea. There drown.

No! Out of the drowning something else gurgles awake. And that's the best of the human consciousness. When you fall into the final sea of *I Don't Know*, then, if you can but gasp *Teach Me*, you turn into a fish, and twiddle your fins and twist your tail and grope in amazement, in a new element.

That's why they called Jesus: the Fish. Pisces. Because he fell, like the weariest river, into the great Ocean that is outside the shore, and there took on a new way of knowledge.

The Proper Study is Man, sure enough. But the proper study of man, like the proper study of anything else, will in the end leave you no option. You'll have to presume to study God. Even the most hard-boiled scientist, if he is a brave and honest man, is landed in this unscientific dilemma. Or rather, he is all at sea in it.

The river of human consciousness, like ancient Ocean, goes in a circle. It starts gaily, bubblingly, fiercely from an inland pool, where it surges up in obvious mystery and Godliness, the human consciousness. And here is the God of the Beginning, call him Jehovah or Ra or Ammon or Jupiter or what you like. One bubbles up in Greece, one in India, one in Jerusalem. From their various God-sources the streams of human consciousness rush variously down. Then begin to meander and to doubt. Then fall slow. Then start to silt up. Then pass into the great Ocean, which is the God of the End.

In the great ocean of the End, most men are lost. But Jesus turned into a fish, he had the other consciousness of the Ocean which is the divine End of us all. And then like a salmon he beat his way up stream again, to speak from the source.

And this is the greater history of man, as distinguished from the lesser history, in which figure Mr Lloyd George and Monsieur Poincaré.

We are in the deep, muddy estuary of our era, and terrified of the emptiness of the sea beyond. Or we are at the end of the great road, that Jesus and Francis and Whitman walked. We are on the brink of a precipice, and terrified at the great void below.

No help for it. We are men, and for men there is no retreat. Over we go.

Over we must and shall go, so we may as well do it voluntarily, keeping our soul alive; and as we drown in our terrestrial nature, transmogrify into fishes. Pisces. That which knows the Oceanic Godliness of the End.

The proper study of mankind is man. Agreed entirely! But in the long run, it becomes again as it was before, man in his relation to the deity. The proper study of mankind is man in his relation to the deity.

And yet not as it was before. Not the specific deity of the inland source. The vast deity of the End. Oceanus whom you can only know by becoming a Fish. Let us become Fishes, and try.

They talk about the sixth sense. They talk as if it were an extension of the other senses. A mere *dimensional* sense. It's nothing of the sort. There is a sixth sense right enough. Jesus had it. The sense of the God that is the End and the Beginning. And the proper study of mankind is man in his relation to this Oceanic God.

We have come to the end, for the time being, of the study of man in his relation to man. Or man in his relation to himself. Or man in his relation to woman. There is nothing more of importance to be said, by us or for us, on this subject. Indeed, we have no more to say.

Of course, there is the literature of perversity. And there is the literature of little playboys and playgirls, not only of the western world. But the literature of perversity is a brief weed. And the playboy–playgirl stuff, like the movies, though a very monstrous weed, won't live long.

As the weariest river winds by no means safely to sea, all the muddy little individuals begin to chirrup: 'Let's play! Let's play at something! We're so god-like when we *play*.'

But it won't do, my dears. The sea will swallow you up, and all your play and perversions and personalities.

You can't get any more literature out of man in his relation to man. Which, of course, should be writ large, to mean man in his relation to woman, to other men, and to the whole environment of men: or woman in her relation to man, or other women, or the whole environment of women. You can't get any more literature out of that. Because any new book must needs be a new stride. And the next stride lands you over the sandbar in the open ocean, where the first and greatest relation of every man and woman is to the Ocean itself, the great God of the

End, who is the All-Father of all sources, as the sea is father of inland lakes and springs of water.

But get a glimpse of this new relation of men and women to the great God of the End, who is the Father, not the Son, of all our beginnings: and you get a glimpse of the new literature. Think of the true novel of St Paul, for example. Not the sentimental looking-backward Christian novel, but the novel looking out to sea, to the great Source, and End, of all beginnings. Not the St Paul with his human feelings repudiated, to give play to the new divine feelings. Not the St Paul violent in reaction against worldliness and sensuality, and therefore a dogmatist with his sheaf of Shalt-Nots ready. But a St Paul two thousand years older, having his own epoch behind him, and having again the great knowledge of the deity, the deity which Jesus knew, the vast Ocean God which is at the end of all our consciousness.

Because, after all, if chemistry winds wearily to sea in the ether, or some such universal, don't we also, not as chemists but as conscious men, also wind wearily to sea in a divine ether, which means nothing to us but space and words and emptiness? We wind wearily to sea in words and emptiness.

But man is a mutable animal. Turn into the Fish, the Pisces of man's final consciousness, and you'll start to swim again in the great life which is so frighteningly godly that you realize your previous presumption.

And then you realize the new relation of man. Men like fishes lifted on a great wave of the God of the End, swimming together, and apart, in a new medium. A new relation, in a new whole.

The Novel and the Feelings

We think we are so civilized, so highly educated and civilized. It is farcical. Because, of course, all our civilization consists in harping on one string. Or at most on two or three strings. Harp, harp, harp, twingle, twingle-twang! That's our civilization, always on one note.

The note itself is all right. It's the exclusiveness of it that is awful. Always the same note, always the same note! 'Ah, how can you run after other women when your wife is so delightful, a lovely plump partridge?' Then the husband laid his hand on his waistcoat, and a frightened look came over his face. 'Nothing but partridge?' he exclaimed.

Toujours perdrix! It was up to that wife to be a goose and a cow, an oyster and an inedible vixen, at intervals.

Wherein are we educated? Come now, in what are we educated? In politics, in geography, in history, in machinery, in soft drinks and in hard, in social economy and social extravagance: ugh! a frightful universality of knowings.

But it's all France without Paris, *Hamlet* without the Prince, and bricks without straw. For we know nothing, or next to nothing, about ourselves. After hundreds of thousands of years we have learned how to wash our faces and bob our hair, and that is about all we *have* learned, *individually*. Collectively, of course, as a species, we have combed the round earth with a tooth-comb, and pulled down the stars almost to within grasp. And then what? Here sit I, a two-legged individual with a risky temper, knowing all about – take a pinch of salt – Tierra del Fuego and Relativity and the composition of celluloid, the appearance of the anthrax bacillus and solar eclipses, and the latest fashion in shoes; and it don't do me *no* good! as the charlady said of near beer. It doesn't leave me feeling no less lonesome inside! as the old Englishwoman said, long ago, of tea without rum.

Our knowledge, like the prohibition beer, is always near. But it never gets there. It leaves us feeling just as lonesome inside.

We are hopelessly uneducated in ourselves. We pretend that when we know a smattering of the Patagonian idiom we have in so far educated ourselves. What nonsense! The leather of my boots is just as effectual in turning me into a bull, or a young steer. Alas! we wear our education just as externally as we wear our boots, and to far less profit. It is all external education, anyhow.

What am I, when I am at home? I'm supposed to be a sensible human being. Yet I carry a whole waste-paper basket of ideas at the top of my head, and in some other part of my anatomy, the dark continent of myself. I have a whole stormy chaos of 'feelings'. And with these self-same feelings I simply don't get a chance. Some of them roar like lions, some twist like snakes, some bleat like snow-white lambs, some warble like linnets, some are absolutely dumb, but swift as slippery fishes, some are oysters that open on occasion: and lo! here am I, adding another scrap of paper to the ideal accumulation in the waste-paper basket, hoping to settle the matter that way.

The lion springs on me! I wave an idea at him. The serpent casts a terrifying glance at me, and I hand him a Moody and Sankey hymn-book. Matters go from bad to worse.

The wild creatures are coming forth from the darkest Africa inside us. In the night you can hear them bellowing. If you are a big game-hunter like Billy Sunday, you may shoulder your elephant gun. But since the forest is inside all of us, and in every forest there's a whole assortment of big game and dangerous creatures, it's one against a thousand. We've managed to keep clear of the darkest Africa inside us, for a long time. We've been so busy finding the North Pole and converting the Patagonians, loving our neighbour and devising new means of exterminating him, listening-in and shutting-out.

But now, my dear, dear reader, Nemesis is blowing his nose. And muffled roarings are heard out of darkest Africa, with stifled shrieks.

I say feelings, not emotions. Emotions are things we more or less recognize. We see love, like a woolly lamb, or like a decorative decadent panther in Paris clothes: according as it is sacred or profane. We see hate, like a dog chained to a kennel. We see fear, like a shivering monkey. We see anger, like a bull with a ring through his nose, and greed, like a pig. Our emotions are our domesticated animals, noble like the horse, timid like the rabbit, but all completely at our service. The rabbit goes into the pot, and the horse into the shafts. For we are creatures of circumstance, and must fill our bellies and our pockets.

Convenience! Convenience! There are convenient emotions and inconvenient ones. The inconvenient ones we chain up, or put a ring through their nose. The convenient ones are our pets. Love is our pet favourite.

And that's as far as our education goes, in the direction of feelings. We have no language for the feelings, because our feelings do not even exist for us.

Yet what is a man? Is he really just a little engine that you stoke with potatoes and beef-steak? Does all the strange flow of life in him come out of meat and potatoes, and turn into the so-called physical energy?

Educated! We are not even *born*, as far as our feelings are concerned.

You can eat till you're bloated, and 'get ahead' till you're a byword, and still, inside you, will be the darkest Africa whence come roars and shrieks.

Man is not a little engine of cause and effect. We must put that out of our minds for ever. The *cause* in man is something we shall never fathom. But there it is, a strange dark continent that we do not explore, because we do not even allow that it exists. Yet all the time, it is within us: the *cause* of us, and of our days.

And our feelings are the first manifestations within the aboriginal jungle of us. Till now, in sheer terror of ourselves, we have turned our backs on the jungle, fenced it in with an enormous entanglement of barbed wire, and declared it did not exist.

But alas! we ourselves only exist because of the life that bounds and leaps into our limbs and our consciousness, from out of the original dark forest within us. We may wish to exclude this inbounding, inleaping life. We may wish to be as our domesticated animals are, tame. But let us remember that even our cats and dogs have, in each generation, to be tamed. They are not now a tame species. Take away the control, and they will cease to be tame. They will not tame *themselves*.

Man is the only creature who has deliberately tried to tame himself. He has succeeded. But alas! it is a process you cannot set a limit to. Tameness, like alcohol, destroys its own creator. Tameness is an effect of control. But the tamed thing loses the power of control, in itself. It must be controlled from without. Man has pretty well tamed himself, and calls his tameness civilization. True civilization would be something very different. But man is now tame. Tameness means the loss of the peculiar power of command. The tame are always commanded by the untame. Man has tamed himself, and so has lost his power for command, the power to give himself direction. He has no choice in himself. He is tamed, like a tame horse waiting for the rein.

Supposing all horses were suddenly rendered masterless, what would they do? They would run wild. But supposing they were left still shut up in their fields, paddocks, corrals, stables, what would they do? They would go insane.

And that is precisely man's predicament. He is tamed. There are no untamed to give the commands and the direction. Yet he is shut up within all his barbed-wire fences. He can only go insane, degenerate.

What is the alternative? It is nonsense to pretend we can untame ourselves in five minutes. That, too, is a slow and strange process, that has to be undertaken seriously. It is nonsense to pretend we can break the fences and dash out into the wilds. There are no wilds left, comparatively, and man is a dog that returns to his vomit.

Yet unless we proceed to connect ourselves up with our own primeval sources, we shall degenerate. And degenerating, we shall break up into a strange orgy of feelings. They will be decomposition feelings, like the colours of autumn. And they will precede whole storms of death, like leaves in a wind.

There is no help for it. Man cannot tame himself and then stay tame. The moment he tries to stay tame he begins to degenerate, and gets the second sort of wildness, the wildness of destruction, which may be autumnal-beautiful for a while, like yellow leaves. Yet yellow leaves can only fall and rot.

Man tames himself in order to learn to un-tame himself again. To be civilized, we must not deny and blank out our feelings. Tameness is not civilization. It is only burning down the brush and ploughing the land. Our civilization has hardly realized yet the necessity for ploughing the soul. Later, we sow wild seed. But so far, we've only been burning off and rooting out the old wild brush. Our civilization, as far as our own souls go, has been a destructive process, up to now. The landscape of our souls is a charred wilderness of burnt-off stumps, with a green bit of water here, and tin shanty with a little iron stove.

Now we have to sow wild seed again. We have to cultivate our feelings. It is no good trying to be popular, to let a whole rank tangle of liberated, degenerate feelings spring up. It will give us no satisfaction.

And it is no use doing as the psychoanalysts have done. The psycho-analysts show the greatest fear of all, of the innermost primeval place in man, where God is, if He is anywhere. The old Jewish horror of the true Adam, the mysterious 'natural man', rises to a shriek in psycho-analysis. Like the idiot who foams and bites his wrists till they bleed. So great is the Freudian hatred of the oldest, old Adam, from whom God is not yet separated off, that the psychoanalyst sees this Adam as nothing but a monster of perversity, a bunch of engendering adders, horribly clotted.

This vision is the perverted vision of the degenerate tame: tamed through thousands of shameful years. The old Adam is the forever un-tamed: he who is of the tame hated, with a horror of fearful hate: but who is held in innermost respect by the fearless.

In the oldest of the old Adam, was God: behind the dark wall of his breast, under the seal of the navel. Then man had a revulsion against himself, and God was separated off, lodged in the outermost space.

Now we have to return. Now again the old Adam must lift up his face and his breast, and un-tame himself. Not in viciousness nor in wanton-ness, but having God within the walls of himself. In the very darkest continent of the body there is God. And from Him issue the first dark rays of our feeling, wordless, and utterly previous to words: the inner-most rays, the first messengers, the primeval, honourable beasts of our being, whose voice echoes wordless and for ever wordless down the darkest avenues of the soul, but full of potent speech. Our own inner meaning.

Now we have to educate ourselves, not by laying down laws and inscribing tables of stone, but by listening. Not listening-in to noises from Chicago or Timbuktu. But listening-in to the voices of the honourable beasts that call in the dark paths of the veins of our body, from the God in the heart. Listening inwards, inwards, not for words nor for inspiration, but to the lowing of the innermost beasts, the feelings, that roam in the forest of the blood, from the feet of God within the red, dark heart.

And how? How? How shall we even begin to educate ourselves in the feelings?

Not by laying down laws, or commandments, or axioms and postulates. Not even by making assertions that such and such is blessed. Not by words at all.

If we can't hear cries far down in our own forests of dark veins, we can look in the real novels, and there listen-in. Not listen to the didactic statements of the author, but to the low, calling cries of the characters, as they wander in the dark woods of their destiny.

Why the Novel Matters

We have curious ideas of ourselves. We think of ourselves as a body with a spirit in it, or a body with a soul in it, or a body with a mind in it. *Mens sana in corpore sano*. The years drink up the wine, and at last throw the bottle away, the body, of course, being the bottle.

It is a funny sort of superstition. Why should I look at my hand, as it so cleverly writes these words, and decide that it is a mere nothing compared to the mind that directs it? Is there really any huge difference between my hand and my brain? Or my mind? My hand is alive, it flickers with a life of its own. It meets all the strange universe in touch, and learns a vast number of things, and knows a vast number of things. My hand, as it writes these words, slips gaily along, jumps like a grasshopper to dot an *i*, feels the table rather cold, gets a little bored if I write too long, has its own rudiments of thought, and is just as much *me* as is my brain, my mind or my soul. Why should I imagine that there is a *me* which is more *me* than my hand is? Since my hand is absolutely alive, me alive.

Whereas, of course, as far as I am concerned, my pen isn't alive at all. My pen *isn't me* alive. Me alive ends at my finger-tips.

Whatever is me alive is me. Every tiny bit of my hands is alive, every little freckle and hair and fold of skin. And whatever is me alive is me.

Only my finger-nails, those ten little weapons between me and an inanimate universe, they cross the mysterious Rubicon between me alive and things like my pen, which are not alive, in my own sense.

So, seeing my hand is all alive, and me alive, wherein is it just a bottle, or a jug, or a tin can, or a vessel of clay, or any of the rest of that nonsense? True, if I cut it it will bleed, like a can of cherries. But then the skin that is cut, and the veins that bleed, and the bones that should never be seen, they are all just as alive as the blood that flows. So the tin can business, or vessel of clay, is just bunk.

And that's what you learn, when you're a novelist. And that's what you are very liable *not* to know, if you're a parson, or a philosopher, or a scientist, or a stupid person. If you're a parson, you talk about souls in heaven. If you're a novelist, you know that paradise is in the palm of your hand, and on the end of your nose, because both are alive; and alive, and man alive, which is more than you can say, for certain, of paradise. Paradise is after life, and I for one am not keen on anything that is *after* life. If you are a philosopher, you talk about infinity, and the pure spirit which knows all things. But if you pick up a novel, you realize immediately that infinity is just a handle to this self-same jug of a body of mine; while as for knowing, if I find my finger in the fire, I know that fire burns, with a knowledge so emphatic and vital, it leaves Nirvana merely a conjecture. Oh, yes, my body, me alive, *knows*, and knows intensely. And as for the sum of all knowledge, it can't be anything more than an accumulation of all the things I know in the body, and you, dear reader, know in the body.

These damned philosophers, they talk as if they suddenly went off in steam, and were then much more important than they are when they're in their shirts. It is nonsense. Every man, philosopher included, ends in his own finger-tips. That's the end of his man alive. As for the words and thoughts and sighs and aspirations that fly from him, they are so many tremulations in the ether, and not alive at all. But if the tremulations reach another man alive, he may receive them into his life, and his life may take on a new colour like a chameleon creeping from a brown rock on to a green leaf. All very well and good. It still doesn't alter the fact that the so-called spirit, the message or teaching of the philosopher or the saint, isn't alive at all, but just a tremulation upon the ether, like a radio message. All this spirit stuff is just tremulations upon the ether. If you, as man alive, quiver from the tremulation of the ether into new life, that is because you are man alive, and you take sustenance and stimulation into your alive man in a myriad ways. But to say that the message, or the spirit which is communicated to you, is more important than your living body, is nonsense. You might as well say that the potato at dinner was more important.

Nothing is important but life. And for myself, I can absolutely see life nowhere but in the living. Life with a capital L is only man alive. Even a cabbage in the rain is cabbage alive. All things that are alive are amazing. And all things that are dead are subsidiary to the living. Better a live dog than a dead lion. But better a live lion than a live dog. *C'est la vie!*

It seems impossible to get a saint, or a philosopher, or a scientist, to stick to this simple truth. They are all, in a sense, renegades. The saint wishes to offer himself up as spiritual food for the multitude. Even Francis of Assisi turns himself into a sort of angel-cake, of which anyone may take a slice. But an angel-cake is rather less than man alive. And poor St Francis might well apologize to his body, when he is dying: 'Oh, pardon me, my body, the wrong I did you through the years!' It was no wafer, for others to eat.

The philosopher, on the other hand, because he can think, decides that nothing but thoughts matters. It is as if a rabbit, because he can make little pills, should decide that nothing but little pills matter. As for the scientist, he has absolutely no use for me so long as I am man alive. To the scientist, I am dead. He puts under the microscope a bit of dead me, and calls it me. He takes me to pieces, and says first one piece, and then another piece, is me. My heart, my liver, my stomach have all been scientifically me, according to the scientist; and nowadays I am either a brain, or nerves, or glands, or something more up-to-date in the tissue line.

Now I absolutely flatly deny that I am a soul, or a body, or a mind, or an intelligence, or a brain, or a nervous system, or a bunch of glands, or any of the rest of these bits of me. The whole is greater than the part. And therefore, I, who am man alive, am greater than my soul, or spirit, or body, or mind, or consciousness, or anything else that is merely a part of me. I am a man, and alive. I am man alive, and as long as I can, I intend to go on being man alive.

For this reason I am a novelist. And being a novelist, I consider myself superior to the saint, the scientist, the philosopher and the poet, who are all great masters of different bits of man alive, but never get the whole hog.

The novel is the one bright book of life. Books are not life. They are only tremulations on the ether. But the novel as a tremulation can make the whole man alive tremble. Which is more than poetry, philosophy, science, or any other book-tremulation can do.

The novel is the book of life. In this sense, the Bible is a great confused novel. You may say, it is about God. But it is really about man alive. Adam, Eve, Sarai, Abraham, Isaac, Jacob, Samuel, David, Bath-Sheba, Ruth, Esther, Solomon, Job, Isaiah, Jesus, Mark, Judas, Paul, Peter: what is it but man alive, from start to finish? Man alive, not mere bits. Even the Lord is another man alive, in a burning bush, throwing the tablets of stone at Moses's head.

I do hope you begin to get my idea, why the novel is supremely important, as a tremulation on the ether. Plato makes the perfect ideal being tremble in me. But that's only a bit of me. Perfection is only a bit, in the strange make-up of man alive. The Sermon on the Mount makes the selfless spirit of me quiver. But that, too, is only a bit of me. The Ten Commandments set the old Adam shivering in me, warning me that I am a thief and a murderer, unless I watch it. But even the old Adam is only a bit of me.

I very much like all these bits of me to be set trembling with life and the wisdom of life. But I do ask that the whole of me shall tremble in its wholeness, some time or other.

And this, of course, must happen in me, living.

But as far as it can happen from a communication, it can only happen when a whole novel communicates itself to me. The Bible – but *all* the Bible – and Homer, and Shakespeare: these are the supreme old novels. These are all things to all men. Which means that in their wholeness they affect the whole man alive, which is the man himself, beyond any part of him. They set the whole tree trembling with a new access of life, they do not just stimulate growth in one direction.

I don't want to grow in any one direction any more. And, if I can help it, I don't want to stimulate anybody else into some particular direction. A particular direction ends in a *cul-de-sac*. We're in a *cul-de-sac* at present.

I don't believe in any dazzling revelation, or in any supreme Word. 'The grass withereth, the flower fadeth, but the Word of the Lord shall stand for ever.' That's the kind of stuff we've drugged ourselves with. As a matter of fact, the grass withereth, but comes up all the greener for that reason, after the rains. The flower fadeth, and therefore the bud opens. But the Word of the Lord, being man-uttered and a mere vibration on the ether, becomes staler and staler, more and more boring, till at last we turn a deaf ear and it ceases to exist, far more finally than any withered grass. It is grass that renews its youth like the eagle, not any Word.

We should ask for no absolutes, or absolute. Once and for all and for ever, let us have done with the ugly imperialism of any absolute. There is no absolute good, there is nothing absolutely right. All things flow and change, and even change is not absolute. The whole is a strange assembly of apparently incongruous parts, slipping past one another.

Me, man alive, I am a very curious assembly of incongruous parts. My yea! of today is oddly different from my yea! of yesterday. My tears of tomorrow will have nothing to do with my tears of a year ago. If the one I love remains unchanged and unchanging, I shall cease to love her. It is only because she changes and startles me into change and defies my inertia, and is herself staggered in her inertia by my changing, that I can continue to love her. If she stayed put, I might as well love the pepper-pot.

In all this change, I maintain a certain integrity. But woe betide me if I try to put my finger on it. If I say of myself, I am this, I am that! – then, if I stick to it, I turn into a stupid fixed thing like a lamp-post. I shall never know wherein lies my integrity, my individuality, my me. I *can* never know it. It is useless to talk about my ego. That only means that I have made up an *idea* of myself, and that I am trying to cut myself out to pattern. Which is no good. You can cut your cloth to fit your coat, but you can't clip bits off your living body, to trim it down to your idea. True, you can put yourself into ideal corsets. But even in ideal corsets, fashions change.

Let us learn from the novel. In the novel, the characters can do nothing but *live*. If they keep on being good, according to pattern, or bad, according to pattern, or even volatile, according to pattern, they cease to live, and the novel falls dead. A character in a novel has got to live, or it is nothing.

We, likewise, in life, have got to live, or we are nothing.

What we mean by living is, of course, just as indescribable as what we mean by *being*. Men get ideas into their heads, of what they mean by Life, and they proceed to cut life out to pattern. Sometimes they go into the desert to seek God, sometimes they go into the desert to seek cash, sometimes it is wine, woman and song, and again it is water, political reform and votes. You never know what it will be next: from killing your neighbour with hideous bombs and gas that tears the lungs, to supporting a Foundlings' Home and preaching infinite Love, and being co-respondent in a divorce.

In all this wild welter, we need some sort of guide. It's no good inventing Thou Shalt Nots!

What then? Turn truly, honourably to the novel, and see wherein you are man alive, and wherein you are dead man in life. You may love a woman as man alive, and you may be making love to a woman as sheer dead man in life. You may eat your dinner as man alive, or as a mere masticating corpse. As man alive you may have a shot at your enemy. But as a ghastly simulacrum of life you may be firing bombs into men who are neither your enemies nor your friends, but just things you are dead to. Which is criminal, when the things happen to be alive.

To be alive, to be man alive, to be whole man alive: that is the point. And at its best, the novel, and the novel supremely, can help you. It can help you not to be dead man in life. So much of a man walks about dead and a carcass in the street and house, today: so much of women is merely dead. Like a pianoforte with half the notes mute.

But in the novel you can see, plainly, when the man goes dead, the woman goes inert. You can develop an instinct for life, if you will, instead of a theory of right and wrong, good and bad.

In life, there is right and wrong, good and bad, all the time. But what is right in one case is wrong in another. And in the novel you see one man becoming a corpse, because of his so-called goodness, another going dead because of his so-called wickedness. Right and wrong is an instinct: but an instinct of the whole consciousness of a man, bodily, mental, spiritual at once. And only in the novel are *all* things given full play, or at least, they may be given full play, when we realize that life itself, and not inert safety, is the reason for living. For out of the full play of all things emerges the only thing that is anything, the wholeness of a man, the wholeness of a woman, man alive, and live woman.

Experiences

Schoolgirl

Ursula had only two more terms at school. She was studying for her matriculation examination. It was dreary work, for she had very little intelligence when she was disjointed from happiness. Stubbornness and a consciousness of impending fate kept her half-heartedly pinned to it. She knew that soon she would want to become a self-responsible person, and her dread was that she would be prevented. An all-containing will in her for complete independence, complete social independence, complete independence from any personal authority, kept her dullishly at her studies. For she knew that she had always her price of ransom – her femaleness. She was always a woman, and what she could not get because she was a human being, fellow to the rest of mankind, she would get because she was a female, other than the man. In her femaleness she felt a secret riches, a reserve, she had always the price of freedom.

However, she was sufficiently reserved about this last resource. The other things should be tried first. There was the mysterious man's world to be adventured upon, the world of daily work and duty, and existence as a working member of the community. Against this she had a subtle grudge. She wanted to make her conquest also of this man's world.

So she ground away at her work, never giving it up. Some things she liked. Her subjects were English, Latin, French, Mathematics and History. Once she knew how to read French and Latin, the syntax bored her. Most tedious was the close study of English Literature. Why should one remember the things one reads? Something in Mathematics, their cold absoluteness, fascinated her, but the actual practice was tedious. Some people in History puzzled her and made her ponder, but the political parts angered her, and she hated ministers. Only in odd streaks did she get a poignant sense of acquisition and enrichment and enlarging from her studies; one afternoon, reading *As You Like It*; once when, with her blood, she heard a passage of Latin, and she knew how the blood beat in a Roman's body; so that ever after she felt she knew the Romans by contact. She enjoyed the vagaries of English Grammar, because it gave her pleasure to detect the live movements of words and sentences; and Mathematics, the very sight of the letters in Algebra, had a real lure for her.

She felt so much and so confusedly at this time, that her face got a queer, wondering, half-scared look, as if she were not sure what might seize upon her at any moment out of the unknown.

Odd little bits of information stirred unfathomable passion in her. When she knew that in the tiny brown buds of autumn were folded, minute and complete, the finished flowers of the summer nine months hence, tiny, folded up, and left there waiting, a flash of triumph and love went over her.

'I could never die while there was a tree,' she said passionately, sententiously, standing before a great ash in worship.

It was the people who, somehow, walked as an upright menace to her. Her life at this time was unformed, palpitating, essentially shrinking from all touch. She gave something to other people, but she was never herself, since she *had* no self. She was not afraid nor ashamed before trees, and birds, and the sky. But she shrank violently from people, ashamed she was not as they were, fixed, emphatic, but a wavering, undefined sensibility only, without form or being.

Assistant Teacher

She was walking down a small, mean, wet street, empty of people. The school squatted low within its railed, asphalt yard, that shone black with rain. The building was grimy, and horrible, dry plants were shadowily looking through the windows.

She entered the arched doorway of the porch. The whole place seemed to have a threatening expression, imitating the church's architecture, for the purpose of domineering, like a gesture of vulgar authority. She saw that one pair of feet had paddled across the flagstone floor of the porch. The place was silent, deserted, like an empty prison waiting the return of tramping feet.

Ursula went forward to the teachers' room that burrowed in a gloomy hole. She knocked timidly.

'Come in!' called a surprised man's voice, as from a prison cell. She entered the dark little room that never got any sun. The gas was lighted naked and raw. At the table a thin man in shirt-sleeves was rubbing a paper on a jelly-tray. He looked up at Ursula with his narrow, sharp face, said 'Good morning', then turned away again, and stripped the paper off the tray, glancing at the violet-coloured writing transferred, before he dropped the curled sheet aside among a heap.

Ursula watched him, fascinated. In the gaslight and gloom and the narrowness of the room, all seemed unreal.

'Isn't it a nasty morning,' she said.

'Yes,' he said, 'it's not much of weather.'

But in here it seemed that neither morning nor weather really existed. This place was timeless. He spoke in an occupied voice, like an echo. Ursula did not know what to say. She took off her waterproof.

'Am I early?' she asked.

The man looked first at the little clock, then at her. His eyes seemed to be sharpened to needle-points of vision.

'Twenty-five past,' he said. 'You're the second to come. I'm first this morning.'

Ursula sat down gingerly on the edge of a chair, and watched his thin red hands rubbing away on the white surface of the paper, then pausing, pulling up a corner of the sheet, peering, and rubbing away again. There was a great heap of curled white-and-scribbled sheets on the table.

'Must you do so many?' asked Ursula.

Again the man glanced up sharply. He was about thirty or thirty-three years old, thin, greenish, with a long nose and a sharp face. His eyes were blue, and sharp as points of steel, rather beautiful, the girl thought.

'Sixty-three,' he answered.

'So many!' she said, gently. Then she remembered.

'But they're not all for your class, are they?' she added.

'Why aren't they?' he replied, a fierceness in his voice.

Ursula was rather frightened by his mechanical ignoring of her, and his directness of statement. It was something new to her. She had never been treated like this before, as if she did not count, as if she were addressing a machine.

'It is too many,' she said sympathetically.

'You'll get about the same,' he said.

That was all she received. She sat rather blank, not knowing how to feel. Still she liked him. He seemed so cross. There was a queer, sharp, keen-edged feeling about him that attracted her and frightened her at the same time. It was so cold, and against his nature.

The door opened, and a short, neutral-tinted young woman of about twenty-eight appeared.

'Oh, Ursula,' the newcomer exclaimed. 'You *are* here early. My word, I'll warrant you don't keep it up. That's Mr Williamson's peg. *This* is yours. Standard Five teacher always has this. Aren't you going to take your hat off?'

Miss Violet Harby removed Ursula's waterproof from the peg on which it was hung, to one a little further down the row. She had already snatched the pins from her own stuff hat, and jammed them through her coat. She turned to Ursula, as she pushed up her frizzed, flat, dun-coloured hair.

'Isn't it a beastly morning,' she exclaimed, 'beastly! And if there's one thing I hate above another it's a wet Monday morning; – pack of kids trailing in anyhow-nohow, and no holding 'em –'

She had taken a black pinafore from a newspaper package, and was tying it round her waist.

'You've brought an apron, haven't you?' she said jerkily, glancing at Ursula. 'Oh – you'll want one. You've no idea what a sight you'll look before half-past four, what with chalk and ink and kids' dirty feet. – Well, I can send a boy down to mamma's for one.'

'Oh, it doesn't matter,' said Ursula.

'Oh, yes – I can send easily,' cried Miss Harby.

Ursula's heart sank. Everybody seemed so cocksure and so bossy. How was she going to get on with such jolty, jerky, bossy people? And Miss Harby had not spoken a word to the man at the table. She simply ignored him. Ursula felt the callous crude rudeness between the two teachers.

The two girls went out into the passage. A few children were already clattering in the porch.

'Jim Richards,' called Miss Harby, hard and authoritative. A boy came sheepishly forward.

'Shall you go down to our house for me, eh?' said Miss Harby, in a commanding, condescending, coaxing voice. She did not wait for an answer. 'Go down and ask mamma to send me one of my school pinas, for Miss Brangwen – shall you?'

The boy muttered a sheepish 'Yes, Miss,' and was moving away.

'Hey,' called Miss Harby. 'Come here – now what are you going for? What shall you say to mamma?'

'A school pina –' muttered the boy.

'Please, Mrs Harby, Miss Harby says will you send her another school pinafore for Miss Brangwen, because she's come without one.'

'Yes, Miss,' muttered the boy, head ducked, and was moving off. Miss Harby caught him back, holding him by the shoulder.

'What are you going to say?'

'Please, Mrs Harby, Miss Harby wants a pinny for Miss Brangwin,' muttered the boy very sheepishly.

'Miss *Brangwen*!' laughed Miss Harby, pushing him away. 'Here, you'd better have my umbrella – wait a minute.'

The unwilling boy was rigged up with Miss Harby's umbrella, and set off.

'Don't take long over it,' called Miss Harby, after him. Then she turned to Ursula, and said brightly:

'Oh, he's a caution, that lad – but not bad, you know.'

'No,' Ursula agreed, weakly.

The latch of the door clicked, and they entered the big room. Ursula glanced down the place. Its rigid, long silence was official and chilling. Half way down was a glass partition, the doors of which were open. A clock ticked re-echoing, and Miss Harby's voice sounded double as she said:

'This is the big room – Standard Five-Six-and-Seven. – Here's your place – Five –'

She stood in the near end of the great room. There was a small high teacher's desk facing a squadron of long benches, two high windows in the wall opposite.

It was fascinating and horrible to Ursula. The curious, unliving light in the room changed her character. She thought it was the rainy morning. Then she looked up again, because of the horrid feeling of being shut in a rigid, inflexible air, away from all feeling of the ordinary day; and she noticed that the windows were of ribbed, suffused glass.

The prison was round her now! She looked at the walls, colour washed, pale green and chocolate, at the large windows with frowsy geraniums against the pale glass, at the long rows of desks, arranged in a squadron, and dread filled her. This was a new world, a new life, with which she was threatened. But still excited, she climbed into her chair at her teacher's desk. It was high, and her feet could not reach the ground, but must rest on the step. Lifted up there, off the ground, she was in office. How queer, how queer it all was! How different it was from the mist of rain blowing over Cossethay. As she thought of her own village, a spasm of yearning crossed her, it seemed so far off, so lost to her.

She was here in this hard, stark reality – *reality*. It was queer that she should call this the reality, which she had never known till today, and which now so filled her with dread and dislike, that she wished she might go away. This was the reality, and Cossethay, her beloved, beautiful, well-known Cossethay, which was as herself unto her, that was minor reality. This prison of a school was reality. Here, then, she would sit in state, the queen of scholars! Here she would realize her dream of being the beloved teacher bringing light and joy to her children! But the desks before her had an abstract angularity that bruised her sentiment and made her shrink. She winced, feeling she had been a fool in her anticipations. She had brought her feelings and her generosity to where neither generosity nor emotion were wanted. And already she felt rebuffed, troubled by the new atmosphere, out of place.

She slid down, and they returned to the teachers' room. It was queer to feel that one ought to alter one's personality. She was nobody, there was no reality in herself, the reality was all outside of her, and she must apply herself to it.

Mr Harby was in the teachers' room standing before a big, open cupboard, in which Ursula could see piles of pink blotting paper, heaps of shiny new books, boxes of chalk, and bottles of coloured inks. It looked a treasure store.

The schoolmaster was a short, sturdy man, with a fine head, and a heavy jowl. Nevertheless, he was good-looking, with his shapely brows and nose, and his great, hanging moustache. He seemed absorbed in his work, and took no notice of Ursula's entry. There was something insulting in the way he could be so actively unaware of another person, so occupied.

When he had a moment of absence, he looked up from the table and said good-morning to Ursula. There was a pleasant light in his brown eyes. He seemed very manly and incontrovertible, like something she wanted to push over.

'You had a wet walk,' he said to Ursula.

'Oh, I don't mind, I'm used to it,' she replied, with a nervous little laugh.

But already he was not listening. Her words sounded ridiculous and babbling. He was taking no notice of her.

'You will sign your name here,' he said to her, as if she were some child – 'and the time when you come and go.'

Ursula signed her name in the time book and stood back. No one took any further notice of her. She beat her brains for something to say, but in vain.

'I'd let them in now,' said Mr Harby to the thin man, who was very hastily arranging his papers.

The assistant teacher made no sign of acquiescence, and went on with what he was doing. The atmosphere in the room grew tense. At the last moment Mr Brunt slipped into his coat.

'You will go to the girls' lobby,' said the schoolmaster to Ursula, with a fascinating, insulting geniality, purely official and domineering.

She went out and found Miss Harby, and another girl teacher, in the porch. On the asphalt yard the rain was falling. A toneless bell tang-tang-tanged drearily overhead, monotonously, insistently. It came to an end. Then Mr Brunt was seen, bareheaded, standing at the other gate of the school yard, blowing shrill blasts on a whistle and looking down the rainy, dreary street.

Boys in gangs and streams came trotting up, running past the master and with a loud clatter of feet and voices, over the yard to the boys' porch. Girls were running and walking through the other entrance.

In the porch where Ursula stood there was a great noise of girls, who were tearing off their coats and hats, and hanging them on the racks bristling with pegs. There was a smell of wet clothing, a tossing out of wet, draggled hair, a noise of voices and feet.

The mass of girls grew greater, the rage around the pegs grew steadier, the scholars tended to fall into little noisy gangs in the porch. Then Violet Harby clapped her hands, clapped them louder, with a shrill 'Quiet, girls, quiet!'

There was a pause. The hubbub died down but did not cease.

'What did I say?' cried Miss Harby, shrilly.

There was almost complete silence. Sometimes a girl, rather late, whirled into the porch and flung off her things.

'Leaders – in place,' commanded Miss Harby shrilly.

Pairs of girls in pinafores and long hair stood separate in the porch.

'Standard Four, Five and Six – fall in,' cried Miss Harby.

There was a hubbub, which gradually resolved itself into three columns of girls, two and two, standing smirking in the passage. In among the peg-racks, other teachers were putting the lower classes into ranks.

Ursula stood by her own Standard Five. They were jerking their shoulders, tossing their hair, nudging, writhing, staring, grinning, whispering and twisting.

A sharp whistle was heard, and Standard Six, the biggest girls, set off, led by Miss Harby. Ursula, with her Standard Five, followed after. She stood beside a smirking, grinning row of girls, waiting in a narrow passage. What she was herself she did not know.

Suddenly the sound of a piano was heard, and Standard Six set off hollowly down the big room. The boys had entered by another door. The piano played on, a march tune, Standard Five followed to the door of the big room. Mr Harby was seen away beyond the desk. Mr Brunt guarded the other door of the room. Ursula's class pushed up. She stood near them. They glanced and smirked and shoved.

'Go on,' said Ursula.

They tittered.

'Go on,' said Ursula, for the piano continued.

The girls broke loosely into the room. Mr Harby, who had seemed immersed in some occupation, away at his desk, lifted his head and thundered,

'Halt!'

There was a halt, the piano stopped. The boys who were just starting through the other door, pushed back. The harsh, subdued voice of Mr Brunt was heard, then the booming shout of Mr Harby, from far down the room:

'Who told Standard Five girls to come in like that?'

Ursula crimsoned. Her girls were glancing up at her, smirking their accusation.

'I sent them in, Mr Harby,' she said, in a clear, struggling voice. There was a moment of silence. Then Mr Harby roared from the distance:

'Go back to your places, Standard Five girls.'

The girls glanced up at Ursula, accusing, rather jeering, furtive. They pushed back. Ursula's heart hardened with ignominious pain.

'Forward – march,' came Mr Brunt's voice, and the girls set off, keeping time with the ranks of boys.

Ursula faced her class, some fifty-five boys and girls who stood filling the ranks of the desks. She felt utterly non-existent. She had no place nor being there. She faced the block of children.

Down the room she heard the rapid firing of questions. She stood before her class not knowing what to do. She waited painfully. Her block of children, fifty unknown faces, watched her, hostile, ready to jeer. She felt as if she were in torture over a fire of faces. And on every side she was naked to them. Of unutterable length and torture the seconds went by.

Then she gathered courage. She heard Mr Brunt asking questions in mental arithmetic. She stood near to her class, so that her voice need not be raised too much, and faltering, uncertain, she said:

'Seven hats at two-pence ha'penny each?'

A grin went over the faces of the class, seeing her commence. She was red and suffering. Then some hands shot up like blades, and she asked for the answer.

The day passed incredibly slowly. She never knew what to do, there came horrible gaps, when she was merely exposed to the children; and when, relying on some pert little girl for information, she had started a lesson, she did not know how to go on with it properly. The children were her masters. She deferred to them. She could always hear Mr Brunt. Like a machine, always in the same hard, high, inhuman voice he went on with his teaching, oblivious of everything. And before this inhuman number of children she was always at bay. She could not get away from it. There it was, this class of fifty collective children, depend-on her for command, for command it hated and resented. It made her feel she could not breathe: she must suffocate, it was so inhuman. They were so many, that they were not children. They were a squadron. She could not speak as she would to a child, because they were not individual children, they were a collective, inhuman thing.

Dinner time came, and stunned, bewildered, solitary, she went into the teachers' room for dinner. Never had she felt such a stranger to life before. It seemed to her she had just disembarked from some strange horrible state where everything was as in hell, a condition of hard, malevolent system. And she was not really free. The afternoon drew at her like some bondage.

The first week passed in a blind confusion. She did not know how to teach, and she felt she never would know. Mr Harby came down every now and then to her class, to see what she was doing. She felt so incompetent as he stood by, bullying and threatening, so unreal, that she wavered, became neutral and non-existent. But he stood there watching with that listening-genial smile of the eyes, that was really threatening; he said nothing, he made her go on teaching, she felt she had no soul in her body. Then he went away, and his going was like a derision. The class was his class. She was a wavering substitute. He thrashed and bullied, he was hated. But he was master. Though she was gentle and always considerate of her class, yet they belonged to Mr Harby, and they did not belong to her. Like some invincible source of the mechanism he kept all power to himself. And the class owned his power. And in school it was power, and power alone that mattered.

Soon Ursula came to dread him, and at the bottom of her dread was a seed of hate, for she despised him, yet he was master of her. Then she began to get on. All the other teachers hated him, and fanned their hatred among themselves. For he was master of them and the children, he stood like a wheel to make absolute his authority over the herd. That seemed to be his one reason in life, to hold blind authority over the school. His teachers were his subjects as much as the scholars. Only, because they had some authority, his instinct was to detest them.

Ursula could not make herself a favourite with him. From the first moment she set hard against him. She set against Violet Harby also. Mr Harby was, however, too much for her, he was something she could not come to grips with, something too strong for her. She tried to approach him as a young, bright girl usually approaches a man, expecting a little chivalrous courtesy. But the fact that she was a girl, a woman, was ignored or used as a matter for contempt against her. She did not know what she was, nor what she must be. She wanted to remain her own responsive, personal self.

So she taught on. She made friends with the Standard Three teacher, Maggie Schofield. Miss Schofield was about twenty years old, a subdued girl who held aloof from the other teachers. She was rather beautiful, meditative, and seemed to live in another, lovelier world.

Ursula took her dinner to school, and during the second week ate it in Miss Schofield's room. Standard Three classroom stood by itself and had windows on two sides, looking on to the playground. It was a passionate relief to find such a retreat in the jarring school. For there were pots of chrysanthemums and coloured leaves, and a big jar of berries: there were pretty little pictures on the wall, photogravure reproductions from Greuze, and Reynolds's *Age of Innocence*, giving an air of intimacy; so that the room, with its window space, its smaller, tidier desks, its touch of pictures and flowers, made Ursula at once glad. Here at last was a little personal touch, to which she could respond.

It was Monday. She had been at school a week and was getting used to the surroundings, though she was still an entire foreigner in herself. She looked forward to having dinner with Maggie. That was the bright spot in the day. Maggie was so strong and remote, walking with slow, sure steps down a hard road, carrying the dream within her. Ursula went through the class teaching as through a meaningless daze.

Her class tumbled out at mid-day in haphazard fashion. She did not yet realize what host she was gathering against herself by her superior tolerance, her kindness and her *laisser-aller*. They were gone, and she was rid of them, and that was all. She hurried away to the teachers' room.

Mr Brunt was crouching at the small stove, putting a little rice-pudding into the oven. He rose then, and attentively poked in a small saucepan on the hob with a fork. Then he replaced the saucepan lid.

'Aren't they done?' asked Ursula gaily, breaking in on his tense absorption.

She always kept a bright, blithe manner, and was pleasant to all the teachers. For she felt like the swan among the geese, of superior heritage and belonging. And her pride at being the swan in this ugly school was not yet abated.

'Not yet,' replied Mr Brunt, laconic.

'I wonder if my dish is hot,' she said, bending down at the oven. She half expected him to look for her, but he took no notice. She was hungry and she poked her finger eagerly in the pot to see if her brussels sprouts and potatoes and meat were ready. They were not.

'Don't you think it's rather jolly bringing dinner?' she said to Mr Brunt.

'I don't know as I do,' he said, spreading a serviette on a corner of the table, and not looking at her.

'I suppose it is too far for you to go home?'

'Yes,' he said. Then he rose and looked at her. He had the bluest, fiercest, most pointed eyes that she had ever met. He stared at her with growing fierceness.

'If I were you, Miss Brangwen,' he said, menacingly, 'I should get a bit tighter hand over my class.'

Ursula shrank.

'Would you?' she asked, sweetly, yet in terror. 'Aren't I strict enough?'

'Because,' he repeated, taking no notice of her, 'they'll get you down if you don't tackle 'em pretty quick. They'll pull you down, and worry you, till Harby gets you shifted – that's how it'll be. You won't be here another six weeks' – and he filled his mouth with food – 'if you don't tackle 'em quick.'

'Oh, but –' Ursula said, resentfully, ruefully. The terror was deep in her.

'Harby'll not help you. This is what he'll do – he'll let you go on, getting worse and worse, till either you clear out or he clears you out. It doesn't matter to me, except that you'll leave a class behind you as I hope *I* shan't have to cope with.'

She heard the accusation in the man's voice, and felt condemned. But still, school had not yet become a definite reality to her. She was shirking it. It was reality, but it was all outside her. And she fought against Mr Brunt's representation. She did not want to realize.

'Will it be so terrible?' she said, quivering, rather beautiful, but with a slight touch of condescension, because she would not betray her own trepidation.

'Terrible?' said the man, turning to his potatoes again. 'I dunno about terrible.'

'I *do* feel frightened,' said Ursula. 'The children seem so –'

'What?' said Miss Harby, entering at that moment.

'Why,' said Ursula, 'Mr Brunt says I ought to tackle my class,' and she laughed uneasily.

'Oh, you have to keep order if you want to teach,' said Miss Harby, hard, superior, trite.

Ursula did not answer. She felt non-valid before them.

'If you want to be let to *live*, you have,' said Mr Brunt.

'Well, if you can't keep order, what good *are* you?' said Miss Harby.

'An' you've got to do it by yourself,' – his voice rose like the bitter cry of the prophets. 'You'll get no *help* from anybody.'

'Oh indeed!' said Miss Harby. 'Some people can't be helped.' And she departed.

The air of hostility and disintegration, of wills working in antagonistic subordination, was hideous. Mr Brunt, subordinate, afraid, acid with shame, frightened her. Ursula wanted to run. She only wanted to clear out, not to understand.

Then Miss Schofield came in, and with her another, more restful note. Ursula at once turned for confirmation to the newcomer. Maggie remained personal within all this unclean system of authority.

'Is the big Anderson here?' she asked of Mr Brunt. And they spoke of some affair about two scholars, coldly, officially.

Miss Schofield took her brown dish, and Ursula followed with her own. The cloth was laid in the pleasant Standard Three room, there was a jar with two or three monthly roses on the table.

'It is so nice in here, you *have* made it different,' said Ursula gaily. But she was afraid. The atmosphere of the school was upon her.

'The big room,' said Miss Schofield, 'ha, it's misery to be in it!'

She too spoke with bitterness. She too lived in the ignominious position of an upper servant hated by the master above and the class beneath. She was, she knew, liable to attack from either side at any minute, or from both at once, for the authorities would listen to the complaints of parents, and both would turn round on the mongrel authority, the teacher.

So there was a hard, bitter withholding in Maggie Schofield even as she poured out her savoury mess of big golden beans and brown gravy.

'It is vegetarian hot-pot,' said Miss Schofield. 'Would you like to try it?'

'I should love to,' said Ursula.

Her own dinner seemed coarse and ugly beside this savoury clean dish.

'I've never eaten vegetarian things,' she said. 'But I should think they can be good.'

'I'm not really a vegetarian,' said Maggie, 'I don't like to bring meat to school.'

'No,' said Ursula, 'I don't think I do either.'

And again her soul rang an answer to a new refinement, a new liberty. If all vegetarian things were as nice as this, she would be glad to escape the slight uncleanness of meat.

'How good!' she cried.

'Yes,' said Miss Schofield, and she proceeded to tell her the receipt. The two girls passed on to talk about themselves. Ursula told all about the High School, and about the matriculation, bragging a little. She felt so poor here, in this ugly place. Miss Schofield listened with brooding, handsome face, rather gloomy.

'Couldn't you have got to some better place than this?' she asked at length.

'I didn't know what it was like,' said Ursula, doubtfully.

'Ah!' said Miss Schofield, and she turned aside her head with a bitter motion.

'Is it as horrid as it seems?' asked Ursula, frowning lightly, in fear.

'It *is*,' said Miss Schofield, bitterly. 'Ha! – is it *hateful*!'

Ursula's heart sank, seeing even Miss Schofield in the deadly bondage.

'It is Mr Harby,' said Maggie Schofield, breaking forth. 'I don't think I *could* live again in the big room – Mr Brunt's voice and Mr Harby – ah –'

She turned aside her head with a deep hurt. Some things she could not bear.

'Is Mr Harby really horrid?' asked Ursula, venturing into her own dread.

'He! – why, he's just a bully,' said Miss Schofield, raising her shamed dark eyes, that flamed with tortured contempt. 'He's not bad as long as you keep in with him, and refer to him, and do everything in his way – but – it's all so *mean*! It's just a question of fighting on both sides – and those great louts –'

She spoke with difficulty and with increased bitterness. She had evidently suffered. Her soul was raw with ignominy. Ursula suffered in response.

'But why is it so horrid?' she asked, helplessly.

'You can't do *anything*,' said Miss Schofield. 'He's against you on one side and he sets the children against you on the other. The children are simply awful. You've got to *make* them do everything. Everything, everything has got to come out of you. Whatever they learn, you've got to force it into them – and that's how it is.'

Ursula felt her heart faint inside her. Why must she grasp all this, why must she force learning on fifty-five reluctant children, having all the time an ugly, rude jealousy behind her, ready to throw her to the mercy of the herd of children, who would like to rend her as a weaker representative of authority. A great dread of her task possessed her. She saw Mr Brunt, Miss Harby, Miss Schofield, all the school-teachers, drudging unwillingly at the graceless task of compelling many children into one disciplined, mechanical set, reducing the whole set to an automatic state of obedience and attention, and then of commanding their acceptance of various pieces of knowledge. The first great task was to reduce sixty children to one state of mind, or being. This state must be produced automatically, through the will of the teacher, and the will of the whole school authority, imposed upon the will of the children. The point was that the headmaster and the teachers should have one will in authority, which should bring the will of the children into accord. But the headmaster was narrow and exclusive. The will of the teachers could not agree with his, their separate wills refused to be so subordinated. So there was a state of anarchy, leaving the final judgement to the children themselves, which authority should exist.

So there existed a set of separate wills, each straining itself to the utmost to exert its own authority. Children will never naturally acquiesce to sitting in a class and submitting to knowledge. They must be compelled by a stronger, wiser will. Against which will they must always strive to revolt. So that the first great effort of every teacher of a large class must be to bring the will of the children into accordance with his own will. And this he can only do by an abnegation of his personal self, and an application of a system of laws, for the purpose of achieving a certain calculable result, the imparting of certain knowledge. Whereas Ursula thought she was going to become the first wise teacher by making the whole business personal, and using no compulsion. She believed entirely in her own personality.

So that she was in a very deep mess. In the first place she was offering to a class a relationship which only one or two of the children were sensitive enough to appreciate, so that the mass were left outsiders, therefore against her. Secondly, she was placing herself in passive antagonism to the one fixed authority of Mr Harby, so that the scholars could more safely harry her. She did not know, but her instinct gradually warned her. She was tortured by the voice of Mr Brunt. On it went, jarring, harsh, full of hate, but so monotonous, it nearly drove her mad: always the same set, harsh monotony. The man was become a mechanism working on and on and on. But the personal man was in subdued friction all the time. It was horrible – all hate! Must she be like this? She could feel the ghastly necessity. She must become the same – put away the personal self, become an instrument, an abstraction, working upon a certain material, the class, to achieve a set purpose of making them know so much each day. And she could not submit. Yet gradually she felt the invincible iron closing upon her. The sun was being blocked out. Often when she went out at playtime and saw a luminous blue sky with changing clouds, it seemed just a fantasy, like a piece of painted scenery. Her heart was so black and tangled in the teaching, her personal self was shut in prison, abolished, she was subjugate to a bad, destructive will. How then could the sky be shining? There was no sky, there was no luminous atmosphere of out-of-doors. Only the inside of the school was real – hard, concrete, real and vicious.

She would not yet, however, let school quite overcome her. She always said, 'It is not a permanency, it will come to an end.' She could always see herself beyond the place, see the time when she had left it. On Sundays and on holidays, when she was away at Cossethay or in the woods where the beech-leaves were fallen, she could think of St Philip's Church School, and by an effort of will put it in the picture as a dirty little low-squatting building that made a very tiny mound under the sky, while the great beech-woods spread immense about her, and the afternoon was spacious and wonderful. Moreover the children, the scholars, they were insignificant little objects far away, oh, far away. And what power had they over her free soul? A fleeting thought of them, as she kicked her way through the beech-leaves, and they were gone. But her will was tense against them all the time.

All the while, they pursued her. She had never had such a passionate love of the beautiful things about her. Sitting on top of the tram-car, at evening, sometimes school was swept away as she saw a magnificent sky settling down. And her breast, her very hands, clamoured for the lovely flare of sunset. It was poignant almost to agony, her reaching for it. She almost cried aloud seeing the sundown so lovely.

For she was held away. It was no matter how she said to herself that school existed no more once she had left it. It existed. It was within her like a dark weight, controlling her movement. It was in vain the high-spirited, proud young girl flung off the school and its association with her. She was Miss Brangwen, she was Standard Five teacher, she had her most important being in her work now.

Constantly haunting her, like a darkness hovering over her heart and threatening to swoop down over it at every moment, was the sense that somehow, somehow she was brought down. Bitterly she denied unto

herself that she was really a school-teacher. Leave that to the Violet
Harbys. She herself would stand clear of the accusation. It was in vain
she denied it.

Within herself some recording hand seemed to point mechanically to
a negation. She was incapable of fulfilling her task. She could never for
a moment escape from the fatal weight of the knowledge.

And so she felt inferior to Violet Harby. Miss Harby was a splendid
teacher. She could keep order and inflict knowledge on a class with
remarkable efficiency. It was no good Ursula's protesting to herself that
she was infinitely, infinitely the superior of Violet Harby. She knew that
Violet Harby succeeded where she failed, and this in a task which was
almost a test of her. She felt something all the time wearing upon her,
wearing her down. She went about in these first weeks trying to deny it,
to say she was free as ever. She tried not to feel at a disadvantage before
Miss Harby, tried to keep up the effect of her own superiority. But a
great weight was on her, which Violet Harby could bear, and she herself
could not.

Though she did not give in, she never succeeded. Her class was getting
in worse condition, she knew herself less and less secure in teaching it.
Ought she to withdaw and go home again? Ought she to say she had
come to the wrong place, and so retire? Her very life was at test.

She went on doggedly, blindly, waiting for a crisis. Mr Harby had
now begun to persecute her. Her dread and hatred of him grew and
loomed larger and larger. She was afraid he was going to bully her and
destroy her. He began to persecute her because she could not keep her
class in proper condition, because her class was the weak link in the
chain which made up the school.

One of the offences was that her class was noisy and disturbed Mr
Harby, as he took Standard Seven at the other end of the room. She was
taking composition on a certain morning, walking in among the scholars.
Some of the boys had dirty ears and necks, their clothing smelled un-
pleasantly, but she could ignore it. She corrected the writing as she went.

'When you say "their fur is brown", how do you write "their"?' she
asked.

There was a little pause; the boys were always jeeringly backward in
answering. They had begun to jeer at her authority altogether.

'Please, Miss, t-h-e-i-r,' spelled a lad, loudly, with a note of mockery.

At that moment Mr Harby was passing.

'Stand up, Hill!' he called, in a big voice.

Everybody started. Ursula watched the boy. He was evidently poor, and rather cunning. A stiff bit of hair stood straight off his forehead, the rest fitted close to his meagre head. He was pale and colourless.

'Who told you to call out?' thundered Mr Harby.

The boy looked up and down, with a guilty air, and a cunning, cynical reserve.

'Please, Sir, I was answering,' he replied, with the same humble insolence.

'Go to my desk.'

The boy set off down the room, the big black jacket hanging in dejected folds about him, his thin legs, rather knocked at the knees, going already with the pauper's crawl, his feet in their big boots scarcely lifted. Ursula watched him in his crawling slinking progress down the room. He was one of *her* boys! When he got to the desk, he looked round, half furtively, with a sort of cunning grin and a pathetic leer at the big boys of Standard Seven. Then, pitiable, pale, in his dejected garments, he lounged under the menace of the headmaster's desk, with one thin leg crooked at the knee and the foot stuck out sideways, his hands in the low-hanging pockets of his man's jacket.

Ursula tried to get her attention back to the class. The boy gave her a little horror, and she was at the same time hot with pity for him. She felt she wanted to scream. She was responsible for the boy's punishment. Mr Harby was looking at her handwriting on the board. He turned to the class.

'Pens down.'

The children put down their pens and looked up.

'Fold arms.'

They pushed back their books and folded arms.

Ursula, stuck among the back forms, could not extricate herself.

'*What* is your composition about?' asked the headmaster. Every hand shot up. 'The –' stuttered some voice in its eagerness to answer.

'I wouldn't advise you to call out,' said Mr Harby. He would have a pleasant voice, full and musical, but for the detestable menace that always tailed in it. He stood unmoved, his eyes twinkling under his bushy black brows, watching the class. There was something fascinating in him, as he stood, and again she wanted to scream. She was all jarred, she did not know what she felt.

'Well, Alice?' he said.

'The rabbit,' piped a girl's voice.

'A very easy subject for Standard Five.'

Ursula felt a slight shame of incompetence. She was exposed before the class. And she was tormented by the contradictoriness of everything.

Mr Harby stood so strong, and so male, with his black brows and clear forehead, the heavy jaw, the big, overhanging moustache: such a man, with strength and male power, and a certain blind, native beauty. She might have liked him as a man. And here he stood in some other capacity, bullying over such a trifle as a boy's speaking out without permission. Yet he was not a little, fussy man. He seemed to have some cruel, stubborn, evil spirit, he was imprisoned in a task too small and petty for him, which yet, in a servile acquiescence, he would fulfil, because he had to earn his living. He had no finer control over himself, only this blind, dogged, wholesale will. He would keep the job going, since he must. And his job was to make the children spell the word 'caution' correctly, and put a capital letter after a full-stop. So at this he hammered with his suppressed hatred, always suppressing himself, till he was beside himself. Ursula suffered bitterly as he stood, short and handsome and powerful, teaching her class. It seemed such a miserable thing for him to be doing. He had a decent, powerful, rude soul. What did he care about the composition on 'The Rabbit'? Yet his will kept him there before the class, threshing the trivial subject. It was habit with him now, to be so little and vulgar, out of place. She saw the shamefulness of his position, felt the fettered wickedness in him which would blaze out into evil rage in the long run, so that he was like a persistent, strong creature tethered. It was really intolerable. The jarring was torture to her. She looked over the silent, attentive class that seemed to have crystallized into order and rigid, neutral form. This he had it in his power to do, to crystallize the children into hard, mute fragments, fixed under his will: his brute will, which fixed them by sheer force. She too must learn to subdue them to her will: she must. For it was her duty, since the school was such. He had crystallized the class into order. But to see him, a strong, powerful man, using all his power for such a purpose, seemed almost horrible. There was something hideous about it. The strange, genial light in his eye was really vicious, and ugly, his smile was one of torture. He could not be impersonal. He could not have a clear, pure purpose, he could only exercise his own brute will. He did not believe in the least in the education he kept inflicting year after year upon the children. So he must bully, only bully, even while it tortured his strong, wholesome nature with shame, like a spur always galling. He was so blind and ugly and out of place. Ursula could not bear it as he stood there. The whole situation was wrong and ugly.

The lesson was finished, Mr Harby went away. At the far end of the room she heard the whistle and the thud of the cane. Her heart stood still within her. She could not bear it, no, she could not bear it when the boy was beaten. It made her sick. She felt that she must go out of this school, this torture-place. And she hated the schoolmaster, thoroughly and finally. The brute, had he no shame? He should never be allowed to continue the atrocity of this bullying cruelty. Then Hill came crawling back, blubbering piteously. There was something desolate about his blubbering that nearly broke her heart. For after all, if she had kept her class in proper discipline, this would never have happened, Hill would never have called out and been caned.

She began the arithmetic lesson. But she was distracted. The boy Hill sat away on the back desk, huddled up, blubbering and sucking his hand. It was a long time. She dared not go near, nor speak to him. She felt ashamed before him. And she felt she could not forgive the boy for being the huddled, blubbering object, all wet and snivelled, which he was.

She went on correcting the sums. But there were too many children. She could not get round the class. And Hill was on her conscience. At last he had stopped crying, and sat bunched over his hands, playing quietly. Then he looked up at her. His face was dirty with tears, his eyes had a curious washed look, like the sky after rain, a sort of wanness. He bore no malice. He had already forgotten, and was waiting to be restored to the normal position.

'Go on with your work, Hill,' she said.

The children were playing over their arithmetic, and, she knew, cheating thoroughly. She wrote another sum on the blackboard. She could not get round the class. She went again to the front to watch. Some were ready. Some were not. What was she to do?

At last it was time for recreation. She gave the order to cease working, and in some way or other got her class out of the room. Then she faced the disorderly litter of blotted, uncorrected books, of broken rulers and chewed pens. And her heart sank in sickness. The misery was getting deeper.

The trouble went on and on, day after day. She had always piles of books to mark, myriads of errors to correct, a heart-wearying task that she loathed. And the work got worse and worse. When she tried to flatter herself that the composition grew more alive, more interesting, she had to see that the handwriting grew more and more slovenly, the books were filthy and disgraceful. She tried what she could, but it was of no use. But she was not going to take it seriously. Why should she? Why should she say to herself, that it mattered, if she failed to teach a class to write perfectly neatly? Why should she take the blame unto herself?

Pay day came, and she received four pounds two shillings and one penny. She was very proud that day. She had never had so much money before. And she had earned it all herself. She sat on top of the tram-car fingering the gold and fearing she might lose it. She felt so established and strong, because of it. And when she got home she said to her mother:

'It is pay day today, mother.'

'Ay,' said her mother coolly.

Then Ursula put down fifty shillings on the table.

'That is my board,' she said.

'Ay,' said her mother, letting it lie.

Ursula was hurt. Yet she had paid her scot. She was free. She paid for what she had. There remained moreover thirty-two shillings of her own. She would not spend any, she who was naturally a spendthrift, because she could not bear to damage her fine gold.

She had a standing ground now apart from her parents. She was something else besides the mere daughter of William and Anna Brangwen. She was independent. She earned her own living. She was an important member of the working community. She was sure that fifty shillings a month quite paid for her keep. If her mother received fifty shillings a month for each of the children she would receive twenty pounds a month and no clothes to provide. Very well then.

Ursula was independent of her parents. She now adhered elsewhere. Now, the 'Board of Education' was a phrase that rang significant to her, and she felt Whitehall far beyond her as her ultimate home. In the government, she knew which minister had supreme control over Education, and it seemed to her that, in some way, he was connected with her, as her father was connected with her.

She had another self, another responsibility. She was no longer Ursula Brangwen, daughter of William Brangwen. She was also Standard Five teacher in St Philip's School. And it was a case now of being Standard Five teacher, and nothing else. For she could not escape.

Neither could she succeed. That was her horror. As the weeks passed on, there was no Ursula Brangwen, free and jolly. There was only a girl of that name obsessed by the fact that she could not manage her class of children. At weekends there came days of passionate reaction, when she went mad with the taste of liberty, when merely to be free in the morning, to sit down at her embroidery and stitch the coloured silks was a passion of delight. For the prison house was always awaiting her! This was only a respite, as her chained heart knew well. So that she seized hold of the swift hours of the weekend, and wrung the last drop of sweetness out of them, in a little, cruel frenzy.

She did not tell anybody how this state was a torture to her. She did not confide, either to Gudrun or to her parents, how horrible she found it to be a school-teacher. But when Sunday night came, and she felt the Monday morning at hand, she was strung up tight with dreadful anticipation, because the strain and the torture was near again.

She did not believe that she could ever teach that great brutish class, in that brutal school; ever, ever. And yet, if she failed, she must in some way go under. She must admit that the man's world was too strong for her, she could not take her place in it; she must go down before Mr Harby. And all her life henceforth, she must go on, never having freed herself of the man's world, never having achieved the freedom of the great world of responsible work. Maggie had taken her place there, she had even stood level with Mr Harby and got free of him: and her soul was always wandering in far-off valleys and glades of poetry. Maggie was free. Yet there was something like subjection in Maggie's very freedom. Mr Harby, the man, disliked the reserved woman, Maggie. Mr Harby, the schoolmaster, respected his teacher, Miss Schofield.

For the present, however, Ursula only envied and admired Maggie. She herself had still to get where Maggie had got. She had still to make her footing. She had taken up a position on Mr Harby's ground, and she must keep it. For he was now beginning a regular attack on her, to drive her away out of his school. She could not keep order. Her class was a turbulent crowd, and the weak spot in the school's work. Therefore she must go, and someone more useful must come in her place, someone who could keep discipline.

The headmaster had worked himself into an obsession of fury against her. He only wanted her gone. She had come, she had got worse as the weeks went on, she was absolutely no good. His system, which was his very life in school, the outcome of his bodily movement, was attacked and threatened at the point where Ursula was included. She was the danger that threatened his body with a blow, a fall. And blindly, thoroughly, moving from strong instinct of opposition, he set to work to expel her.

When he punished one of her children as he had punished the boy Hill, for an offence against *himself*, he made the punishment extra heavy with the significance that the extra stroke came in because of the weak teacher who allowed all these things to be. When he punished for an offence against *her*, he punished lightly, as if offences against her were not significant. Which all the children knew, and they behaved accordingly.

Every now and again Mr Harby would swoop down to examine exercise books. For a whole hour, he would be going round the class, taking book after book, comparing page after page, whilst Ursula stood aside for all the remarks and fault-finding to be pointed at her through the scholars. It was true, since she had come, the composition books had grown more and more untidy, disorderly, filthy. Mr Harby pointed to the pages done before her régime, and to those done after, and fell into a passion of rage. Many children he sent out to the front with their books. And after he had thoroughly gone through the silent and quivering class he caned the worst offenders well, in front of the others, thundering in real passion of anger and chagrin.

'Such a condition in a class, I can't believe it! It is simply disgraceful! I can't think how you have been let to get like it! Every Monday morning I shall come down and examine these books. So don't think that because there is nobody paying any attention to you, that you are free to unlearn everything you ever learned, and go back till you are not fit for Standard Three. I shall examine all books every Monday –'

Then in a rage, he went away with his cane, leaving Ursula to confront a pale, quivering class, whose childish faces were shut in blank resentment, fear and bitterness, whose souls were full of anger and contempt of *her* rather than of the master, whose eyes looked at her with the cold, inhuman accusation of children. And she could hardly make mechanical words to speak to them. When she gave an order they obeyed with an insolent off-handedness, as if to say: 'As for you, do you think we would obey *you*, but for the master?' She sent the blubbering, caned boys to their seats, knowing that they too jeered at her and her authority, holding her weakness responsible for what punishment had overtaken them. And she knew the whole position, so that even her horror of physical beating and suffering sank to a deeper pain, and became a moral judgement upon her, worse than any hurt.

She must, during the next week, watch over her books, and punish any fault. Her soul decided it coldly. Her personal desire was dead for that day at least. She must have nothing more of herself in school. She was to be Standard Five teacher only. That was her duty. In school, she was nothing but Standard Five teacher. Ursula Brangwen must be excluded.

So that, pale, shut, at last distant and impersonal, she saw no longer the child, how his eyes danced, or how he had a queer little soul that could not be bothered with shaping handwriting so long as he dashed down what he thought. She saw no children, only the task that was to be done. And keeping her eyes there, on the task, and not on the child, she was impersonal enough to punish where she could otherwise only have sympathized, understood and condoned, to approve where she would have been merely uninterested before. But her interest had no place any more.

It was agony to the impulsive, bright girl of seventeen to become distant and official, having no personal relationship with the children. For a few days, after the agony of the Monday, she succeeded, and had some success with her class. But it was a state not natural to her, and she began to relax.

Then came another infliction. There were not enough pens to go round the class. She sent to Mr Harby for more. He came in person.

'Not enough pens, Miss Brangwen?' he said, with the smile and calm of exceeding rage against her.

'No, we are six short,' she said, quaking.

'Oh, how is that?' he said, menacingly. Then, looking over the class, he asked:

'How many are there here today?'

'Fifty-two,' said Ursula, but he did not take any notice, counting for himself.

'Fifty-two,' he said. 'And how many pens are there, Staples?'

Ursula was now silent. He would not heed her if she answered, since he had addressed the monitor.

'That's a very curious thing,' said Mr Harby, looking over the silent class with a slight grin of fury. All the childish faces looked up at him blank and exposed.

'A few days ago there were sixty pens for this class – now there are forty-eight. What is forty-eight from sixty, Williams?' There was a sinister suspense in the question. A thin, ferret-faced boy in a sailor suit started up exaggeratedly.

'Please, Sir!' he said. Then a slow, sly grin came over his face. He did not know. There was a tense silence. The boy dropped his head. Then he looked up again, a little cunning triumph in his eyes. 'Twelve,' he said.

'I would advise you to attend,' said the headmaster dangerously. The boy sat down.

'Forty-eight from sixty is twelve: so there are twelve pens to account for. Have you looked for them, Staples?'

'Yes, Sir.'

'Then look again.'

The scene dragged on. Two pens were found: ten were missing. Then the storm burst.

'Am I to have you thieving, besides your dirt and bad work and bad behaviour?' the headmaster began. 'Not content with being the worst-behaved and dirtiest class in the school, you are thieves into the bargain, are you? It is a very funny thing! Pens don't melt into the air: pens are not in the habit of mizzling away into nothing. What has become of them then? They must be somewhere. What has become of them? For they must be found, and found by Standard Five. They were lost by Standard Five, and they must be found.'

Ursula stood and listened, her heart hard and cold. She was so much upset, that she felt almost mad. Something in her tempted her to turn on the headmaster and tell him to stop, about the miserable pens. But she did not. She could not.

After every session, morning and evening, she had the pens counted. Still they were missing. And pencils and india-rubbers disappeared. She kept the class staying behind, till the things were found. But as soon as Mr Harby had gone out of the room, the boys began to jump about and shout, and at last they bolted in a body from the school.

This was drawing near a crisis. She could not tell Mr Harby because, while he would punish the class, he would make her the cause of the punishment, and her class would pay her back with disobedience and derision. Already there was a deadly hostility grown up between her and the children. After keeping in the class, at evening, to finish some work, she would find boys dodging behind her, calling after her: 'Brangwen, Brangwen – Proud-arse.'

When she went into Ilkeston of a Saturday morning with Gudrun, she heard again the voices yelling after her:

'Brangwen, Brangwen.'

She pretended to take no notice, but she coloured with shame at being held up to derision in the public street. She, Ursula Brangwen of Cossethay, could not escape from the Standard Five teacher which she was. In vain she went out to buy ribbon for her hat. They called after her, the boys she tried to teach.

And one evening, as she went from the edge of the town into the country, stones came flying at her. Then the passion of shame and anger surpassed her. She walked on unheeding, beside herself. Because of the darkness she could not see who were those that threw. But she did not want to know.

Only in her soul a change took place. Never more, and never more would she give herself as individual to her class. Never would she, Ursula Brangwen, the girl she was, the person she was, come into contact with those boys. She would be Standard Five teacher, as far away personally from her class as if she had never set foot in St Philip's School. She would just obliterate them all, and keep herself apart, take them as scholars only.

So her face grew more and more shut, and over her flayed, exposed soul of a young girl who had gone open and warm to give herself to the children, there set a hard, insentient thing, that worked mechanically according to a system imposed.

It seemed she scarcely saw her class the next day. She could only feel her will, and what she would have of this class which she must grasp into subjection. It was no good, any more, to appeal, to play upon the better feelings of the class. Her swift-working soul realized this.

She, as teacher, must bring them all, as scholars, into subjection. And this she was going to do. All else she would forsake. She had become hard and impersonal, almost avengeful on herself, as well as on them, since the stone throwing. She did not want to be a person, to be herself any more, after such humiliation. She would assert herself for mastery, be only teacher. She was set now. She was going to fight and subdue.

She knew by now her enemies in the class. The one she hated most was Williams. He was a sort of defective, not bad enough to be so classed. He could read with fluency, and had plenty of cunning intelligence. But he could not keep still. And he had a kind of sickness very repulsive to a sensitive girl, something cunning and etiolated and degenerate. Once he had thrown an ink-well at her, in one of his mad little rages. Twice he had run home out of class. He was a well-known character.

And he grinned up his sleeve at this girl-teacher, sometimes hanging round her to fawn on her. But this made her dislike him more. He had a kind of leech-like power.

From one of the children she took a supple cane, and this she determined to use when real occasion came. One morning, at composition, she said to the boy Williams:

'Why have you made this blot?'

'Please, Miss, it fell off my pen,' he whined out, in the mocking voice that he was so clever in using. The boys near snorted with laughter. For Williams was an actor, he could tickle the feelings of his hearers subtly. Particularly he could tickle the children with him into ridiculing his teacher, or indeed, any authority of which he was not afraid. He had that particular jail instinct.

'Then you must stay in and finish another page of composition,' said the teacher.

This was against her usual sense of justice, and the boy resented it derisively. At twelve o'clock she caught him slinking out.

'Williams, sit down,' she said.

And there she sat, and there he sat, alone, opposite to her, on the back desk, looking up at her with his furtive eyes every minute.

'Please, Miss, I've got to go an errand,' he called out insolently.

'Bring me your book,' said Ursula.

The boy came out, flapping his book along the desks. He had not written a line.

'Go back and do the writing you have to do,' said Ursula. And she sat at her desk, trying to correct books. She was trembling and upset. And for an hour the miserable boy writhed and grinned in his seat. At the end of that time he had done five lines.

'As it is so late now,' said Ursula, 'you will finish the rest this evening.'

The boy kicked his way insolently down the passage.

The afternoon came again. Williams was there, glancing at her, and her heart beat thick, for she knew it was a fight between them. She watched him.

During the geography lesson, as she was pointing to the map with her cane, the boy continually ducked his whitish head under the desk, and attracted the attention of other boys.

'Williams,' she said, gathering her courage, for it was critical now to speak to him, 'what are you doing?'

He lifted his face, the sore-rimmed eyes half smiling. There was something intrinsically indecent about him. Ursula shrank away.

'Nothing,' he replied, feeling a triumph.

'What are you doing?' she repeated, her heart-beat suffocating her.

'Nothing,' replied the boy, insolently, aggrieved, comic.

'If I speak to you again, you must go down to Mr Harby,' she said.

But this boy was a match even for Mr Harby. He was so persistent, so cringing, and flexible, he howled so when he was hurt, that the master hated more the teacher who sent him than he hated the boy himself. For of the boy he was sick of the sight. Which Williams knew. He grinned visibly.

Ursula turned to the map again, to go on with the geography lesson. But there was a little ferment in the class. Williams' spirit infected them all. She heard a scuffle, and then she trembled inwardly. If they all turned on her this time, she was beaten.

'Please Miss –' called a voice in distress.

She turned round. One of the boys she liked was ruefully holding out a torn celluloid collar. She heard the complaint, feeling futile.

'Go in front, Wright,' she said.

She was trembling in every fibre. A big, sullen boy, not bad but very difficult, slouched out to the front. She went on with the lesson, aware that Williams was making faces at Wright, and that Wright was grinning behind her. She was afraid. She turned to the map again. And she was afraid.

'Please Miss, Williams –' came a sharp cry, and a boy on the back row was standing up, with drawn, pained brows, half a mocking grin on his face, half real resentment against Williams – 'Please Miss, he's nipped me,' – and he rubbed his leg ruefully.

'Come in front, Williams,' she said.

The rat-like boy sat with his pale smile and did not move.

'Come in front,' she repeated, definite now.

'I shan't,' he cried, snarling, rat-like, grinning. Something went click in Ursula's soul. Her face and eyes set, she went through the class straight. The boy cowered before her glowering, fixed eyes. But she advanced on him, seized him by the arm, and dragged him from his seat. He clung to the form. It was a battle between him and her. Her instinct had suddenly become calm and quick. She jerked him from his grip, and dragged him, struggling and kicking, to the front. He kicked her several times, and clung to the forms as he passed, but she went on. The class was on its feet in excitement. She saw it, but made no move.

She knew if she let go the boy would dash to the door. Already he had run home once out of her class. So she snatched her cane from the desk, and brought it down on him. He was writhing and kicking. She saw his face beneath her, white, with eyes like the eyes of a fish, stony, yet full of hate and horrible fear. And she loathed him, the hideous writhing thing that was nearly too much for her. In horror lest he should overcome her, and yet at the heart quite calm, she brought down the cane again and again, whilst he struggled making inarticulate noises, and lunging vicious kicks at her. With one hand she managed to hold him, and now and then the cane came down on him. He writhed, like a mad thing. But the pain of the strokes cut through his writhing, vicious, coward's courage, bit deeper, till at last, with a long whimper that became a yell, he went limp. She let him go, and he rushed at her, his teeth and eyes glinting. There was a second of agonized terror in her heart: he was a beast thing. Then she caught him, and the cane came down on him. A few times, madly, in a frenzy, he lunged and writhed, to kick her. But again the cane broke him, he sank with a howling yell on the floor, and like a beaten beast lay there yelling.

Mr Harby had rushed up towards the end of this performance.

'What's the matter?' he roared.

Ursula felt as if something were going to break in her.

'I've thrashed him,' she said, her breast heaving, forcing out the words on the last breath. The headmaster stood choked with rage, helpless. She looked at the writhing, howling figure on the floor.

'Get up,' she said. The thing writhed away from her. She took a step forward. She had realized the presence of the headmaster for one second, and then she was oblivious of it again.

'Get up,' she said. And with a little dart the boy was on his feet. His yelling dropped to a mad blubber. He had been in a frenzy.

'Go and stand by the radiator,' she said.

As if mechanically, blubbering, he went.

The headmaster stood robbed of movement and speech. His face was yellow, his hands twitched convulsively. But Ursula stood stiff not far from him. Nothing could touch her now: she was beyond Mr Harby. She was as if violated to death.

The headmaster muttered something, turned, and went down the room, whence, from the far end, he was heard roaring in a mad rage at his own class.

The boy blubbered wildly by the radiator. Ursula looked at the class. There were fifty pale, still faces watching her, a hundred round eyes fixed on her in an attentive, expressionless stare.

'Give out the history readers,' she said to the monitors.

There was dead silence. As she stood there, she could hear again the ticking of the clock, and the chock of piles of books taken out of the low cupboard. Then came the faint flap of books on the desks. The children passed in silence, their hands working in unison. They were no longer a pack, but each one separated into a silent, closed thing.

'Take page 125, and read that chapter,' said Ursula.

There was a click of many books opened. The children found the page, and bent their heads obediently to read. And they read, mechanically.

Ursula, who was trembling violently, went and sat in her high chair. The blubbering of the boy continued. The strident voice of Mr Brunt, the roar of Mr Harby, came muffled through the glass partition. And now and then a pair of eyes rose from the reading book, rested on her a moment, watchful, as if calculating impersonally, then sank again.

She sat still without moving, her eyes watching the class, unseeing. She was quite still, and weak. She felt that she could not raise her hand from the desk. If she sat there for ever, she felt she could not move again, nor utter a command. It was a quarter past four. She almost dreaded the closing of the school, when she would be alone.

The class began to recover its ease, the tension relaxed. Williams was still crying. Mr Brunt was giving orders for the closing of the lesson. Ursula got down.

'Take your place, Williams,' she said.

He dragged his feet across the room, wiping his face on his sleeve. As he sat down, he glanced at her furtively, his eyes still redder. Now he looked like some beaten rat.

At last the children were gone. Mr Harby trod by heavily, without looking her way, or speaking. Mr Brunt hesitated as she was locking her cupboard.

'If you settle Clarke and Letts in the same way, Miss Brangwen, you'll be all right,' he said, his blue eyes glancing down in a strange fellowship, his long nose pointing at her.

'Shall I?' she laughed nervously. She did not want anybody to talk to her.

As she went along the street, clattering on the granite pavement, she was aware of boys dodging behind her. Something struck her hand that was carrying her bag, bruising her. As it rolled away she saw that it was a potato. Her hand was hurt, but she gave no sign. Soon she would take the tram.

She was afraid, and strange. It was to her quite strange and ugly, like some dream where she was degraded. She would have died rather than admit it to anybody. She could not look at her swollen hand. Something had broken in her; she had passed a crisis. Williams was beaten, but at a cost.

Feeling too much upset to go home, she rode a little farther into the town, and got down from the tram at a small tea-shop. There, in the dark little place behind the shop, she drank her tea and ate bread and butter. She did not taste anything. The taking tea was just a mechanical action, to cover over her existence. There she sat in the dark, obscure little place, without knowing. Only unconsciously she nursed the back of her hand, which was bruised.

When finally she took her way home, it was sunset red across the west. She did not know why she was going home. There was nothing for her there. She had, true, only to pretend to be normal. There was nobody she could speak to, nowhere to go for escape. But she must keep on, under this red sunset, alone, knowing the horror in humanity, that would destroy her, and with which she was at war. Yet it had to be so.

In the morning again she must go to school. She got up and went without murmuring even to herself. She was in the hands of some bigger, stronger, coarser will.

School was fairly quiet. But she could feel the class watching her, ready to spring on her. Her instinct was aware of the class instinct to catch her if she were weak. But she kept cold and was guarded.

Williams was absent from school. In the middle of the morning there was a knock at the door: someone wanted the headmaster. Mr Harby went out, heavily, angrily, nervously. He was afraid of irate parents. After a moment in the passage, he came again into school.

'Sturgess,' he called to one of the larger boys. 'Stand in front of the class and write down the name of anyone who speaks. Will you come this way, Miss Brangwen.'

He seemed vindictively to seize upon her.

Ursula followed him, and found in the lobby a thin woman with a whitish skin, not ill-dressed in a grey costume and a purple hat.

'I called about Vernon,' said the woman, speaking in a refined accent. There was about the woman altogether an appearance of refinement and of cleanliness, curiously contradicted by her half-beggar's deportment, and a sense of her being unpleasant to touch, like something going bad inside. She was neither a lady nor an ordinary working man's wife, but a creature separate from society. By her dress she was not poor.

Ursula knew at once that she was Williams' mother, and that he was Vernon. She remembered that he was always clean, and well-dressed, in a sailor suit. And he had this same peculiar, half transparent unwholesomeness, rather like a corpse.

'I wasn't able to send him to school today,' continued the woman, with a false grace of manner. 'He came home last night *so* ill – he was violently sick – I thought I should have to send for the doctor. – You know he has a weak heart.'

The woman looked at Ursula with her pale, dead eyes.

'No,' replied the girl, 'I did not know.'

She stood still with repulsion and uncertainty. Mr Harby, large and male, with his overhanging moustache, stood by with a slight, ugly smile at the corner of his eyes. The woman went on insidiously, not quite human:

'Oh yes, he has had heart disease ever since he was a child. That is why he isn't very regular at school. And it is very bad to beat him. He was awfully ill this morning – I shall call on the doctor as I go back.'

'Who is staying with him now, then?' put in the deep voice of the schoolmaster, cunningly.

'Oh, I left him with a woman who comes in to help me – and who understands him. But I shall call in the doctor on my way home.'

Ursula stood still. She felt vague threats in all this. But the woman was so utterly strange to her, that she did not understand.

'He told me he had been beaten,' continued the woman, 'and when I undressed him to put him to bed, his body was covered with marks – I could show them to any doctor.'

Mr Harby looked at Ursula to answer. She began to understand. The woman was threatening to take out a charge of assault on her son against her. Perhaps she wanted money.

'I caned him,' she said. 'He was so much trouble.'

'I'm sorry if he was troublesome,' said the woman, 'but he must have been shamefully beaten. I could show the marks to any doctor. I'm sure it isn't allowed, if it was known.'

'I caned him while he kept kicking me,' said Ursula, getting angry because she was half excusing herself, Mr Harby standing there with the twinkle at the side of his eyes, enjoying the dilemma of the two women.

'I'm sure I'm sorry if he behaved badly,' said the woman. 'But I can't think he deserved treating as he has been. I can't send him to school, and really can't afford to pay the doctor. – Is it allowed for the teacher to beat the children like that, Mr Harby?'

The headmaster refused to answer. Ursula loathed herself, and loathed Mr Harby with his twinkling cunning and malice on the occasion. The other miserable woman watched her chance.

'It is an expense to me, and I have a great struggle to keep my boy decent.'

Ursula still would not answer. She looked out at the asphalt yard, where a dirty rag of paper was blowing.

'And it isn't allowed to beat a child like that, I am sure, especially when he is delicate.'

Ursula stared with a set face on the yard, as if she did not hear. She loathed all this, and had ceased to feel or to exist.

'Though I know he is troublesome sometimes – but I think it was too much. His body is covered with marks.'

Mr Harby stood sturdy and unmoved, waiting now to have done, with the twinkling, tiny wrinkles of an ironical smile at the corners of his eyes. He felt himself master of the situation.

'And he was violently sick. I couldn't possibly send him to school today. He couldn't keep his head up.'

Yet she had no answer.

'You will understand, Sir, why he is absent,' she said, turning to Mr Harby.

'Oh yes,' he said, rough and off-hand. Ursula detested him for his male triumph. And she loathed the woman. She loathed everything.

'You will try to have it remembered, Sir, that he has a weak heart. He *is* so sick after these things.'

'Yes,' said the headmaster, 'I'll see about it.'

'I know he is troublesome,' the woman only addressed herself to the male now – 'but if you could have him punished without beating – he is really delicate.'

Ursula was beginning to feel upset. Harby stood in rather superb mastery, the woman cringing to him to tickle him as one tickles trout.

'I had come to explain why he was away this morning, Sir. You will understand.'

She held out her hand. Harby took it and let it go, surprised and angry.

'Good morning,' she said, and she gave her gloved, seedy hand to Ursula. She was not ill-looking, and had a curious insinuating way, very distasteful yet effective.

'Good morning, Mr Harby, and thank you.'

The figure in the grey costume and the purple hat was going across the school yard with a curious lingering walk. Ursula felt a strange pity for her, and revulsion from her. She shuddered. She went into the school again.

The next morning Williams turned up, looking paler than ever, very neat and nicely dressed in his sailor blouse. He glanced at Ursula with a half-smile: cunning, subdued, ready to do as she told him. There was something about him that made her shiver. She loathed the idea of having laid hands on him. His elder brother was standing outside the gate at playtime, a youth of about fifteen, tall and thin and pale. He raised his hat, almost like a gentleman. But there was something subdued, insidious about him too.

'Who is it?' said Ursula.

'It's the big Williams,' said Violet Harby roughly. '*She* was here yesterday, wasn't she?'

'Yes.'

'It's no good her coming – her character's not good enough for her to make any trouble.'

Ursula shrank from the brutality and the scandal. But it had some vague, horrid fascination. How sordid everything seemed! She felt sorry for the queer woman with the lingering walk, and those queer, insidious boys. The Williams in her class was wrong somewhere. How nasty it was altogether.

So the battle went on till her heart was sick. She had several more boys to subjugate before she could establish herself. And Mr Harby hated her almost as if she were a man. She knew now that nothing but a thrashing would settle some of the big louts who wanted to play cat and mouse with her. Mr Harby would not give them the thrashing if he could help it. For he hated the teacher, the stuck-up, insolent high-school miss with her independence.

'Now, Wright, what have you done this time?' he would say genially to the boy who was sent to him from Standard Five for punishment. And he left the lad standing, lounging, wasting his time.

So that Ursula would appeal no more to the headmaster, but, when she was driven wild, she seized her cane, and slashed the boy who was insolent to her, over head and ears and hands. And at length they were afraid of her, she had them in order.

But she had paid a great price out of her own soul, to do this. It seemed as if a great flame had gone through her and burnt her sensitive tissue. She who shrank from the thought of physical suffering in any form, had been forced to fight and beat with a cane and rouse all her instincts to hurt. And afterwards she had been forced to endure the sound of their blubbering and desolation, when she had broken them to order.

Oh, and sometimes she felt as if she would go mad. What did it matter, what did it matter if their books were dirty and they did not obey? She would rather, in reality, that they disobeyed the whole rules of the school, than that they should be beaten, broken, reduced to this crying, hopeless state. She would rather bear all their insults and insolences a thousand times than reduce herself and them to this. Bitterly she repented having got beside herself, and having tackled the boy she had beaten.

Yet it had to be so. She did not want to do it. Yet she had to. Oh why, why had she leagued herself to this evil system where she must brutalize herself to live? Why had she become a school-teacher, why, why?

The children had forced her to the beatings. No, she did not pity them. She had come to them full of kindness and love, and they would have torn her to pieces. They chose Mr Harby. Well then, they must know her as well as Mr Harby, they must first be subjugate to her. For she was not going to be made nought, no, neither by them, nor by Mr Harby, nor by all the system around her. She was not going to be put down, prevented from standing free. It was not to be said of her, she could not take her place and carry out her task. She would fight and hold her place in this state also, in the world of work and man's convention.

She was isolated now from the life of her childhood, a foreigner in a new life, of work and mechanical consideration. She and Maggie, in their dinner hours and their occasional teas at the little restaurant, discussed life and ideas. Maggie was a great suffragette, trusting in the vote. To

Ursula the vote was never a reality. She had within her the strange, passionate knowledge of religion and living far transcending the limits of the automatic system that contained the vote. But her fundamental, organic knowledge had as yet to take form and rise to utterance. For her, as for Maggie, the liberty of woman meant something real and deep. She felt that somewhere, in something, she was not free. And she wanted to be. She was in revolt. For once she were free she could get somewhere. Ah, the wonderful, real somewhere that was beyond her, the somewhere that she felt deep, deep inside her.

In coming out and earning her own living she had made a strong, cruel move towards freeing herself. But having more freedom she only became more profoundly aware of the big want. She wanted so many things. She wanted to read great, beautiful books, and be rich with them; she wanted to see beautiful things, and have the joy of them for ever; she wanted to know big, free people; and there remained always the want she could put no name to.

It was so difficult. There were so many things, so much to meet and surpass. And one never knew where one was going. It was a blind fight. She had suffered bitterly in this school of St Philip's. She was like a young filly that has been broken in to the shafts, and has lost its freedom. And now she was suffering bitterly from the agony of the shafts. The agony, the galling, the ignominy of her breaking in. This wore into her soul. But she would never submit. To shafts like these she would never submit for long. But she would know them. She would serve them that she might destroy them.

She and Maggie went to all kinds of places together, to big suffrage meetings in Nottingham, to concerts, to theatres, to exhibitions of pictures. Ursula saved her money and bought a bicycle, and the two girls rode to Lincoln, to Southwell, and into Derbyshire. They had an endless wealth of things to talk about. And it was a great joy, finding, discovering.

But Ursula never told about Winifred Inger. That was a sort of secret side-show to her life, never to be opened. She did not even think of it. It was the closed door she had not the strength to open.

Once she was broken in to her teaching, Ursula began gradually to have a new life of her own again. She was going to college in eighteen months' time. Then she would take her degree, and she would – ah, she would perhaps be a big woman, and lead a movement. Who knows? – At any rate she would go to college in eighteen months' time. All that mattered now was work, work.

And till college, she must go on with this teaching in St Philip's School, which was always destroying her, but which she could now manage, without spoiling all her life. She would submit to it for a time, since the time had a definite limit.

The class-teaching itself at last became almost mechanical. It was a strain on her, an exhausting wearying strain, always unnatural. But there was a certain amount of pleasure in the sheer oblivion of teaching, so much work to do, so many children to see after, so much to be done, that one's self was forgotten. When the work had become like habit to her, and her individual soul was left out, had its growth elsewhere, then she could be almost happy.

Her real, individual self drew together and became more coherent during these two years of teaching, during the struggle against the odds of class teaching. It was always a prison to her, the school. But it was a prison where her wild, chaotic soul became hard and independent. When she was well enough and not tired, then she did not hate the teaching. She enjoyed getting into the swing of work of a morning, putting forth all her strength, making the thing go. It was for her a strenuous form of exercise. And her soul was left to rest, it had the time of torpor in which to gather itself together in strength again. But the teaching hours were too long, the tasks too heavy, and the disciplinary condition of the school too unnatural for her. She was worn very thin and quivering.

She came to school in the morning seeing the hawthorn flowers wet, the little, rosy grains swimming in a bowl of dew. The larks quivered their song up into the new sunshine, and the country was so glad. It was a violation to plunge into the dust and greyness of the town.

So that she stood before her class unwilling to give herself up to the activity of teaching, to turn her energy, that longed for the country and for joy of early summer, into the dominating of fifty children and the transferring to them some morsels of arithmetic. There was a little absentness about her. She could not force herself into forgetfulness. A jar of buttercups and fool's-parsley in the window-bottom kept her away in the meadows, where in the lush grass the moon-daisies were half-submerged, and a spray of pink ragged robin. Yet before her were faces of fifty children. They were like almost big daisies in a dimness of the grass.

A brightness was on her face, a little unreality in her teaching. She could not quite see her children. She was struggling between two worlds, her own world of young summer and flowers, and this other world of work. And the glimmer of her own sunlight was between her and her class.

Then the morning passed with a strange far-awayness and quietness. Dinner-time came, when she and Maggie ate joyously, with all the windows open. And then they went out into St Philip's churchyard, where was a shadowy corner under red hawthorn trees. And there they talked and read Shelley or Browning or some work about 'Woman and Labour'.

And when she went back to school, Ursula lived still in the shadowy corner of the graveyard, where pink-red petals lay scattered from the hawthorn tree, like myriad tiny shells on a beach, and a church bell sometimes rang sonorously, and sometimes a bird called out, whilst Maggie's voice went on low and sweet.

These days she was happy in her soul: oh, she was so happy, that she wished she could take her joy and scatter it in armfuls broadcast. She made her children happy too, with a little tingling of delight. But to her, the children were not a school class this afternoon. They were flowers, birds, little bright animals, children, anything. They only were not Standard Five. She felt no responsibility for them. It was for once a game, this teaching. And if they got their sums wrong, what matter? And she would take a pleasant bit of reading. And instead of history with dates, she would tell a lovely tale. And for grammar, they could have a bit of written analysis that was not difficult, because they had done it before:

She shall be sportive as the fawn
That wild with glee across the lawn
Or up the mountain springs.

She wrote that from memory, because it pleased her.

So the golden afternoon passed away and she went home happy. She had finished her day of school, and was free to plunge into the glowing evening of Cossethay. And she loved walking home. But it had not been school. It had been playing at school beneath red hawthorn blossom.

She could not go on like this. The quarterly examination was coming, and her class was not ready. It irritated her that she must drag herself away from her happy self, and exert herself with all her strength to force, to compel this heavy class of children to work hard at arithmetic. They did not want to work, she did not want to compel them. And yet, some second conscience gnawed at her, telling her the work was not properly done. It irritated her almost to madness, and she let loose all the irritation in the class. Then followed a day of battle and hate and violence, when she went home raw, feeling the golden evening taken away from her, herself incarcerated in some dark, heavy place, and chained there with a consciousness of having done badly at work.

What good was it that it was summer, that right till evening, when the corncrakes called, the larks would mount up into the light, to sing once more about nightfall. What good was it all, when she was out of tune, when she must only remember the burden and shame of school that day.

And still, she hated school. Still she cried, she did not believe in it. Why should the children learn, and why should she teach them? It was all so much milling the wind. What folly was it that made life into this, the fulfilling of some stupid, factitious duty? It was all so made up, so unnatural. The school, the sums, the grammar, the quarterly examinations, the registers – it was all a barren nothing!

Why should she give her allegiance to this world, and let it dominate her, that her own world of warm sun and growing, sap-filled life was turned into nothing? She was not going to do it. She was not going to be prisoner in the dry, tyrannical man-world. She was not going to care about it. What did it matter if her class did ever so badly in the quarterly examination. Let it – what did it matter?

Nevertheless, when the time came, and the report on her class was bad, she was miserable, and the joy of the summer was taken away from her, she was shut up in gloom. She could not really escape from this world of system and work, out into her fields where she was happy. She must have her place in the working world, be a recognized member with full rights there. It was more important to her than fields and sun and poetry, at this time. But she was only the more its enemy.

It was a very difficult thing, she thought, during the long hours of intermission in the summer holidays, to be herself, her happy self that enjoyed so much to lie in the sun, to play and swim and be content, and also to be a school-teacher getting results out of a class of children. She dreamed fondly of the time when she need not be a teacher any more. But vaguely, she knew that responsibility had taken place in her for ever, and as yet her prime business was to work.

The autumn passed away, the winter was at hand. Ursula became more and more an inhabitant of the world of work, and of what is called life. She could not see her future, but a little way off was college, and to the thought of this she clung fixedly. She would go to college, and get her two or three years' training, free of cost. Already she had applied and had her place appointed for the coming year.

So she continued to study for her degree. She would take French, Latin, English, Mathematics and Botany. She went to classes in Ilkeston, she studied at evening. For there was this world to conquer, this knowledge to acquire, this qualification to attain. And she worked with intensity, because of a want inside her that drove her on. Almost everything was subordinated now to this one desire to take her place in the world.

What kind of place it was to be she did not ask herself. The blind desire drove her on. She must take her place.

She knew she would never be much of a success as an elementary school-teacher. But neither had she failed. She hated it, but she had managed it. . . .

Ursula left school at the end of July, when the summer holiday commenced. The morning outside was bright and sunny, and the freedom got inside the schoolroom this last day. It was as if the walls of the school were going to melt away. Already they seemed shadowy and unreal. It was breaking-up morning. Soon scholars and teachers would be outside, each going his own way. The irons were struck off, the sentence was expired, the prison was a momentary shadow halting about them. The children were carrying away books and inkwells, and rolling up maps. All their faces were bright with gladness and goodwill. There was a bustle of cleaning and clearing away all marks of this last term of imprisonment. They were all breaking free. Busily, eagerly, Ursula made up her totals of attendances in the register. With pride she wrote down the thousands: to so many thousands of children had she given another session's lessons. It looked tremendous. The excited hours passed slowly in suspense. Then at last it was over. For the last time, she stood before her children whilst they said their prayers and sang a hymn. Then it was over.

'Good-bye, children,' she said. 'I shall not forget you, and you must not forget me.'

'No, miss,' cried the children in chorus, with shining faces.

She stood smiling on them, moved, as they filed out. Then she gave her monitors their term sixpences, and they too departed. Cupboards were locked, blackboards washed, inkwells and dusters removed. The place stood bare and vacated. She had triumphed over it. It was a shell now. She had fought a good fight here, and it had not been altogether unenjoyable. She owed some gratitude even to this hard, vacant place, that stood like a memorial or a trophy. So much of her life had been fought for and won and lost here. Something of this school would always belong to her, something of her to it. She acknowledged it. And now came the leave-taking.

In the teachers' room the teachers were chatting and loitering, talking excitedly of where they were going: to the Isle of Man, to Llandudno, to Yarmouth. They were eager, and attached to each other, like comrades leaving a ship.

Then it was Mr Harby's turn to make a speech to Ursula. He looked handsome, with his silver-grey temples and black brows, and his imperturbable male solidity.

'Well,' he said, 'we must say good-bye to Miss Brangwen and wish her all good fortune for the future. I suppose we shall see her again some time, and hear how she is getting on.'

'Oh yes,' said Ursula, stammering, blushing, laughing. 'Oh yes, I shall come and see you.'

Then she realized that this sounded too personal, and she felt foolish.

'Miss Schofield suggested these two books,' he said, putting a couple of volumes on the table: 'I hope you will like them."

Ursula feeling very shy picked up the books. There was a volume of Swinburne's poetry, and a volume of Meredith's.

'Oh I shall love them,' she said. 'Thank you very much – thank you all so much – it is so –'

She stuttered to an end, and very red, turned the leaves of the books eagerly, pretending to be taking the first pleasure, but really seeing nothing.

Mr Harby's eyes were twinkling. He alone was at his ease, master of the situation. It was pleasing to him to make Ursula the gift, and for once extend good feeling to his teachers. As a rule, it was so difficult, each one was so strained in resentment under his rule.

'Yes,' he said, 'we hoped you would like the choice –'

He looked with his peculiar, challenging smile for a moment, then returned to his cupboards.

Ursula felt very confused. She hugged her books, loving them. And she felt that she loved all the teachers, and Mr Harby. It was very confusing.

At last she was out. She cast one hasty glance over the school buildings squatting on the asphalt yard in the hot, glistening sun, one look down the well-known road, and turned her back on it all. Something strained in her heart. She was going away.

'Well, good luck,' said the last of the teachers, as she shook hands at the end of the road. 'We'll expect you back some day.'

He spoke in irony. She laughed, and broke away. She was free. As she sat on the top of the tram in the sunlight, she looked round her with tremendous delight. She had left something which had meant much to her. She would not go to school any more, and do the familiar things. Queer! There was a little pang amid her exultation, of fear, not of regret. Yet how she exulted this morning!

She was tremulous with pride and joy. She loved the two books. They were tokens to her, representing the fruit and trophies of her two years which, thank God, were over.

'To Ursula Brangwen, with best wishes for her future, and in warm memory of the time she spent in St Philip's School,' was written in the headmaster's neat, scrupulous handwriting. She could see the careful hand holding the pen, the thick fingers with tufts of black hair on the back of each one.

He had signed, all the teachers had signed. She liked having all their signatures. She felt she loved them all. They were her fellow-workers. She carried away from the school a pride she could never lose. She had her place as comrade and sharer in the work of the school, her fellow teachers had signed to her, as one of them. And she was one of all workers, she had put in her tiny brick to the fabric man was building, she had qualified herself as co-builder.

Training College

Term began. She went into town each day by train. The cloistered quiet of the college began to close around her.

She was not at first disappointed. The big college built of stone, standing in the quiet street, with a rim of grass and lime-trees all so peaceful: she felt it remote, a magic land. Its architecture was foolish, she knew from her father. Still, it was different from that of all other buildings. Its rather pretty, plaything, Gothic form was almost a style, in the dirty industrial town.

She liked the hall with its big stone chimney-piece and its Gothic arches supporting the balcony above. To be sure the arches were ugly, the chimney-piece of cardboard-like carved stone, with its armorial decoration, looked silly just opposite the bicycle stand and the radiator, whilst the great notice-board with its fluttering papers seemed to slam away all sense of retreat and mystery from the far wall. Nevertheless, amorphous as it might be, there was in it a reminiscence of the wondrous, cloistral origin of education. Her soul flew straight back to medieval times, when the monks of God held the learning of men and imparted it within the shadows of religion. In this spirit she entered college.

The harshness and vulgarity of the lobbies and cloak-rooms hurt her at first. Why was it not all beautiful? But she could not openly admit her criticism. She was on holy ground.

She wanted all the students to have a high, pure spirit, she wanted them to say only the real, genuine things, she wanted their faces to be still and luminous as the nuns' and the monks' faces.

Alas, the girls chattered and giggled and were nervous, they were dressed up and frizzed, the men looked mean and clownish.

Still, it was lovely to pass along the corridor with one's books in one's hands, to push the swinging, glass-panelled door, and enter the big room where the first lecture would be given. The windows were large and lofty, the myriad brown students' desks stood waiting, the great blackboard was smooth behind the rostrum.

Ursula sat beside her window, rather far back. Looking down, she saw the lime-trees turning yellow, the tradesman's boy passing silent down the still, autumn-sunny street. There was the world, remote, remote.

Here, within the great, whispering sea-shell, that whispered all the while with reminiscence of all the centuries, time faded away, and the echo of knowledge filled the timeless silence.

She listened, she scribbled her notes with joy, almost with ecstasy, never for a moment criticizing what she heard. The lecturer was a mouth-piece, a priest. As he stood, black-gowned, on the rostrum, some strands of the whispering confusion of knowledge that filled the whole place seemed to be singled out and woven together by him, till they became a lecture.

At first, she preserved herself from criticism. She would not consider the professors as men, ordinary men, who ate bacon, and pulled on their boots before coming to college. They were the black-gowned priests of knowledge, serving for ever in a remote, hushed temple. They were the beginning and the end of the mystery was in their keeping.

Curious joy she had of the lectures. It was a joy to hear the theory of education, there was such freedom and pleasure in ranging over the very stuff of knowledge, and seeing how it moved and lived and had its being. How happy Racine made her! She did not know why. But as the big lines of the drama unfolded themselves, so steady, so measured, she felt a thrill as of being in the realm of the reality. Of Latin, she was doing Livy and Horace. The curious, intimate, gossiping tone of the Latin class suited Horace. Yet she never cared for him, nor even for Livy. There was an entire lack of sternness in the gossipy class-room. She tried hard to keep her grasp of the Roman spirit. But gradually the Latin became mere gossip-stuff and artificiality to her, a question of manners and verbosities.

Her terror was the mathematics class. The lecturer went so fast, her heart beat excitedly, she seemed to be straining every nerve. And she struggled hard, during private study, to get the stuff into control.

Then came the lovely, peaceful afternoons in the botany laboratory. They were few students. How she loved to sit on her high stool before the bench, with her pith and her razor and her material, carefully mounting her slides, carefully bringing her microscope into focus, then turning with joy to record her observation, drawing joyfully in her book, if the slide were good. . . .

Ursula was relieved to go home. She had still two peaceful years before her. Her future was settled for two years. She returned to college to prepare for her final examination.

But during this year the glamour began to depart from college. The professors were not priests initiated into the deep mysteries of life and knowledge. After all, they were only middle-men handling wares they had become so accustomed to that they were oblivious of them. What was Latin? – So much dry goods of knowledge. What was the Latin class altogether but a sort of second-hand curio shop, where one bought curios and learned the market-value of curios; dull curios too, on the whole. She was as bored by the Latin curiosities as she was by Chinese and Japanese curiosities in the antique shops. 'Antiques' – the very word made her soul fall flat and dead.

The life went out of her studies, why, she did not know. But the whole thing seemed sham, spurious; spurious Gothic arches, spurious peace, spurious Latinity, spurious dignity of France, spurious naïveté of Chaucer. It was a second-hand dealer's shop, and one bought an equipment for an examination. This was only a little side-show to the factories of the town. Gradually the perception stole into her. This was no religious retreat, no seclusion of pure learning. It was a little apprentice-shop where one was further equipped for making money. The college itself was a little, slovenly laboratory for the factory.

A harsh and ugly disillusion came over her again, the same darkness and bitter gloom from which she was never safe now, the realization of the permanent substratum of ugliness under everything. As she came to the college in the afternoon, the lawns were frothed with daisies, the lime-trees hung tender and sunlit and green; and oh, the deep, white froth of the daisies was anguish to see.

For inside, inside the college, she knew she must enter the sham workshop. All the while, it was a sham store, a sham warehouse, with a single motive of material gain, and no productivity. It pretended to exist by the religious virtue of knowledge. But the religious virtue of knowledge was become a flunkey to the god of material success.

A sort of inertia came over her. Mechanically, from habit, she went on with her studies. But it was almost hopeless. She could scarcely attend to anything. At the Anglo-Saxon lecture in the afternoon, she sat looking down, out of the window, hearing no word, of Beowulf or of anything else. Down below, in the street, the sunny grey pavement went beside the palisade. A woman in a pink frock, with a scarlet sunshade, crossed the road, a little white dog running like a fleck of light about her. The woman with the scarlet sunshade came over the road, a lilt in her walk, a little shadow attending her. Ursula watched spellbound. The woman with the scarlet sunshade and the flickering terrier was gone – and whither? Whither?

In what world of reality was the woman in the pink dress walking? To what warehouse of dead unreality was she herself confined?

What good was this place, this college? What good was Anglo-Saxon, when one only learned it in order to answer examination questions, in order that one should have a higher commercial value later on? She was sick with this long service at the inner commercial shrine. Yet what else was there? Was life all this, and this only? Everywhere, everything was debased to the same service. Everything went to produce vulgar things, to encumber material life.

Suddenly she threw over French. She would take honours in Botany. This was the one study that lived for her. She had entered into the lives of the plants. She was fascinated by the strange laws of the vegetable world. She had here a glimpse of something working entirely apart from the purpose of the human world.

College was barren, cheap, a temple converted to the most vulgar, petty commerce. Had she not gone to hear the echo of learning pulsing back to the source of the mystery? The source of mystery! And barrenly, the professors in their gowns offered commercial commodity that could be turned to good account in the examination room; ready-made stuff too, and not really worth the money it was intended to fetch; which they all knew.

All the time in the college now, save when she was labouring in her botany laboratory, for there the mystery still glimmered, she felt she was degrading herself in a kind of trade of sham jewjaws.

Angry and stiff, she went through her last term. She would rather be out again earning her own living. Even Brinsley Street and Mr Harby seemed real in comparison. Her violent hatred of the Ilkeston School was nothing compared with the sterile degradation of college. But she was not going back to Brinsley Street either. She would take her B.A., and become a mistress in some Grammar School for a time.

The last year of her college career was wheeling slowly round. She could see ahead her examination and her departure. She had the ash of disillusion gritting under her teeth. Would the next move turn out the same? Always the shining doorway ahead; and then, upon approach, always the shining doorway was a gate into another ugly yard, dirty and active and dead. Always the crest of the hill gleaming ahead under heaven: and then, from the top of the hill only another sordid valley full of amorphous, squalid activity.

No matter! Every hilltop was a little different, every valley was somehow new. Cossethay and her childhood with her father; the Marsh and the little Church school near the Marsh, and her grandmother and her uncles; the High School at Nottingham and Anton Skrebensky; Anton Skrebensky and the dance in the moonlight between the fires; then the time she could not think of without being blasted, Winifred Inger, and the months before becoming a school-teacher; then the horrors of Brinsley Street, lapsing into comparative peacefulness, Maggie, and Maggie's brother, whose influence she could still feel in her veins, when she conjured him up; then college, and Dorothy Russell, who was now in France, then the next move into the world again!

Already it was a history. In every phase she was so different. Yet she was always Ursula Brangwen. But what did it mean, Ursula Brangwen? She did not know what she was. Only she was full of rejection, of refusal. Always, always she was spitting out of her mouth the ash and grit of disillusion, of falsity. She could only stiffen in rejection, in rejection. She seemed always negative in her action.

That which she was, positively, was dark and unrevealed, it could not come forth. It was like a seed buried in dry ash. This world in which she lived was like a circle lighted by a lamp. This lighted area, lit up by man's completest consciousness, she thought was all the world: that here all was disclosed for ever. Yet all the time, within the darkness she had been aware of points of light, like the eyes of wild beasts, gleaming, penetrating, vanishing. And her soul had acknowledged in a great heave of terror only the outer darkness. This inner circle of light in which she lived and moved, wherein the trains rushed and the factories ground out their machine-produce and the plants and the animals worked by the light of science and knowledge, suddenly it seemed like the area under an arc-lamp, wherein the moths and children played in the security of blinding light, not even knowing there was any darkness, because they stayed in the light.

But she could see the glimmer of dark movement just out of range, she saw the eyes of the wild beast gleaming from the darkness, watching the vanity of the camp fire and the sleepers; she felt the strange, foolish vanity of the camp, which said 'Beyond our light and our order there is nothing', turning their faces always inward towards the sinking fire of illuminating consciousness, which comprised sun and stars, and the Creator, and the System of Righteousness, ignoring always the vast darkness that wheeled round about, with half-revealed shapes lurking on the edge.

Yea, and no man dared even throw a firebrand into the darkness. For if he did he was jeered to death by the others, who cried 'Fool, anti-social knave, why would you disturb us with bogeys? There *is* no darkness. We move and live and have our being within the light, and unto us is given the eternal light of knowledge, we comprise and comprehend the innermost core and issue of knowledge. Fool and knave, how dare you belittle us with the darkness?'

Nevertheless the darkness wheeled round about, with grey shadow-shapes of wild beasts, and also with dark shadow-shapes of the angels, whom the light fenced out, as it fenced out the more familiar beasts of darkness. And some, having for a moment seen the darkness, saw it bristling with the tufts of the hyena and the wolf; and some, having given up their vanity of the light, having died in their own conceit, saw the gleam in the eyes of the wolf and the hyena, that it was the flash of the sword of angels, flashing at the door to come in, that the angels in the darkness were lordly and terrible and not to be denied, like the flash of fangs.

It was a little while before Easter, in her last year at college, when Ursula was twenty-two years old, that she heard again from Skrebensky. He had written to her once or twice from South Africa, during the first months of his service out there in the war, and since had sent her a postcard every now and then, at ever longer intervals. He had become a first lieutenant, and had stayed out in Africa. She had not heard of him now for more than two years.

Often her thoughts returned to him. He seemed like the gleaming dawn, yellow, radiant, of a long, grey, ashy day. The memory of him was like the thought of the first radiant hours of morning. And here was the blank grey ashiness of later daytime. Ah, if he had only remained true to her, she might have known the sunshine, without all this toil and hurt and degradation of a spoiled day. He would have been her angel. He held the keys of the sunshine. Still he held them. He could open to her the gates of succeeding freedom and delight. Nay, if he had remained true to her, he would have been the doorway to her, into the boundless sky of happiness and plunging, inexhaustible freedom which was the paradise of her soul. Ah, the great range he would have opened to her, the illimitable endless space for self-realization and delight for ever.

The one thing she believed in was in the love she had held for him. It remained shining and complete, a thing to hark back to. And she said to herself, when present things seemed a failure:

'Ah, I *was* fond of him,' as if with him the leading flower of her life had died.

Now she heard from him again. The chief effect was pain. The pleasure, the spontaneous joy was not there any longer. But her *will* rejoiced. Her will had fixed itself to him. And the old excitement of her dreams stirred and woke up. He was come, the man with the wondrous lips that could send the kiss wavering to the very end of all space. Was he come back to her? She did not believe.

My dear Ursula, I am back in England again for a few months before going out again, this time to India. I wonder if you still keep the memory of our times together. I have still got the little photograph of you. You must be changed since then, for it is about six years ago. I am fully six years older, – I have lived through another life since I knew you at Cossethay. I wonder if you would care to see me. I shall come up to Derby next week, and I would call in Nottingham, and we might have tea together. Will you let me know? I shall look for your answer.

ANTON SKREBENSKY

Ursula had taken his letter from the rack in the hall at college, and torn it open as she crossed to the Women's room. The world seemed to dissolve away from around her, she stood alone in clear air.

Where could she go to, to be alone? She fled away, upstairs, and through the private way to the reference library. Seizing a book, she sat down and pondered the letter. Her heart beat, her limbs trembled. As in a dream, she heard one gong sound in the college, then, strangely, another. The first lecture had gone by.

Hurriedly she took one of her note-books and began to write.

Dear Anton, Yes, I still have the ring. I should be very glad to see you again. You can come here to college for me, or I will meet you somewhere in the town. Will you let me know? Your sincere friend –

Trembling, she asked the librarian, who was her friend, if he would give her an envelope. She sealed and addressed her letter, and went out, bareheaded, to post it. When it was dropped into the pillar-box, the world became a very still, pale place, without confines. She wandered back to college, to her pale dream, like a first wan light of dawn.

Skrebensky came one afternoon the following week. Day after day, she hurried swiftly to the letter-rack on her arrival at college in the morning, and during the intervals between lectures. Several times, swiftly, with secretive fingers, she had plucked his letter down from its public prominence, and fled across the hall holding it fast and hidden. She read her letters in the botany laboratory, where her corner was always reserved to her.

Several letters, and then he was coming. It was Friday afternoon he appointed. She worked over her microscope with feverish activity, able to give only half her attention, yet working closely and rapidly. She had on her slide some special stuff come up from London that day, and the professor was fussy and excited about it. At the same time, as she focused the light on her field, and saw the plant-animal lying shadowy in a boundless light, she was fretting over a conversation she had had a few days ago with Dr Frankstone, who was a woman doctor of physics in the college.

'No, really,' Dr Frankstone had said, 'I don't see why we should attribute some special mystery to life – do you? We don't understand it as we understand electricity, even, but that doesn't warrant our saying it is something special, something different in kind and distinct from everything else in the universe – do you think it does? May it not be that life consists in a complexity of physical and chemical activities, of the same order as the activities we already know in science? I don't see really, why we should imagine there is a special order of life, and life alone –'

The conversation had ended on a note of uncertainty, indefinite, wistful. But the purpose, what was the purpose? Electricity had no soul, light and heat had no soul. Was she herself an impersonal force, or conjunction of forces, like one of these? She looked still at the unicellular shadow that lay within the field of light, under her microscope. It was alive. She saw it move – she saw the bright mist of its ciliary activity, she saw the gleam of its nucleus, as it slid across the plane of light. What then was its will? If it was a conjunction of forces, physical and chemical, what held these forces unified, and for what purpose were they unified?

For what purpose were the incalculable physical and chemical activities nodalized in this shadowy, moving speck under her microscope? What was the will which nodalized them and created the one thing she saw? What was its intention? To be itself? Was its purpose just mechanical and limited to itself?

It intended to be itself. But what self? Suddenly in her mind the world gleamed strangely, with an intense light, like the nucleus of the creature under the microscope. Suddenly she had passed away into an intensely gleaming light of knowledge. She could not understand what it all was. She only knew that it was not limited mechanical energy, nor mere purpose of self-preservation and self-assertion. It was a consummation, a being infinite. Self was a oneness with the infinite. To be oneself was a supreme, gleaming triumph of infinity.

Ursula sat abstracted over her microscope, in suspense. Her soul was busy, infinitely busy, in the new world. In the new world, Skrebensky was waiting for her – he would be waiting for her. She could not go yet, because her soul was engaged. Soon she would go.

A stillness, like passing away, took hold of her. Far off, down the corridors, she heard the gong booming five o'clock. She must go. Yet she sat still.

The other students were pushing back their stools and putting their microscopes away. Everything broke into turmoil. She saw, through the window, students going down the steps, with books under their arms, talking, all talking.

A great craving to depart came upon her. She wanted also to be gone. She was in dread of the material world, and in dread of her own transfiguration. She wanted to run and meet Skrebensky – the new life, the reality.

Class-Room

A school-day was drawing to a close. In the class-room the last lesson was in progress, peaceful and still. It was elementary botany. The desks were littered with catkins, hazel and willow, which the children had been sketching. But the sky had come over dark, as the end of the afternoon approached: there was scarcely light to draw any more. Ursula stood in front of the class, leading the children by questions to understand the structure, and the meaning of the catkins.

A heavy, copper-coloured beam of light came in at the west window, gilding the outlines of the children's heads with red gold, and falling on the wall opposite in a rich, ruddy illumination. Ursula, however, was scarcely conscious of it. She was busy, the end of the day was here, the work went on as a peaceful tide that is at flood, hushed to retire.

This day had gone by like so many more, in an activity that was like a trance. At the end there was a little haste, to finish what was in hand. She was pressing the children with questions, so that they should know all they were to know, by the time the gong went. She stood in shadow in front of the class, with catkins in her hand, and she leaned towards the children, absorbed in the passion of instruction.

She heard, but did not notice the click of the door. Suddenly she started. She saw, in the shaft of ruddy, copper-coloured light near her, the face of a man. It was gleaming like fire, watching her, waiting for her to be aware. It startled her terribly. She thought she was going to faint. All her suppressed, subconscious fear sprang into being, with anguish.

'Did I startle you?' said Birkin, shaking hands with her. 'I thought you had heard me come in.'

'No,' she faltered, scarcely able to speak. He laughed, saying he was sorry. She wondered why it amused him.

'It is so dark,' he said. 'Shall we have the light?'

And moving aside, he switched on the strong electric lights. The class-room was distinct and hard, a strange place after the soft dim magic that filled it before he came. Birkin turned curiously to look at Ursula. Her eyes were round and wondering, bewildered, her mouth quivered slightly. She looked like one who is suddenly wakened. There was a living, tender beauty, like a tender light of dawn shining from her face. He looked at her with a new pleasure, feeling gay in his heart, irresponsible.

'You are doing catkins?' he asked, picking up a piece of hazel from a scholar's desk in front of him. 'Are they as far out as this? I hadn't noticed them this year.'

He looked absorbedly at the tassel of hazel in his hand.

'The red ones too!' he said, looking at the flickers of crimson that came from the female bud.

Then he went in among the desks, to see the scholars' books. Ursula watched his intent progress. There was a stillness in his motion that hushed the activities of her heart. She seemed to be standing aside in arrested silence, watching him move in another concentrated world. His presence was so quiet, almost like a vacancy in the corporate air.

Suddenly he lifted his face to her, and her heart quickened at the flicker of his voice.

'Give them some crayons, won't you?' he said, 'so that they can make the gynaecious flowers red, and the androgynous yellow. I'd chalk them in plain, chalk in nothing else, merely the red and the yellow. Outline scarcely matters in this case. There is just the one fact to emphasize.'

'I haven't any crayons,' said Ursula.

'There will be some somewhere – red and yellow, that's all you want.' Ursula sent out a boy on a quest.

'It will make the books untidy,' she said to Birkin, flushing deeply.

'Not very,' he said. 'You must mark in these things obviously. It's the fact you want to emphasize, not the subjective impression to record. What's the fact? – red little spiky stigmas of the female flower, dangling yellow male catkin, yellow pollen flying from one to the other. Make a pictorial record of the fact, as a child does when drawing a face – two eyes, one nose, mouth with teeth – so –' And he drew a figure on the blackboard.

At that moment another vision was seen through the glass panels of the door. It was Hermione Roddice. Birkin went and opened to her.

'I saw your car,' she said to him. 'Do you mind my coming to find you? I wanted to see you when you were on duty.'

She looked at him for a long time, intimate and playful, then she gave a short little laugh. And then only she turned to Ursula, who, with all the class, had been watching the little scene between the lovers.

'How do you do, Miss Brangwen,' sang Hermione, in her low, odd, singing fashion, that sounded almost as if she were poking fun. 'Do you mind my coming in?'

Her grey, almost sardonic eyes rested all the while on Ursula, as if summing her up.

'Oh no,' said Ursula.

'Are you *sure*?' repeated Hermione, with complete *sang froid*, and an odd, half-bullying effrontery.

'Oh no, I like it awfully,' laughed Ursula, a little bit excited and bewildered, because Hermione seemed to be compelling her, coming very close to her, as if intimate with her; and yet, how could she be intimate?

This was the answer Hermione wanted. She turned satisfied to Birkin.

'What are you doing?' she sang, in her casual, inquisitive fashion.

'Catkins,' he replied.

'Really!' she said. 'And what do you learn about them?' She spoke all the while in a mocking, half-teasing fashion, as if making game of the whole business. She picked up a twig of the catkin, piqued by Birkin's attention to it.

She was a strange figure in the class-room, wearing a large old cloak of greenish cloth, on which was a raised pattern of dull gold. The high collar, and the inside of the cloak, was lined with dark fur. Beneath she had a dress of fine lavender-coloured cloth, trimmed with fur, and her hat was close-fitting, made of fur and of the dull, green-and-gold figured stuff. She was tall and strange, she looked as if she had come out of some new, bizarre picture.

'Do you know the little red ovary flowers, that produce the nuts? Have you ever noticed them?' he asked her. And he came close and pointed them out to her, on the sprig she held.

'No,' she replied. 'What are they?'

'Those are the little seed-producing flowers, and the long catkins, they only produce pollen, to fertilize them.'

'Do they, do they!' repeated Hermione, looking closely.

'From those little red bits, the nuts come; if they receive pollen from the long danglers.'

'Little red flames, little red flames,' murmured Hermione to herself. And she remained for some moments looking only at the small buds out of which the red flickers of the stigma issued.

'Aren't they beautiful? I think they're so beautiful,' she said, moving close to Birkin, and pointing to the red filaments with her long, white finger.

'Had you never noticed them before?' he asked.

'No, never before,' she replied.

'And now you will always see them,' he said.

'Now I shall always see them,' she repeated. 'Thank you so much for showing me. I think they're so beautiful – little red flames –'

Her absorption was strange, almost rhapsodic. Both Birkin and Ursula were suspended. The little red pistillate flowers had some strange, almost mystic-passionate attraction for her.

The lesson was finished, the books were put away, at last the class was dismissed. And still Hermione sat at the table, with her chin in her hand, her elbow on the table, her long white face pushed up, not attending to anything. Birkin had gone to the window, and was looking from the brilliantly lighted room on to the grey, colourless outside, where rain was noiselessly falling. Ursula put away her things in the cupboard.

At length Hermione rose and came near to her.

'Your sister has come home?' she said.

'Yes,' said Ursula.

'And does she like being back in Beldover?'

'No,' said Ursula.

'No, I wonder she can bear it. It takes all my strength, to bear the ugliness of this district, when I stay here. Won't you come and see me?

D.H.L. – 6

Won't you come with your sister to stay at Breadalby for a few days? –
do –'

'Thank you very much,' said Ursula.

'Then I will write to you,' said Hermione. 'You think your sister will
come? I should be so glad. I think she is wonderful. I think some of her
work is really wonderful. I have two water-wagtails, carved in wood, and
painted – perhaps you have seen it?'

'No,' said Ursula.

'I think it is perfectly wonderful – like a flash of instinct –'

'Her little carvings *are* strange,' said Ursula.

'Perfectly beautiful – full of primitive passion –'

'Isn't it queer that she always likes little things? – she must always
work small things, that one can put between one's hands, birds and tiny
animals. She likes to look through the wrong end of the opera-glasses,
and see the world that way – why is it, do you think?'

Hermione looked down at Ursula with that long, detached scrutiniz-
ing gaze that excited the younger woman.

'Yes,' said Hermione at length. 'It is curious. The little things seem
to be more subtle to her –'

'But they aren't, are they? A mouse isn't any more subtle than a lion,
is it?'

Again Hermione looked down at Ursula with that long scrutiny, as if
she were following some train of thought of her own, and barely attending to the other's speech.

'I don't know,' she replied.

'Rupert, Rupert,' she said mildly, calling him to her. He approached
in silence.

'Are little things more subtle than big things?' she asked, with the odd
grunt of laughter in her voice, as if she were making game of him in the
question.

'Dunno,' he said.

'I hate subtleties,' said Ursula.

Hermione looked at her slowly.

'Do you?' she said.

'I always think they are a sign of weakness,' said Ursula, up in arms,
as if her prestige were threatened.

Hermione took no notice. Suddenly her face puckered, her brow was
knit with thought, she seemed twisted in troublesome effort for utterance.

'Do you really think, Rupert,' she asked, as if Ursula were not present, 'do you really think it is worthwhile? Do you really think the children are better for being roused to consciousness?'

A dark flash went over his face, a silent fury. He was hollow-cheeked and pale, almost unearthly. And the woman, with her serious, conscience-harrowing question, tortured him on the quick.

'They are not roused to consciousness,' he said. 'Consciousness comes to them, willy-nilly.'

'But do you think they are better for having it quickened, stimulated? Isn't it better that they should remain unconscious of the hazel, isn't it better that they should see as a whole, without all this pulling to pieces, all this knowledge?'

'Would you rather, for yourself, know or not know, that the little red flowers are there, putting out for the pollen?' he asked harshly. His voice was brutal, scornful, cruel.

Hermione remained with her face lifted up, abstracted. He hung silent in irritation.

'I don't know,' she replied, balancing mildly. 'I don't know.'

'But knowing is everything to you, it is all your life,' he broke out. She slowly looked at him.

'Is it?' she said.

'To know, that is your all, that is your life – you have only this, this knowledge,' he cried. 'There is only one tree, there is only one fruit, in your mouth.'

Again she was some time silent.

'Is there?' she said at last, with the same untouched calm. And then in a tone of whimsical inquisitiveness: 'What fruit, Rupert?'

'The eternal apple,' he replied in exasperation, hating his own metaphors.

'Yes,' she said. There was a look of exhaustion about her. For some moments there was silence. Then, pulling herself together with a convulsed movement, Hermione resumed, in a sing-song, casual voice.

'But leaving me apart, Rupert; do you think the children are better, richer, happier, for all this knowledge; do you really think they are? Or is it better to leave them untouched, spontaneous. Hadn't they better be animals, simple animals, crude, violent, *anything*, rather than this self-consciousness, this incapacity to be spontaneous?'

They thought she had finished. But with a queer rumbling in her throat she resumed, 'Hadn't they better be anything than grow up crippled, crippled in their souls, crippled in their feelings – so thrown back – so turned back on themselves – incapable –' Hermione clenched her fist like one in a trance – 'of any spontaneous action, always deliberate, always burdened with choice, never carried away.'

Again they thought she had finished. But just as he was going to reply, she resumed her queer rhapsody – 'never carried away, out of themselves, always conscious, always self-conscious, always aware of themselves. Isn't *anything* better than this? Better be animals, mere animals with no mind at all, than this, this *nothingness* –'

'But do you think it is knowledge that makes us unliving and self-conscious?' he asked irritably.

She opened her eyes and looked at him slowly.

'Yes,' she said. She paused, watching him all the while, her eyes vague. Then she wiped her fingers across her brow, with a vague weariness. It irritated him bitterly. 'It is the mind,' she said, 'and that is death.' She raised her eyes slowly to him: 'Isn't the mind –' she said, with the convulsed movement of her body, 'isn't it our death? Doesn't it destroy all our spontaneity, all our instincts? Are not the young people growing up today, really dead before they have a chance to live?'

'Not because they have too much mind, but too little,' he said brutally.

'Are you *sure*?' she cried. 'It seems to me the reverse. They are over-conscious, burdened to death with consciousness.'

'Imprisoned within a limited, false set of concepts,' he cried.

But she took no notice of this, only went on with her own rhapsodic interrogation.

'When we have knowledge, don't we lose everything but knowledge?' she asked pathetically. 'If I know about the flower, don't I lose the flower and have only the knowledge? Aren't we exchanging the substance for the shadow, aren't we forfeiting life for this dead quality of knowledge? And what does it mean to me after all? What does all this knowing mean to me? It means nothing.'

'You are merely making words,' he said; 'knowledge means everything to you. Even your animalism, you want it in your head. You don't want to *be* an animal, you want to observe your own animal functions, to get a mental thrill out of them. It is all purely secondary – and more decadent than the most hide-bound intellectualism. What is it but the worst and last form of intellectualism, this love of yours for passion and the animal instincts? Passion and the instincts – you want them hard enough, but through your head, in your consciousness. It all takes place in your head, under that skull of yours. Only you won't be conscious of what *actually* is: you want the lie that will match the rest of your furniture.'

Hermione set hard and poisonous against this attack. Ursula stood covered with wonder and shame. It frightened her, to see how they hated each other.

'It's all that Lady of Shalott business,' he said, in his strong abstract voice. He seemed to be charging her before the unseeing air. 'You've got that mirror, your own fixed will, your immortal understanding, your own tight conscious world, and there is nothing beyond it. There, in the mirror, you must have everything. But now you have come to all your conclusions, you want to go back and be like a savage, without knowledge. You want a life of pure sensation and "passion".'

He quoted the last word satirically against her. She sat convulsed with fury and violation, speechless, like a stricken pythoness of the Greek oracle.

'But your passion is a lie,' he went on violently. 'It isn't passion at all, it is your *will*. It's your bullying will. You want to clutch things and have them in your power. You want to have things in your power. And why? Because you haven't got any real body, any dark sensual body of life. You have no sensuality. You have only your will and your conceit of consciousness, and your lust for power, to *know*.'

He looked at her in mingled hate and contempt, also in pain because she suffered, and in shame because he knew he tortured her. He had an impulse to kneel and plead for forgiveness. But a bitter red anger burned up to fury in him. He became unconscious of her, he was only a passionate voice speaking.

'Spontaneous!' he cried. 'You and spontaneity! You, the most deliberate thing that ever walked or crawled! You'd be verily deliberately spontaneously – that's you. Because you want to have everything in your own volition, your deliberate voluntary consciousness. You want it all in that loathsome little skull of yours, that ought to be cracked like a nut. For you'll be the same till it *is* cracked, like an insect in its skin. If one cracked your skull perhaps one might get a spontaneous, passionate woman out of you, with real sensuality. As it is, what you want is pornography – looking at yourself in mirrors, watching your naked animal actions in mirrors, so that you can have it all in your consciousness, make it all mental.'

There was a sense of violation in the air, as if too much was said, the unforgivable. Yet Ursula was concerned now only with solving her own problems, in the light of his words. She was pale and abstracted.

'But do you really *want* sensuality?' she asked puzzled.

Birkin looked at her, and became intent in his explanation.

'Yes,' he said, 'that and nothing else, at this point. It is a fulfilment – the great dark knowledge you can't have in your head – the dark involuntary being. It is death to one's self – but it is the coming into being of another.'

'But how? How can you have knowledge not in your head?' she asked, quite unable to interpret his phrases.

'In the blood,' he answered; 'when the mind and the known world is drowned in darkness – everything must go – there must be the deluge. Then you find yourself in a palpable body of darkness, a demon –'

'But why should I be a demon –?' she asked.

'"Woman wailing for her demon lover" –' he quoted – 'why, I don't know.'

Hermione roused herself as from a death – annihilation.

'He is such a *dreadful* satanist, isn't he?' she drawled to Ursula, in a queer resonant voice, that ended in a shrill little laugh of pure ridicule. The two women were jeering at him, jeering him into nothingness. The laugh of the shrill, triumphant female sounded from Hermione, jeering him as if he were a neuter.

'No,' he said. 'You are the real devil who won't let life exist.'

She looked at him with a long, slow look, malevolent, supercilious.

'You know all about it, don't you?' she said, with slow, cold, cunning mockery.

'Enough,' he replied, his face fixing fine and clear like steel. A horrible despair, and at the same time a sense of release, liberation, came over Hermione. She turned with a pleasant intimacy to Ursula.

'You are sure you will come to Breadalby?' she said, urging.

'Yes, I should like to very much,' replied Ursula.

Hermione looked down at her, gratified, reflecting, and strangely absent, as if possessed, as if not quite there.

'I'm so glad,' she said, pulling herself together. 'Some time in about a fortnight. Yes? I will write to you here, at the school, shall I? Yes. And you'll be sure to come? Yes. I shall be so glad. Good-bye! Good-bye!'

Hermione held out her hand and looked into the eyes of the other woman. She knew Ursula as an immediate rival, and the knowledge strangely exhilarated her. Also she was taking leave. It always gave her a sense of strength, advantage, to be departing and leaving the other behind. Moreover she was taking the man with her, if only in hate.

Birkin stood aside, fixed and unreal. But now, when it was his turn to bid good-bye, he began to speak again.

'There's the whole difference in the world,' he said, 'between the actual sensual being and the vicious mental deliberate profligacy our lot goes in for. In our night-time, there's always the electricity switched on, we watch ourselves, we get it all in the head, really. You've got to lapse out before you can know what sensual reality is, lapse into unknowingness, and give up your volition. You've got to do it. You've got to learn not-to-be, before you can come into being.

'But we have got such a conceit of ourselves – that's where it is. We are so conceited, and so unproud. We've got no pride, we're all conceit, so conceited in our own papier-mâché realized selves. We'd rather die than give up our little self-righteous self-opinionated self-will.'

There was silence in the room. Both women were hostile and resentful. He sounded as if he were addressing a meeting. Hermione merely paid no attention, stood with her shoulders tight in a shrug of dislike.

Ursula was watching him as if furtively, not really aware of what she was seeing. There was great physical attractiveness in him – a curious hidden richness, that came through his thinness and his pallor like another voice, conveying another knowledge of him. It was in the curves of his brows and his chin, rich, fine exquisite curves, the powerful beauty of life itself. She could not say what it was. But there was a sense of richness and of liberty.

'But we are sensual enough, without making ourselves so, aren't we?' she asked, turning to him with a certain golden laughter flickering under her greenish eyes, like a challenge. And immediately the queer, careless, terribly attractive smile came over his eyes and brows, though his mouth did not relax.

'No,' he said, 'we aren't. We're too full of ourselves.'

'Surely it isn't a matter of conceit?' she cried.

'That and nothing else.'

She was frankly puzzled.

'Don't you think that people are most conceited of all about their sensual powers?' she asked.

'That's why they aren't sensual – only sensuous – which is another matter. They're *always* aware of themselves – and they're so conceited, that rather than release themselves, and live in another world, from another centre, they'd –'

'You want your tea, don't you,' said Hermione, turning to Ursula with a gracious kindliness. 'You've worked all day –'

Birkin stopped short. A spasm of anger and chagrin went over Ursula. His face set. And he bade good-bye, as if he had ceased to notice her.

They were gone. Ursula stood looking at the door for some moments. Then she put out the lights. And having done so, she sat down again in her chair, absorbed and lost. And then she began to cry, bitterly, bitterly weeping: but whether for misery or joy, she never knew.

Lessford's Rabbits

On Tuesday mornings I have to be at school at half past eight to administer the free breakfasts. Dinners are given in the canteen in one of the mean streets, where the children feed in a Church Mission room appropriately adorned by Sunday School cartoons showing the blessing of the little ones, and the feeding of the five thousand. We serve breakfasts, however, in school, in the woodwork room high up under the roof.

Tuesday morning sees me rushing up the six short flights of stone stairs, at twenty-five minutes to nine. It is my disposition to be late. I generally find a little crowd of children waiting in the 'art' room – so called because it is surrounded with a strip of blackboard too high for the tallest boy to reach – which is a sort of ante-room to the workshop where breakfast is being prepared. I hasten through the little throng to see if things are ready. There are two big girls putting out the basins, and another one looking in the pan to see if the milk is boiling. The room is warm, and seems more comfortable because the windows are high up under the beams of the slanting roof and the walls are all panelled with ruddy gold, varnished wood. The work bench is in the form of three sides of a square – or of an oblong – as the dining tables of the ancients used to be, I believe. At one of the extremities are the three vises, and at the other the great tin pan, like a fish kettle, standing on a gas ring. When the boys' basins are placed along the outer edge of the bench, the girls' on the inner, and the infants' on the lockers against the wall, we are ready. I look at the two rows of assorted basins, and think of the three bears. Then I admit the thirty, who bundle to their places and stand in position, girls on the inside facing boys on the outside, and quaint little infants with their toes kicking the lockers along the walls.

Last week the infant mistress did not come up, so I was alone. She is an impressive woman, who always commands the field. I stand in considerable awe of her. I feel like a reckless pleasure boat with one extravagant sail misbehaving myself in the track of a heavy earnest coaster when she bears down on me. I was considerably excited to find myself in sole charge. As I ushered in the children, the caretaker, a little fierce-eyed man with hollow cheeks and walrus moustache, entered with the large basket full of chunks of bread. He glared around without bidding me good morning.

'Miss Culloch not come?' he asked.

'As you see,' I replied.

He grunted, and put down the basket. Then he drew himself up like a fiery prophet, and stretching forth his hairy arm towards the opposite door, shouted loudly to the children:

'None of you's got to touch that other door there! You hear – you're to leave it alone!'

The children stared at him without answering.

'A brake as I'm making for these doors,' he said confidentially to me, thrusting forward his extraordinarily hairy lean arms, and putting two fingers of one hand into the palm of the other, as if to explain his invention. I bowed.

'Nasty things them swing doors' – he looked up at me with his fierce eyes, and suddenly swished aside his right arm:

'They come to like *that*!' he exclaimed, 'and a child's fingers is cut off – clean!' – he looked at me for ratification. I bowed.

'It'll be a good thing, I think,' he concluded, considerably damped. I bowed again. Then he left me. The chief, almost the only duty of a caretaker, is to review the works of the head and of the staff, as a reviewer does books: at length and according to his superior light.

I told one of the girls to give three chunks of bread to each child, and, having fished a mysterious earwig out of the scalding milk, I filled the large enamelled jug – such as figures and has figured in the drawing lessons of every school in England, I suppose – and doled out the portions – about three-quarters of a pint per senior, and half a pint per infant. Everything was ready. I had to say grace. I dared not launch into the Infant mistress' formula, thanking the Lord for his goodness – 'and may we eat and drink to thine everlasting glory – Amen.' I looked at the boys, dressed in mouldering garments of remote men, at the girls with their rat-tailed hair, and at the infants, quaint little mites on whom I wished, but could not bring myself, to expend my handkerchief, and I wondered what I should say. The only other grace I knew was 'For these and for all good things may the Lord make us truly thankful.' But I wondered whom we should thank for the bad things. I was becoming desperate. I plunged:

'Ready now – hands together, close eyes. "Let us eat, drink and be merry, for tomorrow we die."' I felt myself flushing with confusion – what did I mean? But there was the universal clink of iron spoons on the basins, and a snuffling, slobbering sound of children feeding. They had not noticed, so it was all right. The infants were kneeling and squalling by the lockers, the boys were stretching wide their eyes and their mouths

at the same time, to admit the spoon. They spilled the milk on their
jackets and wiped it off with their sleeves, continuing to eat all the time.

'Don't slobber, lads, be decent,' I said, rebuking them from my
superior sphere. They ate more carefully, glancing up at me when the
spoon was at their mouths.

I began to count the number – nine boys, seven girls, and eleven infants. Not many. We could never get many boys to give in their names
for free meals. I used to ask the Kelletts, who were pinched and pared
thin with poverty:

'Are you sure you don't want either dinner or breakfasts, Kellett?'

He would look at me curiously, and say, with a peculiar small movement of his thin lips,

'No, Sir.'

'But have you plenty – quite plenty?'

'Yes, Sir' – he was very quiet, flushing at my questions. None – or very
few – of the boys could endure to accept the meals. Not many parents
would submit to the indignity of the officer's inquirer and the boys, the
most foolishly sensitive animals in the world, would, many of them,
prefer to go short rather than to partake of charity meals of which all
their school-mates were aware.

'Halket – where is Halket?' I asked.

'Please, Sir, his mother's got work,' replied Lessford, one of my own
boys, a ruddy, bonny lad – many of those at breakfast were pictures of
health. Lessford was brown-skinned and had fine dark eyes. He was a
reticent, irresponsible creature, with a radical incapacity to spell and to
read and to draw, but who sometimes scored at arithmetic. I should
think he came of a long line of unrelievedly poor people. He was skilled
in street lore, and cute at arithmetic, but blunt and blind to everything
that needed a little delicacy of perception. He had an irritating habit of
looking at me furtively, with his handsome dark eyes, glancing covertly
again and again. Yet he was not a sneak; he gave himself the appearance
of one. He was a well-built lad, and he looked well in the blue jersey
he wore – there were great holes at the elbows, showing the whitish shirt
and a brown bit of Lessford. At breakfasts he was a great eater. He
would have five solid pieces of bread, and then ask for more.

We gave them bread and milk one morning, cocoa and currant bread
the next. I happened to go one cocoa morning to take charge. Lessford,
I noticed, did not eat by any means so much as on bread mornings. I
was surprised. I asked him if he did not care for currant loaf, but he said
he did. Feeling curious, I asked the other teachers what they thought of
him. Mr Hayward, who took a currant bread morning, said he was sure

the boy had a breakfast before he came to school; Mr Jephson, who took a milk morning, said the lad was voracious, that it amused him to try to feed him up. I watched – turning suddenly to ask if anyone wanted a little more milk, and glancing over the top of the milk pan as I was emptying it.

I caught him: I saw him push a piece of bread under his jersey, glancing furtively with a little quiver of apprehension up at me. I did not appear to notice, but when he was going downstairs I followed him and asked him to go into the class-room with me. I closed the door and sat down at my table: he stood hanging his head and marking with his foot on the floor. He came to me, very slowly, when I bade him. I put my hand on his jersey, and felt something underneath. He did not resist me, and I drew it out. It was his cap. He smiled, he could not help it, at my discomfiture. Then he pulled his lips straight and looked sulky. I tried again – and this time I found three pieces of bread in a kind of rough pocket inside the waist of his trousers. He looked at them blackly as I arranged them on the table before him, flushing under his brown skin.

'What does this mean?' I asked. He hung his head, and would not answer.

'You may as well tell me – what do you want this for?'

'Eat,' he muttered, keeping his face bent. I put my hand under his chin and lifted up his face. He shut his eyes, and tried to move his face aside, as if from a very strong light which hurt him.

'That is not true,' I said. 'I know perfectly well it is not true. You have a breakfast before you come. You do not come to eat. You come to take the food away.'

'I never!' he exclaimed sulkily.

'No,' I said. 'You did not take any yesterday. But the day before you did.'

'I never, I never!!' he declared, more emphatically, in the tone of one who scores again. I considered.

'Oh no – the day before was Sunday. Let me see. You took some on Thursday – yes, that was the last time – You took four or five pieces of bread. . . .' I hung fire; he did not contradict; 'five, I believe,' I added. He scraped his toe on the ground. I had guessed aright. He could not deny the definite knowledge of a number.

But I could not get another word from him. He stood and heard all I had to say, but he would not look up, or answer anything. I felt angry.

'Well,' I said, 'if you come to breakfasts any more, you will be reported.'

Next day, when asked why he was absent from breakfast, he said his father had got a job.

He was a great nuisance for coming with dirty boots. Evidently he went roaming over fields and everywhere. I concluded he must have a strain of gipsy in him, a mongrel form common in the south of London. Halket was his great friend. They never played together at school, and they had no apparent common interests. Halket was a debonair, clever lad who gave great promise of turning out a ne'er-do-well. He was very lively, soon moved from tears to laughter; Lessford was an inveterate sulker. Yet they always hung together.

One day my bread-stealer arrived at half past two, when the register was closed. He was sweating, dishevelled, and his breast was heaving. He gave no word of explanation, but stood near the great blackboard, his head dropped, one leg loosely apart, panting.

'Well!' I exclaimed, 'this is a nice thing! What have you to say?' I rose from my chair.

Evidently he had nothing to say.

'Come on,' I said finally. 'No foolery! Let me hear it.' He knew he would have to speak. He looked up at me, his dark eyes blazing:

'My rabbits has all gone!' he cried, as a man would announce his wife and children slain. I heard Halket exclaim. I looked at him. He was half-out of the desk, his mercurial face blank with dismay.

'Who's 'ad 'em?' he said, breathing the words almost in a whisper.

'Did you leave th' door open?' Lessford bent forward like a serpent about to strike as he asked this. Halket shook his head solemnly:

'No! I've not been near 'em today.'

There was a pause. It was time for me to reassume my position of authority. I told them both to sit down, and we continued the lesson. Halket crept near his comrade and began to whisper to him, but he received no response. Lessford sulked fixedly, not moving his head for more than an hour.

At playtime I began to question Halket: 'Please, Sir – we had some rabbits in a place on the allotments. We used to gather manure for a man, and he let us have half of his tool-house in the garden –'

'How many had you – rabbits?'

'Please, Sir – they varied. When we had young ones we used to have sixteen sometimes. We had two brown does and a black buck.'

I was somewhat taken back by this.

'How long have you had them?'

'A long time now, Sir. We've had six lots of young ones.'

'And what did you do with them?'

'Fatten them, Sir' – he spoke with a little triumph, but he was reluctant to say much more.

'And what did you fatten them on?'

The boy glanced swiftly at me. He reddened, and for the first time became confused.

'Green stuff, what we had given us out of the gardens, and what we got out of the fields.'

'And bread,' I answered quietly.

He looked at me. He saw I was not angry, only ironical. For a few moments he hesitated, whether to lie or not. Then he admitted, very subdued:

'Yes, Sir.'

'And what did you do with the rabbits?' – he did not answer – 'Come, tell me. I can find out whether or not.'

'Sold them,' – he hung his head guiltily.

'Who did the selling?'

'I, Sir – to a greengrocer.'

'For how much?'

'Eightpence each.'

'And did your mothers know?'

'No, Sir.' He was very subdued and guilty.

'And what did you do with the money?'

'Go to the Empire – generally.'

I asked him a day or two later if they had found the rabbits. They had not. I asked Halket what he supposed had become of them.

'Please, Sir – I suppose somebody must 'a stole them. The door was not broken. You could open our padlock with a hair-pin. I suppose somebody must have come after us last night when we'd fed them. I think I know who it is, too, Sir.' He shook his head widely – 'There's a place where you can get into the allotments off the field –'

A Lesson on a Tortoise

It was the last lesson on Friday afternoon, and this, with Standard Six, was Nature Study from half-past three till half-past four. The last lesson of the week is a weariness to teachers and scholars. It is the end; there is no need to keep up the tension of discipline and effort any longer, and, yielding to weariness, a teacher is spent.

But Nature Study is a pleasant lesson. I had got a big old tortoise, who had not yet gone to sleep, though November was darkening the early afternoon, and I knew the boys would enjoy sketching him. I put him under the radiator to warm while I went for a large empty shell that I had sawn in two to show the ribs of some ancient tortoise absorbed in his bony coat. When I came back I found Joe, the old reptile, stretching slowly his skinny neck, and looking with indifferent eyes at the two intruding boys who were kneeling beside him. I was too good-tempered to send them out again into the playground, too slack with the great relief of Friday afternoon. So I bade them put out the Nature books ready. I crouched to look at Joey, and stroke his horny, blunt head with my finger. He was quite lively. He spread out his legs and gripped the floor with his flat hand-like paws, then he slackened again as if from a yawn, drooping his head meditatively.

I felt pleased with myself, knowing that the boys would be delighted with the lesson. 'He will not want to walk,' I said to myself, 'and if he takes a sleepy stride, they'll be just in ecstasy, and I can easily calm him down to his old position.' So I anticipated their entry. At the end of play-time I went to bring them in. They were a small class of about thirty – my own boys. A difficult, mixed class, they were, consisting of six London Home boys, five boys from a fairly well-to-do Home for the children of actors, and a set of commoners varying from poor lads who hobbled to school, crippled by broken enormous boots, to boys who brought soft, light shoes to wear in school on snowy days. The Gordons were a difficult set; you could pick them out: crop haired, coarsely dressed lads, distrustful, always ready to assume the defensive. They would lie till it made my heart sick, if they were charged with offence, but they were willing, and would respond beautifully to an appeal. The actors were of different fibre: some gentle, a pleasure even to look at; others polite and obedient, but indifferent, covertly insolent and vulgar; all of them more or less gentlemanly.

The boys crowded round the table noisily as soon as they discovered Joe. 'Is he alive? – Look, his head's coming out! He'll bite you? – He *won't*!' – with much scorn – 'Please, Sir, do tortoises bite?' I hurried them off to their seats in a little group in front, and pulled the table up to the desks. Joe kept fairly still. The boys nudged each other excitedly, making half-audible remarks concerning the poor reptile, looking quickly from me to Joe and then to their neighbours. I set them sketching, but in their pleasure at the novelty they could not be still:

'Please, Sir – shall we draw the marks on the shell? Please, Sir, has he only got four toes?' – 'Toes!' echoes somebody, covertly delighted at the absurdity of calling the grains of claws 'toes'. 'Please, Sir, he's moving – Please, Sir!'

I stroked his neck and calmed him down:

'Now don't make me wish I hadn't brought him. That's enough. Miles – you shall go to the back and draw twigs if I hear you again! Enough now – be still, get on with the drawing, it's hard!'

I wanted peace for myself. They began to sketch diligently. I stood and looked across at the sunset, which I could see facing me through my window, a great gold sunset, very large and magnificent, rising up in immense gold beauty beyond the town, that was become a low dark strip of nothingness under the wonderful up-building of the western sky. The light, the thick, heavy golden sunlight which is only seen in its full dripping splendour in town, spread on the desks and the floor like gold lacquer. I lifted my hands, to take the sunlight on them, smiling faintly to myself, trying to shut my fingers over its tangible richness.

'Please, Sir!' – I was interrupted – 'Please, Sir, can we have rubbers?'

The question was rather plaintive. I had said they should have rubbers no more. I could not keep my stock, I could not detect the thief among them, and I was weary of the continual degradation of bullying them to try to recover what was lost among them. But it was Friday afternoon, very peaceful and happy. Like a bad teacher, I went back on my word:

'Well –!' I said, indulgently.

My monitor, a pale, bright, erratic boy, went to the cupboard and took out a red box.

'Please, Sir!' he cried, then he stopped and counted again in the box. 'Eleven! There's only eleven, Sir, and there was fifteen when I put them away on Wednesday –!'

The class stopped, every face upturned. Joe sunk, and lay flat on his shell, his legs limp. Another of the hateful moments had come. The sunset was smeared out, the charm of the afternoon was smashed like a fair glass that falls to the floor. My nerves seemed to tighten, and to vibrate with sudden tension.

'Again!' I cried, turning to the class in passion, to the upturned faces, and the sixty watchful eyes.

'Again! I am sick of it, sick of it I am! A thieving, wretched set! – a skulking, mean lot!' I was quivering with anger and distress.

'Who is it? You must know! You are all as bad as one another, you hide it – a miserable –!' I looked round the class in great agitation. The 'Gordons', with their distrustful faces, were noticeable:

'Marples!' I cried to one of them, 'where are those rubbers?'

'I don't know where they are – I've never 'ad no rubbers' – he almost shouted back, with the usual insolence of his set. I was more angry:

'You must know! They're gone – they don't melt into air, they don't fly – who took them then? Rawson, do you know anything of them?'

'No, Sir!' he cried, with impudent indignation.

'No, you intend to know nothing! Wood, have you any knowledge of these four rubbers?'

'No!' he shouted, with absolute insolence.

'Come here!' I cried, 'come here! Fetch the cane, Burton. We'll make an end, insolence and thieving and all.'

The boy dragged himself to the front of the class, and stood slackly, almost crouching, glaring at me. The rest of the 'Gordons' sat upright in their desks, like animals of a pack ready to spring. There was tense silence for a moment. Burton handed me the cane, and I turned from the class to Wood. I liked him best among the Gordons.

'Now my lad!' I said. 'I'll cane you for impudence first.'

He turned swiftly to me; tears sprang to his eyes.

'Well,' he shouted at me, 'you always pick on the Gordons – you're always on to us –!' This was so manifestly untrue that my anger fell like a bird shot in a mid-flight.

'Why!' I exclaimed, 'what a disgraceful untruth! I am always excusing you, letting you off –!'

'But you pick on us – you start on us – you pick on Marples, an' Rawson, an' on me. You always begin with the Gordons.'

'Well,' I answered, justifying myself, 'isn't it natural? Haven't you boys stolen – haven't these boys stolen – several times – and been caught?'

'That doesn't say as we do now,' he replied.

'How am I to know? You don't help me. How do I know? Isn't it natural to suspect you –?'

'Well, it's not us. We know who it is. Everybody knows who it is – only they won't tell.'

'Who knows?' I asked.

'Why Rawson, and Maddock, and Newling, and all of 'em.'

I asked these boys if they could tell me. Each one shook his head, and said 'No, Sir.' I went round the class. It was the same. They lied to me every one.

'You see,' I said to Wood.

'Well – they won't own up,' he said. 'I shouldn't 'a done if you hadn't 'a been goin' to cane me.'

This frankness was painful, but I preferred it. I made them all sit down. I asked Wood to write his knowledge on a piece of paper, and I promised not to divulge. He would not. I asked the boys he had named, all of them. They refused. I asked them again – I appealed to them.

'Let them all do it then!' said Wood. I tore up scraps of paper, and gave each boy one.

'Write on it the name of the boy you suspect. He is a thief and a sneak. He gives endless pain and trouble to us all. It is your duty.'

They wrote furtively, and quickly doubled up the papers. I collected them in the lid of the rubber box, and sat at the table to examine them. There was dead silence, they all watched me. Joe had withdrawn into his shell, forgotten.

A few papers were blank; several had 'I suspect nobody' – these I threw in the paper basket; two had the name of an old thief, and these I tore up; eleven bore the name of my assistant monitor, a splendid, handsome boy, one of the oldest of the actors. I remembered how deferential and polite he had been when I had asked him, how ready to make barren suggestions; I remembered his shifty, anxious look during the questioning; I remembered how eager he had been to do things for me before the monitor came in the room. I knew it was he – without remembering.

'Well!' I said, feeling very wretched when I was convinced that the papers were right. 'Go on with the drawing.'

They were very uneasy and restless, but quiet. From time to time they watched me. Very shortly, the bell rang. I told the two monitors to collect up the things, and I sent the class home. We did not go into prayers. I, and they, were in no mood for hymns and the evening prayer of gratitude.

When the monitors had finished, and I had turned out all the lights but one, I sent home Curwen, and kept my assistant-monitor a moment.

'Ségar, do you know anything of my rubbers?'

'No, Sir' – he had a deep, manly voice, and he spoke with earnest pro-testation – flushing.

'No? Nor my pencils? – nor my two books?'

'No, Sir! I know nothing about the books.'

'No? The pencils then –?'

'No, Sir! Nothing! I don't know anything about them.'

'Nothing, Ségar?'

'No, Sir.'

He hung his head, and looked so humiliated, a fine, handsome lad, that I gave it up. Yet I knew he would be dishonest again, when the opportunity arrived.

'Very well! You will not help as monitor any more. You will not come into the classroom until the class comes in – any more. You understand?'

'Yes, Sir' – he was very quiet.

'Go along then.'

He went out, and silently closed the door. I turned out the last light, tried the cupboards, and went home.

I felt very tired, and very sick. The night had come up, the clouds were moving darkly, and the sordid streets near the school felt like disease in the lamplight.

Last Lesson of the Afternoon

When will the bell ring, and end this weariness?
How long have they tugged the leash, and strained apart,
My pack of unruly hounds! I cannot start
Them again on a quarry of knowledge they hate to hunt,
I can haul them and urge them no more.

No longer now can I endure the brunt
Of the books that lie out on the desks; a full threescore
Of several insults of blotted pages, and scrawl
Of slovenly work that they have offered me.
I am sick, and what on earth is the good of it all?
What good to them or me, I cannot see!

       So, shall I take
My last dear fuel of life to heap on my soul
And kindle my will to a flame that shall consume
Their dross of indifference; and take the toll
Of their insults in punishment? – I will not! –

I will not waste my soul and my strength for this.
What do I care for all that they do amiss!
What is the point of this teaching of mine, and of this
Learning of theirs? It all goes down the same abyss.

What does it matter to me, if they can write
A description of a dog, or if they can't?
What is the point? To us both, it is all my aunt!
And yet I'm supposed to care, with all my might.

I do not, and will not; they won't and they don't;
    and that's all!
I shall keep my strength for myself; they can keep
    theirs as well.
Why should we beat our heads against the wall
Of each other? I shall sit and wait for the bell.

Arguments

Men Must Work and
Women as Well

Supposing that circumstances go on pretty much in the same way they're going on in now, then men and women will go on pretty much in the same way they are now going on in. There is always an element of change, we know. But change is of two sorts: the next step, or a jump in another direction. The next step is called progress. If our society continues its course of gay progress along the given lines, then men and women will do the same: always along the given lines.

So what is important in that case is not so much men and women, but the given lines. The railway train doesn't matter particularly in itself. What matters is where it is going to. If I want to go to Crewe, then a train to Bedford is supremely uninteresting to me, no matter how full it may be. It will only arouse a secondary and temporal interest if it happens to have an accident.

And there you are with men and women today. They are not particularly interesting, and they are not, in themselves, particularly important. All the thousands and millions of bowler hats and neat handbags that go bobbing to business every day may represent so many immortal souls, but somehow we feel that is not for us to say. The clergyman is paid to tickle our vanity in these matters. What all the bowler hats and neat handbags represent to you and me and to each other is business, my dear, and a job.

So that, granted the present stream of progress towards better business and better jobs continues, the point is, not to consider the men and women bobbing in the stream, any more than you consider the drops of water in the Thames – but where the stream is flowing. Where is the stream flowing, indeed, the stream of progress? Everybody hopes, of course, it is flowing towards bigger business and better jobs. And what does that mean, again, to the man under the bowler hat and the woman who clutches the satchel?

It means, of course, more money, more congenial labours, and fewer hours. It means freedom from all irksome tasks. It means, apart from the few necessary hours of highly paid and congenial labour, that men and women shall have nothing to do except enjoy themselves. No beastly housework for the women, no beastly homework for the men. Free! free to enjoy themselves. More films, more motor-cars, more dances, more golf, more tennis and more getting completely away from yourself. And the goal of life is enjoyment.

Now if men and women want these things with sufficient intensity, they may really get them, and go on getting them. While the game is worth the candle, men and women will go on playing the game. And it seems today as if the motor-car, the film, the radio and the jazz were worth the candle. This being so, progress will continue from business to bigger business, and from job to better job. This is, in very simple terms, the plan of the universe laid down by the great magnates of industry like Mr Ford. And they know what they are talking about.

But – and the 'but' is a very big one – it is not easy to turn business into bigger business, and it is sometimes *impossible* to turn uncongenial jobs into congenial ones. This is where science really leaves us in the lurch, and calculation collapses. Perhaps in Mr Ford's super-factory of motor-cars all jobs may be made abstract and congenial. But the woman whose cook falls foul of the kitchen range, heated with coal, every day, hates that coal range herself even more darkly than the cook hates it. Yet many housewives can't afford electric cooking. And if everyone could, it still doesn't make housework entirely congenial. All the inventions of modern science fail to make housework anything but uncongenial to the modern woman, be she mistress or servantmaid. Now the only decent way to get something done is to get it done by somebody who quite likes doing it. In the past, cooks really enjoyed cooking and housemaids enjoyed scrubbing. Those days are over; like master, like man, and still more so, like mistress, like maid. Mistress loathes scrubbing; in two generations, maid loathes scrubbing. But scrubbing must be done. At what price? – raise the price. The price is raised, the scrubbing goes a little better. But after a while, the loathing of scrubbing becomes again paramount in the kitchenmaid's breast, and then ensues a general state of tension, and a general outcry: is it worth it? Is it really worth it?

What applies to scrubbing applies to all labour that cannot be mechanized or abstracted. A girl will slave over shorthand and typing for a pittance because it is not muscular work. A girl will not do housework well, not for a good wage. Why? Because, for some mysterious or obvious reason, the modern woman and the modern man hate physical work. Ask your husband to peel the potatoes, and earn his deep resentment. Ask your wife to wash your socks, and earn the same. There is still a certain thrill about 'mental' and purely mechanical work like attending a machine. But actual labour has become to us, with our education, abhorrent.

And it is here that science has not kept pace with human demand. It is here that progress is fatally threatened. There is an enormous, insistent demand on the part of the human being that mere labour, such as scrubbing, hewing and loading coal, navvying, the crude work that is the basis of all labour, shall be done away with. Even washing dishes. Science hasn't even learned how to wash dishes for us yet. The mistress who feels so intensely bitter about her maid who will not wash the dishes properly does so because she herself so loathes washing them. Science has rather left us in the lurch in these humble but basic matters. Before babies are conveniently bred in bottles, let the scientist find a *hey presto!* trick for turning dirty teacups into clean ones; since it is upon science we depend for our continued progress.

Progress, then, which proceeds so smoothly, and depends on science, does not proceed as rapidly as human feelings change. Beef-steaks are beef-steaks still, though all except the eating is horrible to us. A great deal must be done about a beef-steak besides the eating of it. And this great deal is done, we have to face the fact, unwillingly. When the mistress loathes trimming and grilling a beef-steak, or paring potatoes, or wringing the washing, the maid will likewise loathe these things, and do them at last unwillingly, and with a certain amount of resentment.

The one thing we don't sufficiently consider, in considering the march of human progress, is also the very dangerous march of human feeling that goes on at the same time and not always parallel. The change in human feeling! And one of the greatest changes that has ever taken place in man and woman is the revulsion from physical effort, physical labour and physical contact, which has taken place within the last thirty years. This change hits woman even harder than man, for she has always had to keep the immediate physical side going. And now it is repellent to her – just as nearly all physical activity is repellent to modern man. The film, the radio, the gramophone were all invented because physical effort and physical contact have become repulsive to man and woman alike. The aim is to abstract as far as possible. And science is our only help. And science still can't wash the dinner-things or darn socks or even mend the fire. Electric heaters or central heating, of course! But that's not all.

What, then, is the result? In the abstract we sail ahead to bigger business and better jobs and babies bred in bottles and food in tabloid form. But meanwhile science hasn't rescued us from beef-steaks and dish-washing, heavy labour and howling babies. There is a great hitch. And owing to the great hitch, a great menace to progress. Because every day mankind hates the business of beef-steaks and dish-washing, heavy labour and howling babies more bitterly.

The housewife is full of resentment – she can't help it. The young husband is full of resentment – he can't help it, when he has to plant potatoes to eke out the family income. The housemaid is full of resentment, the navvy is full of resentment, the collier is full of resentment, and the collier's wife is full of resentment, because her man can't earn a proper wage. Resentment grows as the strange fastidiousness of modern men and women increases. Resentment, resentment, resentment – because the basis of life is still brutally physical, and that has become repulsive to us. Mr Ford, being in his own way a genius, has realized that what the modern workman wants, just like the modern gentleman, is abstraction. The modern workman doesn't *want* to be 'interested' in his job. He wants to be as little interested, as nearly perfectly mechanical as possible. This is the great will of the people, and there is no gainsaying it. It is precisely the same in woman as in man. Woman demands an electric cooker because it makes no call on her attention or her 'interest' at all. It is almost a pure abstraction, a few switches, and no physical contact, no *dirt*, which is the inevitable result of physical contact, at all. If only we could make housework a real abstraction, a matter of turning switches and guiding a machine, the housewife would again be more or less content. But it can't quite be done, even in America.

And the resentment is enormous. The resentment against *eating*, in the breast of modern woman who has to prepare food, is profound. Why all this work and bother about *mere eating*? Why, indeed? Because neither science nor evolution has kept up with the change in human feeling, and beef-steaks are beef-steaks still, no matter how detestable they may have become to the people who have to prepare them. The loathsome fuss of food continues, and will continue, in spite of all talk about tabloids. The loathsome digging of coal out of the earth, by half-naked men, continues, deep underneath Mr Ford's super-factories. There it is, and there it will be, and you can't get away from it. While men quite enjoyed hewing coal, which they did, and while women really enjoyed cooking, even with a coal range, which they did – then all was well. But suppose society *en bloc* comes to hate the thought of sweating cooking over a hot range, or sweating hacking at a coal-seam, then what are you to do? You have to ask, or to demand that a large section of society shall do something they have come to hate doing, and which you would hate to do yourself. What then? Resentment and ill-feeling!

Social life means all classes of people living more or less harmoniously together. And private life means men and women, man and woman living together more or less congenially. If there is serious discord between the social classes, then society is threatened with confusion. If there is serious discord between man and woman, then the individual, and that means practically everybody, is threatened with internal confusion and unhappiness.

Now it is quite easy to keep the working classes in harmonious working order, so long as you don't ask them to do work they simply do not want to do. The board-schools, however, did the fatal deed. They said to the boys: 'work is noble, but what you want is to *get on*, you don't want to stick down a coal-mine all your life. Rise up, and do *clean* work! Become a school-teacher or a clerk, not a common collier.'

This is sound board-school education, and is in keeping with all the noblest social ideals of the last century. Unfortunately it entirely overlooks the unpleasant effect of such teaching on those who *cannot* get on, and who must perforce stick down a coal-mine all their lives. And these, in the board-school of a mining district, are at least 90 per cent of the boys; it must be so. So that 90 per cent of these board-school scholars are deliberately taught, at school, to be malcontents, taught to despise themselves for not having 'got on', for not having 'got out of the pit', for sticking down all their lives doing 'dirty work' and being 'common colliers'. Naturally, every collier, doomed himself, wants to get his boys out of the pit, to be gentlemen. And since this again is *impossible* in 90 per cent of the cases, the number of 'gentlemen', or clerks and school-teachers, being strictly proportionate to the number of colliers, there comes again the sour disillusion. So that by the third generation you have exactly what you've got today, the young malcontent collier. He has been deliberately produced by modern education coupled with modern conditions, and is logically, inevitably and naturally what he is: a malcontent collier. According to all the accepted teaching, he ought to have risen and bettered himself: equal opportunity, you know. And he hasn't risen and bettered himself. Therefore he is more or less a failure in his own eyes even. He is doomed to do dirty work. He is a malcontent. Now even Mr Ford can't make coal-mines clean and shiny and abstract. Coal won't be abstracted. Even a Soviet can't do it. A coal-mine remains a hole in the black earth, where blackened men hew and shovel and sweat. You can't abstract it, or make it an affair of pulling levers, and, what is even worse, you can't abandon it, you can't do away with it. There it is, and it has got to be. Mr Ford forgets that his clean and pure and harmonious super-factory, where men only pull shining levers or turn bright handles, has all had to be grossly mined and smelted before it could come into existence. Mr Ford's is one of the various heavens of industry. But these heavens rest on various hells of labour, always did and always will. Science rather leaves us in the lurch in these matters. Science is supposed to remove these hells for us. And – it doesn't. Not at all!

If you had never taught the blackened men down the various hells that they *were* in hell, and made them despise themselves for being there – a *common* collier, a *low* labourer – the mischief could never have developed so rapidly. But now we have it, all society resting on a labour basis of smouldering resentment. And the collier's question: how would *you* like to be a collier? – is unanswerable. We know perfectly well we should dislike it intensely. – At the same time, my father, who never went to a board-school, quite liked it. But he has been improved on. Progress! Human feeling has changed, changed rapidly and radically. And science has not changed conditions to fit.

What is to be done? We all loathe brute physical labour. We all think it is horrible to have to do it. We consider those that actually do it low and vile, and we have told them so, for fifty years, urging them to get away from it and 'better themselves', which would be very nice, if everybody *could* get on, and brute labour could be abandoned, as, scientifically, it ought to be. But actually, not at all. We are forced to go on forcing a very large proportion of society to remain 'unbettered', 'low and common', 'common colliers, common labourers', since a very large portion of humanity must still spend its life labouring, now and in the future, science having let us down in this respect. You can't teach mankind to 'better himself' unless you'll better the gross earth to fit him. And the gross earth remains what it was, and man its slave. For neither science nor evolution shows any signs of saving us from our gross necessities. The labouring masses are and will be, even if all else is swept away: because they must be. They represent the gross necessity of man, which science has failed to save us from.

So then, what? The only thing that remains to be done is to make labour as likeable as possible, and try to teach the labouring masses to like it: which, given the trend of modern feeling, not only sounds, but is, fatuous. Mankind *en bloc* gets more fastidious and more 'nice' every day. Every day it loathes dirty work more deeply. And every day the whole pressure of social consciousness works towards making everybody more fastidious, more 'nice', more refined, and more unfit for dirty work. Before you make all humanity unfit for dirty work, you should first remove the necessity for dirty work.

But such being the condition of men and women with regard to work

– a condition of repulsion in the breasts of men and women for the work that has got to be done – what about private life, the relation between man and woman? How does the new fastidiousness and nicety of mankind affect this?

Profoundly! The revulsion from physical labour, physical effort, physical contact has struck a death-blow at marriage and home-life. In the great trend of the times, a woman cannot save herself from the universal dislike of housework, housekeeping, rearing children and keeping a home going. Women make the most unselfish efforts in this direction, because it is generally expected of them. But this cannot remove the *instinctive* dislike of preparing meals and scouring saucepans, cleaning baby's bottles or darning the man's underwear, which a large majority of women feel today. It is something which there is no denying, a real physical dislike of doing these things. Many women school themselves and are excellent housewives, physically disliking it all the time. And this, though admirable, is wearing. It is an exhaustive process, with many ill results.

Can it be possible that women actually ever did like scouring saucepans and cleaning the range? – I believe some few women still do. I believe that twenty years ago, even, the majority of women enjoyed it. But what, then, has happened? Can human instincts really change?

They can, and in the most amazing fashion. And this is the great problem for the sociologist: the violent change in human instinct, especially in women. Woman's instinct used to be all for home, shelter, the protection of the man, and the happiness of running her own house. Now it is all against. Woman *thinks* she wants a lovely little home of her own, but her instinct is all against it, when it means matrimony. She *thinks* she wants a man of her own, but her instinct is dead against having him around all the time. She would like him on a long string, that she can let out or pull in, as she feels inclined. But she just doesn't want him inevitably and insidiously there all the time – not even every evening – not even for weekends, if it's got to be a fixture. She wants him to be merely intermittent in her landscape, even if he is always present in her soul, and she writes him the most intimate letters every day. All well and good! But her instinct is against him, against his permanent and perpetual physical presence. She doesn't want to feel his presence as something material, unavoidable and permanent. It goes dead against her grain, it upsets her instinct. She loves him, she loves, even, being faithful to him. But she doesn't want him substantially around. She doesn't want his actual physical presence – except in snatches. What she *really* loves is the thought of him, the idea of him, the *distant* communion with him – varied with snatches of actually being together, like little festivals, which we are more or less glad when they are over.

Now a great many modern girls feel like this, even when they force themselves to behave in the conventional side-by-side fashion. And a great many men feel the same – though perhaps not so acutely as the women. Young couples may force themselves to be conventional husbands and wives, but the strain is often cruel, and the result often disastrous.

Now then we see the trend of our civilization in terms of human feeling and human relation. It is, and there is no denying it, towards a greater and greater abstraction from the physical, towards a further and further physical separateness between men and women, and between individual and individual. Young men and women today are together all the time, it will be argued. Yes, but they are together as good sports, good chaps, in strange independence of one another, intimate one moment, strangers the next, hands-off! all the time and as little connected as the bits in a kaleidoscope.

The young have the fastidiousness, the nicety, the revulsion from the physical, intensified. To the girl today, a man whose physical presence she is aware of, especially a bit *heavily* aware of, is or becomes really abhorrent. She wants to fly away from him to the uttermost ends of the earth. And as soon as women or girls get a bit female physical, young men's nerves go all to pieces. The sexes can't stand one another. They adore one another as spiritual or personal creatures, all talk and wit and back-chat, or jazz and motor-cars and machines, or tennis and swimming – even sitting in bathing-suits all day on a beach. But this is all peculiarly non-physical, a flaunting of the body in its non-physical, merely optical aspect. So much nudity, fifty years ago, would have made man and woman quiver through and through. Now, not at all! People flaunt their bodies to show how unphysical they are. The more the girls are not desired, the more they uncover themselves.

And this means, when we analyse it out, repulsion. The young are, in a subtle way, physically repulsive to one another, the girl to the man and the man to the girl. And they rather enjoy the feeling of repulsion, it is a sort of contest. It is as if the young girl said to the young man today: I rather like you, you know. You are so thrillingly repulsive to me. – And as if the young man replied: Same here! – There may be, of course, an intense bodiless sort of affection between young men and women. But as soon as either becomes a positive physical presence to the other, immediately there is repulsion.

And marriages based on the thrill of physical repulsion, as so many are today, even when coupled with mental 'adoring' or real wistful, bodiless affection, are in the long run – not so very long, either – catastrophic. There you have it, the great 'spirituality', the great 'betterment' or refinement; the great fastidiousness; the great 'niceness' of feeling; when a girl must be a flat, thin, bodiless stick, and a boy a correct mannequin, each of them abstracted towards real caricature. What does it all amount to? What is its motive force?

What it amounts to, really, is physical repulsion. The great spirituality of our age means that we are all physically repulsive to one another. The great advance in refinement of feeling and squeamish fastidiousness means that we hate the *physical* existence of anybody and everybody, even ourselves. The amazing move into abstraction on the part of the whole of humanity – the film, the radio, the gramophone – means that we loathe the physical element in our amusements, we don't *want* the physical contact, we want to get away from it. We don't *want* to look at flesh and blood people – we want to watch their shadows on a screen. We don't *want* to hear their actual voices: only transmitted through a machine. We must get away from the physical.

The vast mass of the lower classes – and this is most extraordinary – are even more grossly abstracted, if we may use the term, than the educated classes. The uglier sort of working man today truly has no body and no real feelings at all. He eats the most wretched food, because taste has left him, he only *sees* his meal, he never *really* eats it. He drinks his beer by idea, he no longer tastes it at all. This must be so, or the food and beer could not be as bad as they are. And as for his relation to his women – his poor women – they are pegs to hang clothes on, and there's an end of them. It is a horrible state of feelingless depravity, atrophy of the senses.

But under it all, as ever, as everywhere, vibrates the one great impulse of our civilization, physical recoil from every other being and from every form of physical existence. Recoil, recoil, recoil. Revulsion, revulsion, revulsion. Repulsion, repulsion, repulsion. This is the rhythm that underlies our social activity, everywhere, with regard to physical existence.

Now we are all basically and permanently physical. So is the earth, so even is the air. What then is going to be the result of all this recoil and repulsion, which our civilization has deliberately fostered?

The result is really only one and the same: some form of collective social madness. Russia, being a very physical country, was in a frantic state of physical recoil and 'spirituality' twenty years ago. We can look on the revolution, really, as nothing but a great outburst of anti-physical insanity; we can look on Soviet Russia as nothing but a logical state of society established in anti-physical insanity. – Physical and material are, of course, not the same; in fact, they are subtly opposite. The machine is absolutely material, and absolutely anti-physical – as even our fingers know. And the Soviet is established on the image of the machine, 'pure' materialism. The Soviet hates the real physical body far more deeply than it hates Capital. It mixes it up with the bourgeois. But it sees very little danger in it, since all western civilization is now mechanized, materialized and ready for an outburst of insanity which shall throw us all into some purely machine-driven unity of lunatics.

What about it, then? What about it, men and women? The only thing to do is to get your bodies back, men and women. A great part of society is irreparably lost: abstracted into non-physical, mechanical entities whose motive power is still recoil, revulsion, repulsion, hate and, ultimately, blind destruction. The driving force *underneath* our society remains the same: recoil, revulsion, hate. And let this force once run out of hand, and we know what to expect. It is not only in the working class. The well-to-do classes are just as full of the driving force of recoil, revulsion, which ultimately becomes hate. The force is universal in our spiritual civilization. Let it once run out of hand, and then –

It only remains for some men and women, individuals, to try to get back their bodies and preserve the other flow of warmth, affection and physical unison. There is nothing else to do.

Education of the People

1

What is education all about? What is it doing? Does anybody know? It doesn't matter so much for people with money. For them social intercourse is an end in itself, a sort of charming game for which they need a little polish of manner, a trifle of social grace, and a certain amount of accomplishments, mental and otherwise. Even supposing they look on life as a serious affair, it only means they intend, in some way or other, to devote themselves to the service of the nation. And the service of the nation, though an important matter surely, is by now a somewhat cut-and-dried business.

The point is, the nation which is served. And what is the nation? Without attempting a high-flown definition, it is the people. And who are the people? Why, they are the proletariat. For according to the modern democratic ideal under which we still march, *ideally*, the upper classes exist only for the purpose of devoting themselves to the good of the people. Everything works back to the people, to the proletariat, strictly. If a man justifies his existence nowadays – and what man doesn't? – he proclaims that he is a servant and benefactor of the people, the vast proletariat. From the King downwards, this is so.

And the people, the proletariat. What about them and their education? They are the be-all and the end-all. To them everything is *ideally* devoted (mind, we are only writing now of education as it exists for us as an ideal, or an idea). There is not an idealist, or a man of ideas living who does not ostensibly come forward, like the Pope in Holy Week, with a basin and a towel to bathe the feet of the poor. And the poor sit aloft while their feet are laved. And then what? What *are* the poor, actually?

Because, before you can educate the people, you must know what the people are. We know well enough they are the proletariat, the human implements of industry. But that, we argue, is in their utilitarian aspect only. They have a higher reality. Their proletarian or laborious nature is their mundane nature. When the Pope washes the feet of the poor men, it is not because the poor men have been shunting trucks on the railway and got their feet hot and dirty. Not at all. He washes their feet as an act of symbolic recognition of the divine nature which is alive in each of these poor men. In this world, we are content to recognize divinity only in those that serve. The whole world screams *Ich dien*. Heaven knows *what* it serves! And yet, if we go back to the Pope, we shall realize that it is not in the *service*, the *labour* that he recognizes the divinity, but in the actual nature of the *servant*, the labourer, the humble individual. He washes the feet of the humble, not the feet of trades-unionistic, strike-menacing truck-shunters.

The man and his job. You've got to make a distinction between the two. If Louis Quatorze was content to be a State, we can't allow (ideally, at least) our dustman Jim Shepherd to regard himself as the apotheosis of dustbins. When Louis Quatorze said that He was the State, or the State was Him, he belittled himself really. For after all, it is a much rarer and more difficult thing to be oneself than to be either a State or a dustbin. At his best, a man is himself; his job, even if it be State-swaying, comes a long way after. For almost anybody could sway a State or swing a dust tub. But no man can take on another man's self. If you want to be unique, be yourself. And the spark of divinity in each being, however humble, is what the Pope recognizes in Holy Week.

The job is not by any means holy: and the man, in some degree, is. No doubt here we shall raise the wind of opposition from labour units and employer's units. But we don't care. We represent the true idealists who even now sit on the Board of Education and foggily but fervently enact their ideals. The job is not at all divine, the labour in some measure *is*. So let technical education remain apart.

But here comes the first dilemma. Because, however cloistral our elementary schools may be, sheltering the eternal flame of the high ideal of human existence, Jimmy Shepherd, aged twelve, and Nancy Shepherd, aged thirteen, know very well that the eternal flame of the high ideal is all my-eye. It's all toffee, my dear sirs. What you've got to do is to *get a job*, and when you've got your job then you must *make a decent screw*. First and last, this is the state of man. So says little Jimmy Shepherd, and so says his sister Nancy. She's got her thirteen-year-old eye on a laundry, and he's got his twelve-year-old eye on a bottle factory. Headmaster and headmistress and all the teachers know perfectly well that the high goal of all *their* endeavours is the laundry and the bottle-factory. They try to stunt a bit sometimes about the high ideal of human existence, the dignity of human life or the nobility of labour. But if they *really* want to put the fear of the Lord into Jimmy or Nancy they say: 'You'll break more bottles than you'll make, my young genius,' or else 'You'll burn more shirt-fronts than you'll brighten, my girl: and *then* you'll know what you're in for, at the weekend.' This mystic weekend is not the sacred Sabbath of Holy Communion, it is *payday*, and nothing else.

The high idealists up in Whitehall may preserve some illusion around themselves. But there is absolutely no illusion for the elementary school-teachers. They know what the end will be. And they know that they've got to keep their *own* job, and they've got to struggle for a headship. And between the disillusion of their scholars' destiny, on the one hand, and the disillusion of their own mean and humiliating destiny, on the other, they haven't much breath left for the fanning of the high flame of noble human existence.

If ever there is a poor devil on the face of the earth it is the elementary school-teacher. He is invested with a wretched idealist sort of authority over a pack of children, an authority which parents jeer at and despise. For they know the teacher is under *their* thumb. '*I* pay for you, I'll let you know, out of the rates. *I'm* your employer. And therefore you'll treat my child properly, or I'm going up to the Town Hall.' All of which Jimmy and Nancy exultingly hear, and the teacher, guardian of the high flame of human divinity, quakes because he knows his job is in danger. He is insulted from above and from below. Comes along an inspector of schools, a university man himself, with no respect for the sordid promiscuity of the elementary school. For elementary schools know no remoteness and dignity of the rostrum. The teacher is on a level with the scholars, or inferior to them. And an elementary school knows no code of honour, no *esprit de corps*. There is the profound cynicism of the laundry and the bottle-factory at the bottom of everything. How should a refined soul down from Oxford fail to find it a little sordid and common?

The elementary school-teacher is in a vile and false position. Set up as representative of an ideal which is all toffee, invested in an authority which has absolutely no base except in the teacher's own isolate will, he is sneered at by the idealists above and jeered at by the materialists below, and ends by being a mongrel who is neither a wage-earner nor a professional, neither a head-worker nor a hand-worker, neither living by his brain nor by his physical toil, but a bit of both, and despised for both. He is caught between the upper and nether millstones of idealism and materialism, and every shred of natural pride is ground out of him, so that he has to die or to cultivate some unpleasant *suffisance* which makes him objectionable for ever.

Yet who dare say that the idealists are wrong? And who dare say the materialists are right? The elementary school is where the two meet, like millstones. And teacher and scholars are ground between the two.

It is absolutely fatal for the manhood of the teacher. And it is bitterly detrimental for the scholars. You can hardly keep a boy for ten years in the elementary schools, 'educating him' to be himself, 'educating him' up to the high ideal of human existence, with the bottle-factory outside the gate all the time, without producing a state of cynicism in the child's soul. Children are wonderfully subtle at dodging a hateful conclusion. If they are going to live, they must keep some illusions. But alas, they know the shoddiness of their illusions. What boy of fourteen, in an elementary school, but is a subtle cynic about all ideals?

What is wrong, then? The system. But when you've said that you've said nothing. The system, after all, is only the outcome of the human psyche, the human desires. We shout and blame the machine. But who on earth makes the machine, if we don't? And any alterations in the system are only modifications in the machine. The system is *in us*, it is not something external to us. The machine is in us, or it would never come out of us. Well then, there's nothing to blame but ourselves, and there's nothing to change except inside ourselves.

For instance, you may exclude technical training from the elementary schools; you may prolong the school years to the age of sixteen – or to the age of twenty, if you like. And what then? At the gate of the school lies the sphinx who puts this question to every emerging scholar, boy or girl: 'How are you going to make your living?' And every boy or girl must answer or die: so the poor things believe.

We call this the system. It isn't, really. The trouble lies in us who are so afraid of this particular sphinx. 'My dear sphinx, my wants are very small, my needs still smaller. I wonder you trouble yourself about so trivial a matter. I am going to get a job in a bottle factory, where I shall have to spend a certain number of hours a day. But that is the least of my concerns. My dear sphinx, you are a kitten at riddles. If you asked me, now, what I'm going to do with my life, apart from the bottle factory, you might have frightened me. As it is, really, every smoky tall chimney is an answer to you.'

Curious that when the toothless old sphinx croaks 'How are you going to get your living?' our knees give way beneath us. What has happened to us, that we are so frightened by that toothless old lion of *want*? Do we really think we might not be able to earn our bread and butter? – bread and margarine, at the worst? Why are we so frightened? Out of fifty million people, about ten thousand can't obtain their bread and butter without the workhouse or some such aid. But what's the odds? The odds against earning your living are one in five thousand. There are not so many odds against your dying of typhoid or being killed in a street-accident. Yet you don't really care a snap about street-accidents or typhoid. Then why are you so afraid of dying of starvation? You'll never die of starvation, anyhow. So what *are* you afraid of?

The fear of penury is very curious, in our age. In really poor ages, men did not fear penury. They didn't care. But we are abjectly terrified of it. Why? It isn't any such awful thing, if you don't care about keeping up appearances.

There is no cure for this craven terror of poverty save in human courage and insouciance. A sphinx has you by your cravenness. Oedipus and all those before him might just have easily answered the sphinx by saying, 'Oh, my dear sphinx, that's quite easy. A Borogrove, of course. What, don't you know what a Borogrove is? My dear sphinx, go to school, go to school. I knew all about Borogroves before I was out of the cradle, and here you are, heaven knows how old, propounding silly riddles to which Borogrove is the answer, and you admit you've never heard of one. I absolutely refuse to concern myself with *your* solution, if you know nothing of mine.' Exit the sphinx with its tail between its legs.

And so with the sphinx of our material existence. She'll never go off with her tail between her legs till we simply jeer at her. 'Earn my living, you crazy old bitch? Why, I'm going Jimmy-Shepherding. No, not sheep at all. *Jimmishepherding*. You don't understand. Worse luck for you, old bird.'

You can set up State Aid and Old Age Pensions and Young Age Pensions till you're black in the face. But if you can't cure people of being frightened for their own existence, you'll educate them in vain. You may as well let a frightened little Jimmy Shepherd go bottle-blowing at the age of four. If he's frightened for his own existence, he'll never do more than keep himself assertively materially alive. And that's the end of it. So he might just as well start young, and avoid those lying years of idealistic education.

So that the first thing to be done, in the education of the people, is to cure them of the fear of not earning their own living. This won't be easy. The fear goes deep, in our nervous age. Men will go through all the agonies of war, and come out more frightened still of not being able to earn their living. It is a mystery. They will face guns and shells and unspeakable horrors, almost with equanimity. After all, that's merely death. It's not life. Life is the thing to be afraid of – and having enough money to live on is the anguished soul-problem. It has become an *idée fixe*, the idea of earning, or not earning, a living. And we are all monomaniacs in it.

And yet, the only way to solve the whole problem is to cure mankind, from the inside, of the fear. And this is the business of our reformed education. At present, we are all in the boat because our idealists are just as terrified of not earning their living as are the materialists. Even more.

That's the point. The idealists are more terrified than the materialists about not being able to earn their living. The materialists are brutal about it. They don't have to excuse themselves. They handle the tools and do the graft. But the idealists, those that sit in the Olympus of Whitehall, for example? It is they who tremble. They are earning their living tooth-and-nail, by promulgating up there in the clouds. But the material world cocks its eye on them. It keeps them as a luxury, as the Greeks kept their Olympic gods. After all, the idealists butter our motives with fair words and their own parsnips. When we have at last decided that our motives are none the better for the fair-word buttering of idealism, then the idealists will have to eat their Olympic parsnips very dry. Which is what they are afraid of. So they churn fair words, up there, and the proletariat churns margarine and a little butter down below, and so far there is an exchange. But as the price of butter rises the price of fair words depreciates, till the idealists are in a fair way of doing no trade at all, up on Olympus. Which is what they are afraid of. So they churn phrases like mad, hoping to bring out something that will catch the market.

And there we are. Between the idealists and the materialists our poor 'elementary' children have their education shaken into them. Which is a shame. It is a shame to treat children as we treat them in school, to a lot of highfalutin and lies, and to a lot of fear and humiliation. Instead of putting the fear of the Lord into them we put the fear of the job. After which the job rises up and gives us a nasty knock in the eye; we get strikes and labour menaces, and idealism is in a fair way of being kicked off Olympus altogether. Materialism threatens to sit aloft. And Olympus fawns and cringes, and is terrified, because it doesn't know how it will earn its living.

Idealism would be all right if it weren't frightened. But it *is* frightened: frightened to death. It is terrified that it won't be able to butter its parsnips. It is terrified that it won't be able to make a living. Curious thing, but rich people are inwardly more terrified of poverty, want, destitution, even than poor people. Even the proletariat is not so agonized with fear of not being able to make a living as are millionaires and dukes. The more the money the more intense the fear.

So there we are, all living in an agony and nightmare of fear of not being able to make a living. But we actually *are* the living. We live, and therefore everything is ours. Whence, then, the fear? Just a sort of irrational mob-panic.

Idealism *must* get over its fright. It is most to blame. There it sits in a fog, promulgating ideas and ideals, and all the time in a mad panic for fear of losing its job. There it sits decreeing that our children shall be educated pure from the taint of materialism and industrialism, and all the time it is fawning and cringing before industrialism and materialism, and having throes and spasms of agony about its own salary. Certainly even idealists must have a salary. But why are they in such agonies of fear lest it be not forthcoming? After all, if they draw a salary, it is because they are *not* frightened. Their salary is the tithe due to their living fearlessness. And so, cadging their screw in panic, they are a swindle. And they cause our children to be educated to the tune of their swindlery.

And then no wonder that our children, the children of the people, look down their nose at ideals. It is no wonder the young workmen sneer at all idealism, all idealists, and at everything higher than wages and short hours. They are having their own back on the lie, and on the liars, that educated them in school. They've been educated in the lie, and therefore

they also can spout idealism at will. But by their deeds ye shall know
them: both parties.

Here's the end, then, of the first word on Education. Idealism is no
good without fearlessness. To follow a high aim, you must be fearless of
the consequences. To promulgate a high aim, and to be fearful of the
consequences – as our idealists today – is much worse than leaving high
aims alone altogether. Teach the three R's and leave the children to look
out for their own aims. That's the very best thing we can do at the
moment, since we are all cowards.

But later, when we've plucked a bit of our courage up, we'll embark
on a new course of education, and *vogue la galère*. Those of us that are
going to starve, why, we'll take our chance. Who has wits, and *guts*,
doesn't starve: neither does he care about starving. *Courage, mes amis*.

2

Elementary education today assumes two responsibilities. It has in its
hands the moulding of the nation. And elementary school-teachers are
taught that they are to mould the young nation to two ends. They are
to strive to produce in the child under their charge: 1. the perfect citizen; 2. the perfect individual.

Unfortunately the teachers are not enlightened as to what we mean
by a perfect citizen and a perfect individual. When they are, during their
training, instructed and lectured upon the teaching of history, they are
told that the examples of history teach us the virtues of citizenship: and
when drawing and painting and literary composition are under discussion, these subjects are supposed to teach the child self-expression.

Citizenship has been an indefinite *Fata Morgana* to the elementary
school-teacher: but self-expression has been a worse. Before the war we
sailed serene under this flag of self-expression. Each child was to *express
himself*: why, nobody thought necessary to explain. But infants were to
express themselves, and nothing but themselves. Here was a pretty task
for a teacher: he was to make his pupil *express himself*. Which *self* was
left vague. A child was to be given a lump of soft clay and told to express
himself, presumably in the pious hope that he might model a Tanagra
figure or a Donatello plaque, all on his little lonely-o.

Now it is obvious that every boy's first act of self-expression would
be to throw the lump of soft clay at something: preferably at the teacher.
This impulse is to be suppressed. On what grounds, metaphysically? since
the soft clay was given for self-expression. To this just question there
is no answer. Self-expression in infants means, presumably, incipient
Tanagra figurines and Donatello plaques, incipient *Iliads* and *Macbeths*

and 'Odes to the Nightingale': a world of infant prodigies, in short. And the responsibility for all this foolery was heaped on the shoulders of that public clown, the elementary school-teacher.

The war, however, brought us to our senses a little, and we ran the flag of citizenship up above the flag of self-expression. This was much easier for the teacher. At least, now, the ideal was *service*, not self-expression. 'Work, and learn how to serve your country.' Service means authority: while self-expression means pure negation of all authority. So that teaching became a somewhat simpler matter under the ideal of national service.

However, the war is over, and there is a slump in national service. The public isn't inspired by the ideal of serving its country any more: it has had its whack. And the idealists, who must run to give the public the inspiration it fancies at the moment, are again coming forward with trayfuls of infant prodigies and 'self-expression'.

Now citizenship and self-expression are all right, as ideals for the education of the people, if only we knew what we meant by the two terms. The interpretation we give them is just ludicrous. Self-sacrifice in time of need; disinterested nobility of heart to enable each one to vote properly at a general election; an understanding of what is meant by income-tax and money interest; all vague and fuzzy. Nobody pretends to enlighten the teacher as to the mysteries of citizenship. Nobody attempts to instruct *him* in the relationship of the individual to the community. Nothing at all. There is a little gas about *esprit de corps* and national interest – but it is all gas.

None of which would matter if we would just leave the ideals out of our educational system. If we were content to teach a child to read and write and do his modicum of arithmetic, just as at an earlier stage his mother teaches him to walk and to talk, so that he may toddle his little way upon the face of the earth by himself, it would be all right. It would be a thousand times better, as things stand, to chuck overboard all your drawing and painting and music and modelling and pseudo-science and 'graphic' history and 'graphic' geography and 'self-expression', all the lot. Pitch them overboard, teach the three Rs, and then proceed with a certain amount of technical instruction, in preparation for the coming job. For all the rest, for all that concerns the child himself, leave him alone. If he likes to learn, the means of learning are in his hands. Brilliant scholars could be drafted into secondary schools. If he doesn't like to learn, it is his affair. The quality of learning is not strained. Is not radical *unlearnedness* just as true a form of self-expression, and just as desirable a state, for many natures (even the bulk), as learnedness? Here we talk of free self-expression, and we proceed to force all natures into ideal and aesthetic expression. We talk about individuality, and try to drag up every weed into a rose-bush. If a nettle likes to be a nettle, if it likes to have no flowers to speak of, why, that's the nettle's affair. Why should we force some poor devil of an elementary school-teacher to sting his fingers to bits trying to graft the obstreperous nettle-stem with rose and vine? We, who sail under the flag of freedom, are bullies such as the world has never known before: idealist bullies; bullying idealism, which will allow nothing except in terms of itself.

Every teacher knows that it is worse than useless trying to educate at least 50 per cent of his scholars. Worse than useless: it is dangerous; perilously dangerous. What is the result of it? Drag a lad who has no capacity for true learning or understanding through the processes of education, and what do you produce in him, in the end? A profound contempt for education, and for all educated people. It has meant nothing to him but irritation and disgust. And that which a man finds irritating and disgusting he finds odious and contemptible.

And this is the point to which we are bringing the nation, inevitably. Everybody is educated: and what is education? A sort of *unmanliness*. Go down in the hearts of the masses of the people and this is what you'll find: the cynical conviction that every educated man is unmanly, less manly than an uneducated man. Every little Jimmy Shepherd has dabbled his bit in pseudo-science and in the arts; he has seen a test-tube and he has handled plasticine and a camel's-hair brush; he knows that $a+a+b=2a+b$. What more is there for him to know? Nothing. Pfui to your learning.

A little learning *is* a dangerous thing: how dangerous we are likely to be finding out. A man who has not the soul, or the spirit, to learn and to *understand*, he whose whole petty education consists in the acquiring of a few tricks, will inevitably, in the end, come to regard all educated or understanding people as tricksters. And once *that* happens, what becomes of your State? It is inevitably at the mercy of your bottle-washing Jimmy Shepherds and his parallel Nancys. For the uninstructible outnumber the instructible by a very large majority. Behold us then in the grimy fist of Jimmy Shepherd, the uninstructible Brobdingnag. Fools we are, we've put ourselves there: so if he pulls all our heads off, serves us right. He is Brobdingnagian because he is legion. Whilst we poor instructible mortals are Lilliputian in comparison. And the one power we had, the power of commanding reverence or respect in the Brobdingnag, a power God-given to us, we ourselves have squandered and degraded. On our own heads be it.

For a sensible system of education, then. Begin at the age of seven –
five is too soon – and teach reading, writing, arithmetic as the only
necessary mental subjects: reading to include geography, map-practice,
history and so on. Three hours a day is enough for these. Another hour
a day might be devoted to physical and domestic training. Leave a child
alone for the rest: out of sight and out of mind.

At the age of twelve, make a division. Teachers, schoolmasters, school-
inspectors and parents will carefully decide what children shall be educated further. These shall be drafted to secondary schools, where an
extended curriculum includes Latin or French, and some true science.
Secondary scholars will remain till the age of sixteen.

The children who will not be drafted to the secondary schools will,
at the age of twelve, have their 'mental' education reduced to two hours,
whilst three hours will be devoted to physical and domestic training;
that is, martial exercises and the rudiments of domestic labour, such as
boot-mending, plumbing, soldering, painting and paper-hanging, garden-
ing – all those minor trades on which domestic life depends, and in which
every working man should have some proficiency. This is to continue
for three years.

Then on the completion of the fourteenth year, these scholars will be
apprenticed half-time to some trade to which they are judged fitting, by
a consensus of teachers and parents and the scholars themselves. For
two years these half-timers shall spend the morning at their own trade,
and some two hours in the afternoon at martial exercises and reading
and at what we call domestic training, boot-mending, etc. At the age of
sixteen they enter on their regular labours, as artisans.

The secondary scholars shall for two years, from the age of twelve to
the age of fourteen, follow the curriculum of the secondary school for
four hours a day, but shall put in one hour a day at the workshops and
at physical training. At the completion of the fourteenth year a division
shall be made among these secondary scholars. Those who are apparently 'complete' as far as mental education can make them, according
to their own nature and capacity, shall be drafted into some apprentice-
ship for some sort of semi-profession, such as school-teaching, and all
forms of clerking. Like the elementary scholars, however, all secondary
scholars put in two hours in the afternoon at reading and in the workshops or at physical training: one hour for the mental education, one
hour for the physical. At the age of sixteen, clerks, school-teachers, etc.
shall enter their regular work, or the regular training for their work.

The remaining scholars, of the third or highest class, shall at the age of
sixteen be drafted into colleges. Those that have scientific bent shall be

trained scientifically, those that incline to the liberal arts shall be educated according to their inclination, and those that have gifts in the pure arts or in the technical arts shall find artistic training. But an hour a day shall be devoted to some craft, and to physical training. Every man shall have a craft at which finally he is expert – or two crafts if he choose – even if he be destined for professional activity as a doctor, a lawyer, a priest, a professor and so on.

The scholars of the third class shall remain in their colleges till the age of twenty, receiving there a general education as in our colleges today, although emphasis is laid on some particular branch of the education. At the age of twenty these scholars shall be drafted for their years of final training – as doctors, lawyers, priests, artists and so on. At the age of twenty-two they shall enter the world.

All education should be State education. All children should start together in the elementary schools. From the age of seven to the age of twelve boys and girls of every class should be educated together in the elementary schools. This will give us a common human basis, a common radical understanding. All children, boys and girls, should receive a training in the respective male and female domestic crafts. Every man should finally be expert at some craft, and should be a trained *free* soldier, no matter what his profession. Every woman also should have her chosen, expert craft, so that each individual is master of some kind of work.

Of course a great deal will depend on teachers and headmasters. The elementary teachers will not be so terribly important, but they will be carefully selected for their power to control and instruct children, not for their power to pass examinations. Headmasters will always be men of the highest education, invested with sound authority. A headmaster, once established, will be like a magistrate in a community.

Because one of the most important parts in this system of education will be the judging of the scholars. Teachers, masters, inspectors and parents will all of them unite to decide the next move for the child. The child will be consulted – but the last decision will be left to the headmaster and the inspector – the final word to the inspector.

Again, no decision will be final. If at any time it shall become apparent that a child is unfit for the group he occupies, then, after a proper consultation, he shall be removed to his own natural group. Again, if a child has no capacity for arithmetic, we shall not persist for five years in drilling arithmetic into him. Some form of useful manual work will be substituted for the arithmetic lesson: and so on.

Such is a brief sketch of a sensible system of education for a civilized people. It may be argued that it puts too much power into the hands of schoolmasters and school-inspectors. But better there than in the hands of factory-owners and trades unions. The position of masters and inspectors will be discussed later.

Again, it may be argued that there is too much rule and government here. As a matter of fact, we are all limited to our own natures. And the aim above all others in this system is to recognize the true nature in each child, and to give each its natural chance. If we want to be free, we cannot be free to do otherwise than follow our own soul, our own true nature, to its fulfilment. And for this purpose primarily the suggested scheme would exist. Each individual is to be helped, wisely, reverently, towards its own natural fulfilment. Children can't choose for themselves. They are not sufficiently conscious. A choice is made, even if nobody makes it. The bungle of circumstance decrees the fate of almost every child today. Which is why most men hate their fates, circumstantial and false as they are.

And then, as to cost: which is always important. Our present system of education is extravagantly expensive, and simply dangerous to our social existence. It turns out a lot of half-informed youth who despise the whole business of understanding and wisdom, and who realize that in a world like ours nothing but money matters. Our system of education tacitly grants that nothing but money matters, but puts up a little parasol of human ideals under which human divinity can foolishly masquerade for a few hours during school life, and on Sundays. Coming from under this parasol, little Jimmy Shepherd knows that he's quite as divine as anybody else. He's quite as much a little god as anybody else, because he's been told so in school from the age of five till the age of fifteen, so he ought to know. Nobody's any better than he is: he's quite as good as anybody else, and, because he's a poor dustman's son, even more acceptable in the eyes of God. And therefore why hasn't he got as much money? since money is all that he can make any use of. His own human divinity is no more use to him than anybody else's human divinity, and once it comes to fighting for shillings he's absolutely not going to be put off by any toffee about ideals. And there we are with little Jimmy Shepherd, aged fifteen. He's a right dangerous little party, all of our own making: and his name is legion.

Our system of education today threatens our whole social existence tomorrow. We should be wise if by decree we shut up all elementary schools at once, and kept them shut. Failing that, we must look round for a better system, one that will work.

But if we try a new system, we must know what we're about. No good floundering into another muddle. While education was strictly a religious process, it had a true goal. While it existed for governing classes, it had a goal. And *universal elementary* education has had a goal. But a fatal one.

We have assumed that we could educate Jimmy Shepherd and make him a Shelley or an Isaac Newton. At the very least we were sure we could make him a highly intelligent being. And we're just beginning to find our mistake. We can't make a highly intelligent being out of Jimmy Shepherd. Why should we, if the Lord created him only moderately intelligent? Why do we want always to go one better than the Creator?

So now, having gone a very long way downhill on a very dangerous road, and having got ourselves thoroughly entangled in a vast mob which may at any moment start to bolt down to the precipice Gadarene-wise, why, the best we can do is to try to steer uphill.

We've got first to find which way *is* uphill. We've got to shape our course by some just idea. We shaped it by a faulty idea of equality and the perfectibility of man. Now for the true idea: either that or the precipice edge.

3

It is obvious that the old ideal of Equality won't do. It is landing us daily deeper in a mess. And yet no idea which has passionately swayed mankind can be altogether wrong: not even the most fallacious-seeming. Therefore, before we can dispose of the equality ideal, the ideal that all men are essentially equal, we have got to find how far it is true.

In no sense whatever are men actually equal. Physically, some are big and some are small, some weak, some strong; mentally, some are intelligent, some are not, and the degrees of difference are infinite; spiritually, some are rare and fine, some are vulgar; morally, some are repulsive and some attractive. True, all men have noses, mouths, stomachs and so on. But then this is a mere abstraction. Every nose, every stomach is different, actually, from every other nose and stomach. It is all according to the individual. Noses and stomachs are not interchangeable. You might perhaps graft the end of one man's nose on the nose of another man. But the grafted gentleman would not thereby have a dual identity. His essential self would remain the same: a little disfigured, perhaps, but not metamorphosed. Whatever tricks you may perform, of grafting one bit of an individual on another, you don't produce a new individual, a new type. You only produce a disfigured, patched-up old individual. It isn't like grafting roses. You couldn't graft bits of Lord Northcliffe on a thousand journalists and produce a thousand Napoleons of the Press. Every journalist would remain himself: a little disfigured or mutilated, maybe.

It is quite sickening to hear scientists rambling on about the interchange of tissue and members from one individual to another. They have at last reached the old alchemistic fantasy of producing the homunculus. They hope to take the hind leg of a pig and by happy grafting produce a marvellous composite individual, a fused erection of living tissue which will at last prove that man can *make* man, and that therefore he isn't divine at all, he is a purely human marvel, only so extraordinarily clever and marvellous that the sun will stop still to look at him.

When science begins to generalize from its own performances it is puerile as the alchemists were, at last. The truth about man, before he falls into imbecility, is that each one is just himself. That's the first, the middle truth. Every man has his own identity, which he preserves till he falls into imbecility or worse. Upon this clue of his own identity every man is fashioned. And the clue of a man's own identity is a man's own self or soul, that which is incommutable and incommunicable in him. Every man, while he remains a man and does not lapse into disintegration, becoming a lump of chaos, is truly himself, only himself, no matter how many fantastic attitudes he may assume. True it is that man goes and gets a host of ideas in his head, and proceeds to reconstruct himself according to those ideas. But he never actually succeeds in this business of reconstructing himself out of his own head, until he has gone cracked. And then he may prance on all fours like Nebuchadnezzar, or do as he likes. But whilst he remains sane the buzzing ideas in his head will never allow him to change or metamorphose his own identity: modify, yes; but never change. While a man remains sane he remains himself and nothing but himself, no matter how fantastically he may attitudinize according to some pet idea. For example, this of equality. St Francis was ready to fall in rapture at the feet of the peasant. But he wasn't ready to take the muck-rake from the peasant's hands and start spreading manure at twopence a day, an insignificant and forgotten nobody, a serf. Not at all. St Francis kept his disciples and was a leader of men, in spite of all humility, poverty and equality. Quite right, because St Francis was by nature a leader of men, and what has any creed or theory of equality to do with it? He was born such: it was his own intrinsic being. In his soul he was a leader. Where does equality come in? Why, by his poverty, St Francis wished to prove his own intrinsic superiority, not his equality. And if a man is a born leader, what does it matter if he hasn't got twopence, or if he has got two million? His own nature is his destiny, not his purse.

All a man can be, at the very best, is himself. At the very worst he can be something a great deal less than himself, a money-grubber, a millionaire, a State, like Louis Quatorze, a self-conscious ascetic, a spiritual prig, a grass-chewing Nebuchadnezzar.

So where does equality come in? Men are palpably unequal in *every* sense except the mathematical sense. Every man counts one: and this is the root of all equality: here, in a pure intellectual abstraction.

The moment you come to compare them, men are unequal, and their inequalities are infinite. But supposing you *don't* compare them. Supposing, when you meet a man, you have the pure decency not to compare him either with yourself or with anything else. Supposing you can meet a man with this same singleness of heart. What then? Is the man your equal, your inferior, your superior? He can't be, if there is no comparison. If there is no comparison, he is the incomparable. He is the incomparable. He is single. He is himself. When I am single-hearted, I don't compare myself with my neighbour. He is immediate to me, I to him. He is not my *equal*, because this presumes comparison. He is incomparably himself, I am incomparably myself. We behold each other in our pristine and simple being. And this is the first, the finest, the perfect way of human intercourse.

And on this great first-truth of the pristine incomparable nature of every individual soul is founded, mistakenly, the theory of equality. Every man, when he is incontestably himself, is single, incomparable, beyond compare. But to deduce from this that all men are equal is a sheer false deduction: a simple *non sequitur*. Let every man be himself, purely himself. And then, in the evil hour when you *do* start to compare, you will see the endless inequality between men.

In the perfect human intercourse, a relation establishes itself happily and spontaneously. No two men meet one another direct without a spontaneous equilibrium taking place. Doubtless there is inequality between the two. But there is no *sense* of inequality. The give-and-take is perfect; without knowing, each is adjusted to the other. It is as the stars fall into their place, great and small. The small are as perfect as the great, because each is itself and in its own place. But the great are none the less the great, the small the small. And the joy of each is that it is so.

The moment I begin to pay direct mental attention to my neighbour, however; the moment I begin to scrutinize him and attempt to set myself over against him, the element of comparison enters. Immediately I am aware of the inequalities between us. But even so, it is inequalities and not inequality. There is *never* either any equality or any inequality between me and my neighbour. Each of us is himself, and as such is

single, alone in the universe, and not to be compared. Only in our parts
are we comparable. And our parts are vastly unequal.

Which finishes equality for ever, as an ideal. Finishes also fraternity.
For fraternity implies a consanguinity which is almost the same as
equality. Men are not equal, neither are they brothers. They are themselves. Each one is himself, and each one is essentially, starrily responsible
for himself. Any assumption by one person of responsibility for another
person is an interference, and a destructive tyranny. No person is responsible for the *being* of any other person. Each one is starrily single,
starrily self-responsible, not to be blurred or confused.

Here then is the new ideal for society: not that all men are equal, but
that each man is himself: 'one is one and all alone and ever more shall
be so.' Particularly this is the ideal for a new system of education. Every
man shall be himself, shall have every opportunity to come to his own
intrinsic fullness of being. There are unfortunately many individuals to
whom these words mean nothing: mere verbiage. We must have a
proper contempt and defiance of these individuals, though their name
be legion.

How are we to obtain that a man shall come to his own fullness of
being; that a child shall grow up true to his own essential self? It is no
use just letting the child do as it likes. Because the human being, more
than any other living thing, is susceptible to falsification. We alone have
mental consciousness, speech and thought. And this mental consciousness is our greatest peril.

A child in the bath sees the soap, and wants it, and won't be happy
till he gets it. When he gets it he rubs it into his eyes and sucks it, and is
in a far more unhappy state. Why? To see the soap and to want it is a
natural act on the part of any young animal, a sign of that wonderful
naïve curiosity which is so beautiful in young life. But the 'he won't be
happy till he gets it' quality is, alas, purely human. A young animal, if
diverted, would forget the piece of soap at once. It is only an accident
in his horizon. Or, given the piece of soap, he would sniff it, perhaps
turn it over, and then merely abandon it. Beautiful to us is the pure non-
chalance of a young animal which *forgets* the piece of soap the moment
it has sniffed it and found it no good. Only the intelligent human baby
proceeds to fill its mouth, stomach and eyes with acute pain, on account
of the piece of soap. Why? Because the poor little wretch got an idea, an
incipient idea into its little head. The rabbit never gets an idea into its
head, so it can sniff the soap and turn away. But the human baby, poor,
tormented little creature, *can't help* getting an idea into his young head.
And then he *can't help* acting on his idea: no matter what the con-

sequences. And this bit of soap shows us what a bitter responsiblity our mental consciousness is to us, and how it leads astray even the infant in his bath. Poor innocent: we like to imagine him a spontaneous, unsophisticated little creature. But what do we mean by sophistication? We mean that a being is at the mercy of some idea which it has got into its head, and which has no true relation to its actual desire or need. Witness the piece of soap. The baby saw the piece of soap, and got an idea into its head that the soap was immeasurably desirable. Acting on this simple idea, it nearly killed itself, and filled an hour or so of its young life with horrid misery.

It is only when we grow up that we learn not to be run away with by ideas which we get in our heads and which don't correspond to any true natural desire or need. At least, education and growing-up is supposed to be a process of learning to escape the automatism of ideas, to live direct from the spontaneous, vital centre of oneself.

Anyhow, it is criminal to expect children to 'express themselves' and to bring themselves up. They will eat the soap and pour the treacle on their hair and put their fingers in the candle-flame, in the acts of physical self-expression, and in the wildness of spiritual self-expression they will just go to pieces. All because, really, they have enough mental intelligence to obliterate their instinctive intelligence and to send them to destruction. A little animal that can crawl will manage to live, if abandoned. Abandon a child of five years and it won't merely die, it will almost certainly maim and kill itself. This mental consciousness we are born with is the most double-edged blessing of all, and grown-ups must spend years and years guarding their children from the disastrous effects of this blessing.

Now let us go back to the maxim that every human being must come to the fullness of himself. It is part of our sentimental and trashy creed today that a little child is most purely himself, and that growing up perverts him away from himself. We assume he starts as a spontaneous little soul, limpid, purely self-expressive, and grows up to be a sad, sophisticated machine. Which is all very well, and might easily be so, if the mind of the little innocent didn't start to work so soon, and to interfere with all his little spontaneity. Nothing is so subject to small, but fatal automatization as a child: some little thing it sets its *mind* on, and the game is up. And a child is always setting its little mind on something, usually something which doesn't at all correspond with the true and restless desire of its living soul. And then, which will win, the little mind or the little soul? We all know, to our sorrow. When a child sets its little mind on the soap, its little soul, not to speak of its little eyes and stomach, is thrown to the winds. And yet the desire for the soap is only the misdirection of the eternally yearning, desirous soul of an infant.

Here we are, then. Instead of waiting for the wisdom out of the mouths of babes and sucklings, let us see that we keep the soap-tablet out of the same mouths. We've got to educate our children, and it's no light responsibility. We've got to try to educate them to that point where at last there will be a perfect correspondence between the spontaneous, yearning, impulsive-desirous soul and the automatic *mind* which runs on little wheels of ideas. And this is the hardest job we could possibly set ourselves. For man just doesn't know how to interpret his own soul-promptings, and therefore he sets up a complicated arrangement of ideas and ideals and works himself automatically till he works himself into the grave or the lunatic-asylum.

We've got to educate our children. Which means, we've got to decide for them: day after day, year after year, we've got to go on deciding for our children. It's not the slightest use asking little Jimmy 'What would you like, dear?' because little Jimmy doesn't know. And if he *thinks* he knows, it's only because, as a rule, he's got some fatal little idea into his head, like the soap-tablet. Yet listen to the egregious British parent solemnly soliciting his young son: 'What would you like to be, dear? A doctor or a clergyman?' – 'An engine-driver,' replies Jimmy, and the comedy of babes-and-sucklings continues.

We've got to decide for our children: for years and years we have to make their decisions. And we've got to take the responsibility on to ourselves, as a community. It's no good feeding our young with a sticky ideal education till they are fourteen years old, then pitching them out, pap-fed, into the whirling industrial machine and the warren of back streets. It's no good expecting parents to do anything. Parents don't know how to decide; they go to little Jimmy as if he were the godhead. And even if they did know how to decide, they can do nothing in face of the factory and the trades union and the back streets.

We, the educators, have got to decide for the children: decide the steps of their young fates, seriously and reverently. It is a sacred business, and unless we can act from our deep, believing souls, we'd best not act at all, but leave it to Northcliffe and trades unions.

We must choose, with this end in view. We want quality of life, not quantity. We don't want swarms and swarms of people in back streets. We want distinct individuals, and these are incompatible with swarms and masses. A small, choice population, not a horde of hopeless units.

And every man to be himself, to come to his own fullness of being. Not every man a little wonder of cleverness or high ideals. Every man himself, according to his true nature. And those who are comparatively non-mental can form a vigorous, passionate proletariat of indomitable individuals; and those who will work as clerks to be free and energetic, not humiliated as they are now, but fierce with their own freedom of beings; and the *man* will be always more than his job; the job will be a minor business.

We must have an ideal. So let our ideal be living, spontaneous individuality in every man and woman. Which living, spontaneous individuality, being the hardest thing of all to come at, will need most careful rearing. Educators will take a grave responsibility upon themselves. They will be the priests of life, deep in the wisdom of life. They will be the life-priests of the new era. And the leaders, the inspectors, will be men deeply initiated into the mysteries of life, adepts in the dark mystery of living, fearing nothing but life itself, and subject to nothing but their own reverence for the incalculable life-gesture.

4

It is obvious that a system of education such as the one we so briefly sketched out in our second chapter will inevitably produce distinct classes of society. The basis is the great class of workers. From this class will rise also the masters of industry, and, probably, the leading soldiers. Second comes the clerkly caste, which will include elementary teachers and minor professionals, and which will produce the local government bodies. Thirdly we have the class of the higher professions, legal, medical, scholastic: and this class will produce the chief legislators. Finally, there is the small class of the supreme judges: not merely legal judges, but judges of the destiny of the nation.

These classes will not arise accidentally, through the accident of money, as today. They will not derive through heredity, as the great oriental castes. There will be no automatism. A man will not be chosen to a class, or a caste, because he is exceptionally fitted for a particular job. If a child shows an astonishing aptitude, let us say, for designing clocks, and at the same time has a profound natural life-understanding, then he will pass on to the caste of professional masters, or even to that of supreme judges, and his skill in clocks will only be one of his accomplishments, his *private* craft. The whole business of educators will be to estimate, not the particular faculty of the child for some particular job: not at all; nor even a specific intellectual capacity; the whole business will be to estimate the profound life-quality, the very nature of the child, that which makes him ultimately what he is, his soul-strength and his soul-wisdom, which cause him to be a natural master of life. Technical

capacity is all the time subsidiary. The highest quality is living understanding – not intellectual understanding. Intellectual understanding
belongs to the technical activities. But vital understanding belongs to the
masters of life. And all the professionals in our new world are not mere
technical experts: they are life-directors. They combine with their soul-
power some great technical skill. But the first quality will be the soul-
quality, the quality of being, and the power for the directing of life itself.

Hence we shall see that the system is primarily religious, and only
secondarily practical. Our supreme judges and our master professors
will be primarily *priests*. Let us not take fright at the word. The true
religious faculty is the most powerful and the highest faculty in man,
once he exercises it. And by the religious faculty we mean the inward
worship of the creative life-mystery: the implicit knowledge that life is
unfathomable and unsearchable in its motives, not to be described,
having no ascribable goal save the bringing-forth of an ever-changing,
ever-unfolding creation; that new creative being and impulse surges up
all the time in the deep fountains of the soul, from some great source
which the world has known as God; that the business of man is to become so spontaneous that he shall utter at last direct the act and the
state which arises in him from his deep being; and finally, that the mind
with all its great powers is only the servant of the inscrutable, unfathomable soul. The *idea* or the *ideal* is only instrumental in the unfolding of
the soul of man, a tool, not a goal. Always simply a tool.

We should have the courage to refrain from dogma. Dogma is the
translation of the religious impulse into an intellectual term. An intellectual term is a finite, fixed, mechanical thing. We must be content for
ever to live from the undescribed and indescribable impulse. Our god is
the Unnamed, the Veiled, and any attempt to give names, or to remove
veils, is just a mental impertinence which ends in nothing but futility and
impertinencies.

So, the new system will be established upon the living religious faculty
in men. In some men this faculty has a more direct expression in consciousness than in other men. Some men are aware of the deep troublings
of the creative sources of their own souls, they are aware, they find
speech or utterance in act, they come forth in consciousness. In other
men the troublings are dumb, they will never come forth in expression,
unless they find a mediator, a minister, an interpreter.

And this is how the great castes naturally arrange themselves. Those
whose souls are alive and strong but whose voices are unmodulated, and
whose thoughts unformed and slow, these constitute the great base of all
peoples at all times: and it will always be so. For the creative soul is for

ever charged with the potency of still unborn speech, still unknown thoughts. It is the everlasting source which surges everlastingly with the massive, subterranean fires of creation, new creative being: and whose fires find issue in pure jets and bubblings of unthinkable newness only here and there, in a few, or comparatively few, individuals.

It must always be so. We cannot imagine the deep fires of the earth rushing out everywhere, in a myriad myriad jets. The great volcanoes stand isolate. And at the same time the life-issues concentrate in certain individuals. Why it is so, we don't know. But why should we know? We are, after all, *only* individuals, we are not the eternal life-mystery itself.

And therefore there will always be the vast, living masses of mankind, incoherent and almost expressionless by themselves, carried to perfect expression in the great individuals of their race and time. As the leaves of a tree accumulate towards blossom, so will the great bulk of mankind at all time accumulate towards its leaders. We don't want to turn every leaf of an apple tree into a flower. And so why should we want to turn every individual human being into a unit of complete expression? Why should it be our goal to turn every coal-miner into a Shelley or a Parnell? We can't do either. Coal-miners are consummated in a Parnell, and Parnells are consummated in a Shelley. That is how life takes its way: rising as a volcano rises to an apex, not in a countless multiplicity of small issues.

Time to recognize again this great truth of human life, and to put it once more into practice. Democracy is gone beyond itself. The true democracy is that in which a people gradually cumulate, from the vast base of the populace upwards through the zones of life and understanding to the summit where the great man, or the most perfect utterer, is alone. The false democracy is that wherein every issue, even the highest, is dragged down to the lowest issue, the myriad-multiple lowest human issue: today, the wage.

Mankind may have a perverse, self-wounding satisfaction in this reversal of the life-course. But it is a poor, spiteful, ignominious satisfaction.

In its living periods mankind accumulates upwards, through the zones of life-expression and passionate consciousness, upwards to the supreme utterer, or utterers. In its disintegrating periods the reverse is the case. Man accumulates downwards, down to the lowest issue. And the great men of the downward development are the men who symbolize the gradually sinking zones of being, till the final symbol, the great man who represents the wage-reality, rises up and is hailed as the supreme. No doubt he is the material, mechanical universal of mankind, a unit of automatized existence.

It is a pity that democracy should be identified with this downward tendency. We who believe that every man's soul is single and incomparable, we thought we were democrats. But evidently democracy is a question of the integral wage, not the integral soul. If everything comes down to the wage, then down it comes. When it is a question of the human soul, the direction must be a cumulation upwards: upwards from the very roots, in the vast Demos, up to the very summit of the supreme judge and utterer, the first of men. There is a first of men; and there is the vast, basic Demos; always, at every age in every continent. The people is an organic whole, rising from the roots, through trunk and branch and leaf, to the perfect blossom. This is the tree of human life. The supreme blossom utters the whole tree, supremely. Roots, stem, branch, these have their own being. But their perfect climax is in the blossom which is beyond them, and which yet is organically one with them.

We see mankind through countless ages trying to express this truth. There is the rising up through degrees of aristocracy up to kings or emperors; there is a rising up through degrees of church dignity, to the Pope; there is a rising up through zones of priestly and military elevation, to the Egyptian King-God; there is the strange accumulation of caste.

And what is the fault mankind has had to find with all these great systems? The fact that *somewhere*, the individual soul was discounted, abrogated. And when? Usually at the bottom. The slave, the serf, the vast populace, had no soul. It has been left to our era to put the populace in possession of its own soul. But no populace will ever know, by itself, what to do with its own soul. Left to itself, it will never do more than demand a pound a day, and so on. The populace finds its living soul-expression cumulatively through the rising up of the classes above it, towards pure utterance or expression or being. And the populace has its supreme satisfaction in the up-flowing of the sap of life, from its vast roots and trunk, up to the perfect blossom. The populace partakes of the flower of life: but it can never *be* the supreme, lofty flower of life: only leaves of grass. And shall we hew down the Tree of Life for the sake of the leaves of grass?

It is time to start afresh, and we need system. Those who cry out against our present system, blame it for all evils of modern life, call it the Machine which devours us all, and demand the abolition of all systems, these people confuse the issue. They actually desire the disintegration of mankind into amorphousness and oblivion: like the parched dust of Babylon. Well, that is a goal, for those that want it.

As a matter of fact, all life is organic. You can't have the merest speck of rudimentary life, without organic differentiation. And men who are collectively active in organic life-production must be organized. Men who are active purely in material production must be mechanized. There is the duality.

Obviously a system which is established for the purposes of pure material production, as ours today, is in its very nature a mechanism, a social machine. In this system we live and die. But even such a system as the great Popes tried to establish was palpably not a machine, but an organization, a social organism. There is nothing at all to be gained from disunion, disintegration and amorphousness. From mechanical systematization there is vast material productivity to be gained. But from an organic system of human life we shall produce the real blossoms of life and being.

There must be a system; there *must* be classes of men; there *must* be differentiation: either that, or amorphous nothingness. The true choice is not between system and no-system. The choice is between system and system, mechanical or organic.

We have blamed the great aristocratic systems of the past, because of the automatic principle of heredity upon which they were established. A great man does not necessarily have a son at all great. We have blamed the great ecclesiastical system of the Church of Rome for the automatic principle of mediation on which it was established; we blame the automatism of caste, and of dogma. And then what? What do we put in place of all these semi-vital principles? The utterly non-vital, completely automatized system of material production. The ghosts of the great dead must turn on us.

What good is our intelligence to us, if we will not use it in the greatest issues? Nothing will excuse us from the responsibility of living: even death is no excuse. We have to live. So we may as well live fully. We are doomed to live. And therefore it is not the smallest use running into *pis allers* and trying to shirk the responsibility of living. We can't get out of it.

And therefore the only thing to do is to undertake the responsibility with good grace. What responsibility? The responsibility of establishing a new system: a new, organic system, free as far as ever it can be from automatism or mechanism: a system which depends on the profound spontaneous soul of men.

How to begin? Is it any good having revolutions and cataclysms?

Who knows? Revolutions and cataclysms may be inevitable. But they are merely hopeless and catastrophic unless there come to life the germ of a new mode. And the new mode must be incipient somewhere. And therefore, let us start with education.

Let us start at once with a new system of education: a system which will cost us no more, nay, less than the dangerous present system. At least we shall produce capable individuals. Let us first of all have compulsory instruction of all teachers in the new idea. Then let us begin with the schools. Life can go on just the same. It is not a cataclysmic revolution. It is a forming of new buds upon the tree, under the harsh old foliage.

What do we want? We want to produce the new society of the future, gradually, livingly. It will be a slow job, but why not? We cut down the curriculum for the elementary school at once. We abolish all the smatterings. The smatterings of science, drawing, painting and music are only the absolute death-blow to real science and song and artistic capacity. Folk-song lives till we have schools; and then it is dead, and the shrill shriek of self-conscious scholars is supposed to take its place.

Away with all smatterings. Away with the imbecile pretence of culture in the elementary schools. Remember the back streets, remember that the souls of the working people are only rendered neurasthenic by your false culture. We want to keep the young populace robust and sufficiently nonchalant. Teach a boy to read, to write and to do simple sums, and you have opened the door of all culture to him, if he wants to go through.

Even if we do no more, let us do so much. Away with all smatterings. Three hours a day of reading, writing and arithmetic, and that's the lot of mental education, until the age of twelve. When we say three hours a day, we mean the three hours of the morning. What it will amount to will be two hours of work: two intervals of absolutely free play, twenty minutes each interval; and twenty minutes for assembly and clearing-up and dismissal.

In the afternoon, actual *martial* exercises, swimming and games, actual gymnasium *games*, but no Swedish drill. None of that physical-exercise business, that meaningless, vicious self-automatization; no athleticism. Never let physical movement be didactic, didactically performed from the mind.

Thus doing, we shall reduce the cost of our schools hugely, and we can hope to get some children, not the smirking, self-conscious, nervous little creatures we do produce. If we dare to have workshops, let us convert some of our schools into genuine work-sheds, where boys learn to mend boots and do joinering and carpentry and plumbing such as they will need in their own homes; other schools into kitchens, sculleries and sewing-rooms for the girls. But let this be definite technical instruction for practical use, not some nonsense of fancy wood-carving and model churches. And let the craft-instructors be actual craftsmen, not school-teachers. Separate the workshop entirely from the school. Let there be no connection. Avoid all 'correlation', it is most vicious. Craftsmanship is a physical spontaneous intelligence, quite apart from *ideal* intelligence, and ruined by the introduction of the deliberate mental act.

And all the time, watch the *being* in each scholar. Let the school-master and the crafts-master and the games-master all watch the individual lads, to find out the living nature in each child, so that, ultimately, a man's destiny shall be shaped into the natural form of that man's being, not as now, where children are rammed down into ready-made destinies, like so much canned fish.

You can cut down the expenses of the morning school to one-half. Big classes will not matter. The *personal* element, personal supervision is of no moment.

5

State education has a dual aim: 1. the production of the desirable citizen; 2. the development of the individual.

You can obtain one kind of perfect citizen by suppressing individuality and cultivating the public virtues: which has been the invariable tendency of reform, and of social idealism in modern days. A real individual has a spark of danger in him, a menace to society. Quench this spark and you quench the individuality, you obtain a social unit, not an integral man. All modern progress has tended, and still tends, to the production of quenched social units: dangerless beings, ideal creatures.

On the other hand, by the over-development of the individualistic qualities, you produce a disintegration of all society. This was the Greek danger, as the quenching of the individual in the social unit was the Roman danger.

You must have a harmony and an inter-relation between the two modes. Because, though man is first and foremost an individual being, yet the very accomplishing of his individuality rests upon his fulfilment in social life. If you isolate an individual you deprive him of his life; if you leave him no isolation you deprive him of himself. And there it is! Life consists in the interaction between a man and his fellows, from the individual, integral love in each.

And upon what does human relationship rest? It rests upon our accepted attitude to life, our belief in the life-aims, and in our conception of right and wrong. No matter how we may pretend, for example, to be free from moral dogma, every one of our actions, and even our emotions, is under the influence of our ingrown moral creed. We cannot act without moral bias. Still more, we are influenced by our conception of the nature of man. We believe that, being men and women, we are therefore such and such and such. Without formulating or putting into any conscious expression what our idea of a man and a woman, a white man and a white woman *is*, we still have a large, potent idea, accumulated in our psyche through the course of ages. And according to this *idea* of what we ourselves are, and of what our neighbour is, we take up our attitude to the world, and we model all our behaviour. Lastly, though we express it or not, we believe that life has some great goal, of happiness and peace and harmony, and all our judgements are biased by this belief.

Here we are, then, born and swaddled in fixed beliefs, no matter how we may deny our beliefs, with lip-denial. There they are, in our very tissue. And they are not to be ousted save by new beliefs.

Such is man: a creature of beliefs and of foregone conclusion. As a matter of fact, we should never put one foot before the other, save for the foregone conclusion that we shall find the earth beneath the outstretched foot. Man travels a long journey through time. And the nature of his travels varies from time to time. Sometimes even he discovers himself upon the brink of a precipice, on the shore of a sea. Remains then to adopt a new conclusion, to take a new direction, to put the foot down differently. When we pass from Arabia Felix to Arabia Petrea, it needs must be with a different tread. Man *must* walk. And to walk he must believe that he will find the ground there under his feet at every stride. That is, he must have beliefs and foregone conclusions, and conceptions of what the nature of life is, and the goal thereof. Only, as the land changes, his beliefs must change. It is no use charging on over the edge of a precipice. It is no use plunging on from stony ground into soft sand, and keeping the same hob-nailed boots on. Man is given mental intelligence in order that he many effect quick changes, quick readjustments, preserving himself alive and integral through a myriad environments and adverse circumstances which would exterminate a non-adaptable animal.

So now that the human soul is drawing near the conclusion of one of its great phases: now it has suddenly blundered out of Arabia Felix into Arabia Deserta, and is passing beyond the zone of grass and green trees altogether into the magic of the sands, it behoves us all to readjust ourselves. We can't go back to the fleshpots of the old fat peace, because the old fat peace is not within us. Let us go on, then, and adjust ourselves to the new stage.

We have got to discover a new mode of human relationship – for man is the world to man. We have blundered blind into a new world, and we don't know how to get on. It behoves us to find out.

We have got to discover a new mode of human relationship. Which means, incidentally, that we have got to get a new conception of man and of ourselves. And we have then to establish a new morality.

It is useless to think that we can get along without a conception of what man is, and without a belief in ourselves, and without the morality to support this belief. The only point is that our conception, our belief and our morality, though valid for the time being, is valid only for the time being. We are a million things which we don't know we are. Now and again we make new and shocking discoveries in ourselves: our right hand suddenly becomes a new and monstrous-seeming member to us, our right eye has the iniquity to see those things which were never before seen. Hence a dilemma. We have either to cut off and pluck out the eye, and remain virtuously *in statu quo*. Or we have to accept the eye and accept the hand, and admit that our virtue has lost its validity. In this latter issue, we must know a new virtue as a snake grows a new skin. Which we can do, if we will, with much *éclat*.

Now the good old creed we have been suckled in teaches us that man is *essentially* and *finally* an ideal being; essentially and finally a pure spirit, an abstraction, a term of abstract consciousness. As such he has his immortality and his identity with the infinite. This identity with the infinite is the goal of life. And it is reached through love, self-abandoning love. All that is truly love is good and holy; all that is not truly love is evil.

There is the creed, in a nutshell. And any creed which is to be found in a nutshell is a creed which had dropped off the Tree of Life, and is finished.

Now it is according to this creed that we proceed, at present, to educate our children. Sentimentally, we like to assume that a child is a little pure spirit arrived out of the infinite and clothed in innocent, manna-like flesh. This pure little spirit only needs to be fed on beauty, truth and light, and it will grow up into a creature so near the angels that we'd best not mention it. Little stories full of love and sacrifice, little acts full of grace, little productions, little models in plasticine more spiritual than Donatello, little silver-point drawings more ethereal than Botticelli, little water-colour blobs that will suggest the world's dawn:

all these things we quite seriously expect of small children, and in this expectation Whitehall gravely elaborates the educational system.

Ideal and innocent little beings, their minds only need to be *led* into the Canaan of their promise, and we shall have a world of *blameless* Shelleys and *superior* Botticellis. The degree of blamelessness and ideal superiority we set out to attain, in educating our children, is unimaginable. Pure little spirits, unblemished darlings! So sad that as they grow up some of the grossness of the world creeps in! *How* it creeps in, heaven knows, unless it is through the Irish stew and rice pudding at dinner. Or perhaps *somewhere* there are evil communications to corrupt good manners: time itself seems the great corrupter.

Whatever the end may be – and the end is bathos – our children *must* be regarded as ideal little beings, and their little minds must be *led* into blossom. Of course their little bodies are important: most important. Because, of course, their little bodies are the instruments of their dear little minds. And therefore you can't have a good sweet mind without a sweet healthy body. Give *every* attention to the body, for it is the sacred ark, the holy vessel which contains the holy of holies, the *mind* of the ideal little creature. *Mens sana in corpore sano.*

And therefore the child is taught to cherish its own little body, to do its little exercises and its little drill, so that it can become a fine man, or a fine woman. Let it only turn its *mind* to its own physique, and it will produce a physique that would shame Phidias. Let only the mind take up the body, and it will produce a body as a show gardener produces carrots, something to take your breath away. For the mind, the ideal reality, this is omnipotent and everything. The body is but a lower extension from the mind, diminishing in virtue as it descends. What is noble is near the brain: the ignoble is near the earth. A child is an ideal little creature, a term of ideal consciousness, pure spirit.

Any ideal, once it is really established, becomes ridiculous, so ridiculous that we begin to feel a certain mistrust of mankind's collective sense of humour. A man is never half such a fool as mankind makes of him. Mankind is a sententious imbecile without misgiving. When an individual reaches this stage, we put him away.

Well, our ideal little darlings, our innocents from the infinite, our sweet and unspoiled little natures, our little spirits straight from the hands of the Maker, our idealized little children, what are we making of them, as we lead their pure little minds into the Canaan of promise, as we educate them up to all that is pure and spiritual and ideal? What are we making of them? Fools, bitter fools. Bitter fools. If you want to know, ask them.

What is a child? A breath of the spirit of God? Well then, the breath of the spirit of God is something that still needs defining. It isn't like the waft of a handkerchief perfumed with *Ess-Bouquet*.

But, seriously, before we can dream of pretending to educate a child, we must get a different notion of the nature of children. When we see a seed putting forth its fat cotyledon, do we rhapsodize about the pure beauty of the divine issue? When we see a foal on stalky legs creaking after its mother, are we smitten with dazzled revelation of the hidden God? If we want to be dazzled with revelation, look at a mature tree in full blossom, a mature stallion in the full pride of spring. Look at a man or a woman in the magnificence of their full-grown powers, not at a tubby infant.

What is an infant? What is its holy little mind? An infant is a new clue to an as-yet-unformed human being, and its little mind is a pulp of undistinguished memory and cognition. A little child has one clue to itself, central within itself. For the rest, it is new pulp, busy with differentiation towards the great goal of fulfilled being. Instead of worshipping the child, and seeing in it a divine emission which time will stale, we ought to realize that here is a new little clue to a human being, laid soft and vulnerable on the face of the earth. Here is our responsibility, to see that this unformed thing shall come to its own final form and fullness, both physical and mental.

Which is a long and difficult business. We have to feed the little creature in more ways than one: not only its little stomach and its little mind, but its little passions and will, its senses. Long experience has taught us that a baby should be fed on milk and pap: though we're not *quite* sure even now whether carrot-water wouldn't be better. Our ancient creed makes us insist on awaking the little 'mind'. We are all quite agreed that we have serious responsibilities with regard to the infant stomach and the infant mind. But we don't even know, yet, that there is anything else.

We think that all the reaction goes on within the stomach and the little brain. All that is wonderful, under the soft little skull; all that is tiresome, under the tubby wall of the abdomen. A set of organs which *ought* to work beautifully and automatically, considering the care we take: and a marvellous little mind which, we are sure, is full of invisible celestial blossoms of consciousness.

Poor baby: no wonder it is queer. That self-same little stomach isn't half so automatic as we and and our precious doctors would like to have it. The 'instrument' of the human body isn't half so instrumental as it might be. Imagine a kettle, for instance, suddenly refusing to sit on the fire, and not to be persuaded. Think of a sewing-machine that insisted on sewing cushions, nothing but cushions, and would not be pacified. What a world! And yet we go on expecting the baby's stomach to cook the food and boil the water automatically, as if it were a kettle. And when it refuses, we still talk to it as if it *were* a kettle. Anything rather than depart from our foregone conclusion that the human body is a complicated instrument, a sort of system of retorts and generators which will finally produce the electric messages of ideas.

The body is not an instrument, but a living organism. And the goal of life is not the idea, the mental consciousness is not the sum and essence of a human being. Human consciousness is not only ideal; cognition, or knowing, is not only a mental act. Acts of emotion and volition are acts of primary cognition and may be almost entirely non-mental.

Even apart from this, it is obvious to anyone who handles a baby that the vital activity is neither mental nor stomachic. Wherein lies the mystery of a baby, for us adults? From what has grown the legend of the adoration of the infant? From the fact that in the infant the great affective centres, volitional and emotional, act direct and spontaneous, without mental cognition or interference. When mental cognition starts, it only puts a spoke in the wheel of the great affective centres. This forever baffles us. We can see that it is not mental reaction which constitutes the true consciousness of a baby. Neither perception nor apperception, nor conception, nor any form of cognition, such as is recognized by our psychology, is to be ascribed to the infant mind. And yet there *is* consciousness, and even cognition: here, as in the mindless animals.

What kind of consciousness is it? We must look to the great affective centres, emotional and volitional. And we shall find that in the tiny infant there are two emotional centres primal and intensely active, with two corresponding volitional centres. We need go through no tortures of scientific psychology to get at the truth. We need only take direct heed of the infant.

And then we shall realize that the busy business of consciousness is not taking place beneath the soft little skull, but beneath the little navel, and in the midst of the little breast. Here are the two great affective centres of the so-called emotional consciousness. Which emotional consciousness, according to our idealistic psychology, is only some sort of *force*, like imagination, heat or electric current. This force which arises and acts from the primal emotional-affective centres is supposed to be impersonal, general, truly a mechanical universal force, like electricity or heat or any kinetic force.

Impersonal, and having nothing to do with the individual. The personal and the individual element does enter until we reach mental consciousness. Personality, individuality, depends on mentality. So our psychology assumes. In the *mind*, a child is personal and individual, it is itself. Outside the mind, it is an instrument, a dynamo, if you like, a unit of difficult kinetic force betraying a sort of automatic consciousness, the same in every child, undifferentiated. In the same way, according to our psychology, animals have no personality and no individuality, be-cause they have no mental cognition. They have a certain psyche which they hold in common. What is true of one rabbit is true of another. All we can speak of is 'the psychology of the rabbit', one rabbit having just the same psyche as another. Why? Because it has no recognizable cogni-tion: it has only instinct.

We know this is all wrong, because, having met a rabbit or two, we have seen quite clearly that each separate rabbit was a separate, distinct rabbit – individual, with a specific nature of his own. We should be sorry to attribute a *mind* to him. But he has consciousness, and quite an indi-vidual consciousness too. It is notorious that human beings see foreigners all alike. To an English sailor the faces of a crowd of Chinese are all alike. But that is because the English sailor doesn't *see* the difference, not because the difference doesn't exist. Why, each fat domestic sheep, mere clod as it seems, has a distinct individual nature of its own, known to a shepherd after a very brief acquaintance.

So here we are with the great affective centres, volitional and emo-tional. The two chief emotional centres in the baby are the solar plexus of the abdomen and the cardiac plexus of the breast. The corresponding ganglia of the volitional system are the lumbar ganglion and the thoracic ganglion.

And we may as well leave off at once regarding these great affective centres as merely instrumental, like little dynamos and accumulators and so on. Nonsense. They are primary, integral mind-centres, each of a specific nature. There is a specific form of *knowing* takes place at each of these centres, without any mental reference at all. And the specific form of knowing at each of the great affective centres in the infant is of an individual and personal nature, peculiar to the very soul and being of that infant.

That is, at the great solar plexus an infant *knows*, in primary, mindless knowledge; and from this centre he acts and reacts directly, individually and self-responsibly. The same from the cardiac plexus, and the two corresponding ganglia, lumbar and thoracic. The brain at first acts only as a switchboard which keeps these great active centres in circuit of com-munication. The process of idealization, mental consciousness, is a subsidiary process. It is a second form of conscious activity. Mental activity, final cognition, ideation, is only set up secondarily from the perfect interaction and inter-communication of the primary affective centres, which remain all the time our dynamic first-minds.

6

How to begin to educate a child. First rule, leave him alone. Second rule, leave him alone. Third rule, leave him alone. That is the whole beginning.

Which doesn't mean we are to let him starve, or put his fingers in the fire, or chew broken glass. That is mere neglect. As a little organism, he must have his proper environment. As a little individual he has his place and his limits: we also are individuals, and as such cannot allow him to make an unlimited nuisance of himself. But as a little person and a little mind, if you please, he does not exist. Personality and mind, like moustaches, belong to a certain age. They are a deformity in a child.

It is in this respect that we repeat, *leave him alone*. Leave his sensibilities, his emotions, his spirit and his mind severely alone. There is the devil in mothers, that they must try to provoke *personal* recognition and *personal* response from their infants. They might as well start rubbing *Tatcho* on the tiny chin, to provoke a beard. Except that the *Tatcho* provocation will have no effect, unless perhaps a blister: whereas the emotional or psychic provocation has, alas, only too much effect.

For this reason babies should invariably be taken away from their modern mothers and given, not to yearning and maternal old maids, but to rather stupid fat women who can't be bothered with them. There should be a league for the prevention of maternal love, as there is a society for the prevention of cruelty to animals. The stupid fat woman may not guard so zealously against germs. But all the germs in the list of bacteriology are not so dangerous for a child as mother-love.

And why? Not for any thrilling Freudian motive, but because our now deadly idealism insists on idealizing every human relationship, but particularly that of mother and child. Heaven, how we all prostrate ourselves before the mother–child relationship, in all the grovelling degeneracy of Mariolatry! Highest, purest, most ideal of relationships, mother and child!

What nasty drivel! The mother–child relationship is certainly deep and important, but to make it high, or pure, or ideal is to make a nauseous perversion of it. A healthy, natural child has no high nature, no purity and no ideal being. To stimulate these qualities in the infant is to produce psychic deformity, just as ugly as if we stimulated the growth of a beard on the baby face.

As far as all these high and personal matters go, *leave the child alone*. Personality and spiritual being mean with us our *mental consciousness* of our *own self*. A mother is to a high degree, alas, mentally conscious of her own self, her own exaltedness, her own mission, in these miserable days. And she wants her own mental consciousness reciprocated in the child. The child must *recognize* and respond. Alas, that the child cannot give her the greatest smack in the eye, every time she smirks and yearns for recognition and response. If we are to save the ultimate sanity of our children, it is *down with mothers! A bas les mères!*

Down to the right level. Pull them down from their exalted perches. No more of this Madonna smirking and yearning. No more soul. A mother should have ten strokes with the birch every time she 'comes over' with soul or yearning love or aching responsibility. Ten hard, stinging strokes on her bare back, each time. Because White Slave Traffic is a cup of tea compared with yearning mother-love. It should be knocked out of her, for it is a vice which threatens the ultimate sanity of our race.

The relation between mother and child is not personal at all, until it becomes perverted. Personal means mental consciousness of self. And a child has *no* mental consciousness and no *self*, and ten times less than no mental consciousness of self until that fiend, its mother, followed by a string of personally affected females, proceeds to provoke this mental consciousness in the small psyche. Worst luck of all, the emotional female fiends succeed. Sometimes they produce an *obvious* derangement in the psyche of the infant, and then they receive all the pity in the world, instead of a good barbaric thrashing. Usually the derangement is only incipient, due to develop later as morbid self-consciousness and neurosis. How can we help being neurotic when our mothers provoked self-consciousness in us at the breast: provoked our self-conscious reciprocity, in order to satisfy their own spiritual and ideal lust for communion in self-consciousness?

Down with exalted mothers, and down with the exaltation of motherhood, for it threatens the sanity of our race. The relation of mother and child, while it remains natural, is non-personal, non-ideal, non-spiritual. It is effective at the great primary centres, the solar plexus and the cardiac plexus, and from these centres it acts *direct*, without the so-called conscious knowledge: that is, without any transfer into the mind. Nothing is so strange as the remote look of recognition, remote, heavy and potent, which is seen in the eyes of an infant. This wonderful remote look should be magic and sacred to a mother. Her whole instinct should revolt against disturbing it.

But no creature so perverse as the human mother today. No creature so delights in the traducing of the deepest instincts. Show me a woman who can be satisfied with the remote, deep, far-off baby-recognition. Show me the woman who can rest without provoking the look of *present* recognition in the eyes of a baby; that winsome, pathetic smile of infant recognition which is murder to a child so young. Why, even in the eyes of a child of seven the look of recognition is still remote and impersonal; it has a certain heavy far-offness which is its beauty. The self does not stand fully present in the eyes until maturity, look does not actually meet look until then.

The old, instinctive mother instinctively cast off her personal consciousness in her communication with her child, and entered into that state of deep, unformed or untranslated consciousness, non-mental, on a lower, more primal plane. For this the idealists despised her, and hence the idealizing, the making mental and self-conscious of the naturally non-mental, spontaneous state of motherhood.

Remains now for the perverted, idealized mother deliberately to cast off her ideal, self-conscious motherhood, to return to the old deeps. Or else man must drag her ideal robes off her, by force. But back she must go, to the old mindlessness, the old unconsciousness, the despised animality of motherhood. Our spiritualizing processes have been sheer perversion, when they have influenced the basic human affections.

The true relation between mother and child is established between the primary affective centres in each, without mental, self-conscious intervention. At the primary centres, the solar plexus and the cardiac plexus, the dynamic individual consciousness stirs and flushes and seeks an object. The primary dynamic consciousness is like a living force which moves from its own polarized centre seeking an object, the object being chiefly some other corresponding pole of vitality in another living being. So from the solar plexus of the infant sympathetic system moves a pristine conscious-force, seeking an object, a corresponding pole. This corresponding pole is found in the solar plexus of the mother.

As a matter of fact, the first polarity between the essential clue of the infant and the essential clue of the mother, located in the solar plexus, was established long before birth, at the moment of conception. But during all the period of gestation, the infant had no actual separate existence. It is only after birth, after the break of the navel-string, that the child's polar vitality becomes separate and distinct.

And at the same time, as soon as the child is liberated into separate and distinct existence, it craves at once for the readjustment of the old connection, the fitting together of the wound of the navel with its origin

in the mother. We don't mean that the child has any idea of what has
happened. We don't mean that it summons its little wits to effect the
desired restitution.

What actually happens is that, once the child is born and divided into
separate existence, then at the solar plexus there surges a current of free
vital consciousness, like a wave of electricity seeking its correspondent
pole. The correspondent pole is found naturally in the great affective
centre, the solar plexus of the mother. But failing the mother, the
corresponding pole may be found in another being, or even as in
the legend, in a she-wolf. Suffice it that the two great dynamic centres,
the solar plexus in the infant and the solar plexus in some external being,
are seized into correspondence, and a vital circuit set up.

The vital circuit, we remark, is set up between two extraneous and
individual beings, each separately existing. Yet the circuit embraces the
two in a perfectly balanced unison. The mother and child are on the
same plane. The mother is one in vital correspondence with the child.
That is, in all her direct intercourse with the child she is as rudimentary
as the child itself, her dynamic consciousness is as undeveloped and non-
mental as the child's.

Herein we have the true mother: she who corresponds with her child
on the deep, rudimentary plane of the first dynamic consciousness. This
correspondence is a sightless, mindless correspondence of touch and
sound. The two dark poles of vital being must be kept constant in mother
and infant, so that the flow is uninterrupted. The constancy is preserved
by intimacy of contact, physical immediacy. But this physical immediacy
does not make the two beings any less distinct and separate. It makes
them more so. The child develops its own single, incipient self at its own
primary centre; the mother develops her own separate, matured female
self. The circuit of dynamic polarity which keeps the two equilibrized
also produces each of them, produces the infant's developing body and
psyche, produces the perfected womanhood of the mother.

All this, so long as the circuit is not broken, the flow perverted. The
circuit, the flow, is kept as the child lies against the bosom of its mother,
just as the circle of magnetic force is kept constant in a magnet, by the
'keeper' which unites the two poles. The child which sleeps in its
mother's arms, the child which sucks its mother's breast, the child which
screams and kicks on its mother's knee is established in a vital circuit
with its parent, out of which circuit its being arises and develops. From
pole to pole, direct, the current flows: from the solar plexus in the
abdomen of the child to the solar plexus in the abdomen of the mother,
from the cardiac plexus in the breast of the child to the cardiac plexus

in the breast of the mother. The mouth which sucks, the little voice which calls and cries, both issue from the deep centres of the breast and bowels, giving expression from these centres, and not from the brain. The baby is not mentally vocal. It utters itself from the great affective centres. And this is why it has such power to charm or to madden us. The mother in her response utters herself from the same affective centres; her coos and callings also are unintelligible. Not the mind speaks, but the deep, happy bowels, the lively breast.

Introduce one grain of self-consciousness into the mother, as she chuckles and coos to her baby, and what then? The good life-flow instantly breaks. The sounds change. She begins to produce them deliberately, under mental control. And what then? The deep affective centre in the baby is suddenly robbed, as when the mouth still sucking is suddenly snatched from the full breast. The vital flow is suddenly interrupted, and a new stimulus is applied to the child. There is a new provocation, a provocation for mental response from the infantile self-consciousness. And what then? The child either howls, or turns pale and makes this convulsed effort at mental-conscious, or self-conscious response. After which it is probably sick.

The same with the baby's eyes. They do not see, mentally. Mentally, they are sightless and dark. But they have the remote, deep vision of the deep affective centres. And so a mother, laughing and clapping to her baby, has the same half-sightless, glaucous look in her eyes, vision non-mental and non-critical, the primary affective centres corresponding through the eyes, void of idea or mental cognition.

But rouse the devil of a woman's self-conscious will, and she, clapping and cooing and laughing apparently just as before, will try to force a personal, *conscious* recognition into the eyes of the baby. She will try and try and try, fiendishly. And the child will blindly, instinctively resist. But with the cunning of seven legions of devils and the persistency of hell's most hellish fiend, the cooing, clapping, devilish modern mother traduces the child into the personal mode of consciousness. She succeeds, and starts this hateful 'personal' love between herself and her excited child, and the unspoken but unfathomable hatred between the violated infant and her own assaulting soul, which together make the bane of human life, and give rise to all the neurosis and neuritis and nervous troubles we are all afflicted with.

With children we must absolutely leave out the self-conscious and personal note. Communication must be remote and impersonal, a correspondence direct between the deep affective centres. And this is the reason why we must kick out all the personal fritter from the elementary schools. Stories must be *tales*, fables. They may have a flat *moral* if you like. But they must never have a personal, self-conscious note, the little-Mary-who-dies-and-goes-to-heaven touch, or the little-Alice-who-saw-a-fairy. This is the most vicious element in our canting infantile education today. 'And you will all see fairies, dears, if you know how to look for them.'

It is perversion of the infant mind at the start. This continual introduction of a little child-heroine or -hero, with whom the little girl or the little boy can self-consciously identify herself or himself, stultifies all development at the true centres. Fairies are not a personal, *mental* reality. Alice Jenkinson, who lives in 'The Laburnums', Leslie Road, Brixton, knows quite well that fairies are all 'my-eye'. But she is quite content to smirk self-consciously and say, 'Yes, miss', when teacher asks her if she'd like to see a fairy. It's all very well playing games of pretence, so long as you enter right into the game, robustly, and forget your own pretensive self. But when, like the little Alices of today, you keep a constant self-conscious smirk on your nose all the time you're 'playing fairies', then to hell with you and your fairies. And ten times to hell with the smirking, self-conscious 'teacher' who encourages you. A hateful, self-tickling, self-abusive affair, the whole business.

And this is what is wrong, first and foremost, with our education: this attempt deliberately to provoke reactions in the great affective centres and to dictate these reactions from the mind. Fairies are true embryological realities of the human psyche. They are true and real for the great affective centres, which see as through a glass, darkly, and which have direct correspondence with living and naturalistic influences in the surrounding universe, correspondence which cannot have mental, rational utterance, but must express itself, if it be expressed, in preternatural forms. Thus fairies are true, and Little Red Riding Hood is most true.

But they are not true for Alice Jenkinson, smirking little minx. Because Alice Jenkinson is an incurably self-conscious little piece of goods, and she *cannot* act direct from the great affective centres, she *can* only act perversely, by reflection, from her *personal* consciousness. And therefore, for her, all fairies and princesses and Peters and Wendys should be put on the fire, and she should be spanked and transported to Newcastle, to have some of her self-consciousness taken out of her.

An inspector should be sent round *at once* to burn all pernicious Little Alice and Little Mary literature in the elementary schools, and empowered to cut down to one-half the salary of any teacher found smirking or smuggling or indulging in any other form of pretty self-consciousness and personal grace. Abolish all the bunkum, go back to the three Rs. Don't cultivate any more imagination at all in children: it only means pernicious self-consciousness. Let us, for heaven's sake, have children without imagination and without 'nerves', for the two are damnably inseparable.

Down with imagination in school, down with self-expression. Let us have a little severe hard work, good, clean, well-written exercises, well-pronounced words, well-set-down sums: and as far as headwork goes, no more. No more self-conscious dabblings and smirkings and lispings of 'The silver birch is a dainty lady' (so is little Alice, of course). The silver birch must be finely downcast to see itself transmogrified into a smirky little Alice. The owl and the pussy-cat may have gone to sea in the pea-green boat, and the little girl may well have said: 'What long teeth you've got, Grandmother!' This is well within the bounds of natural pristine experience. But that dainty-lady business is only self-conscious smirking.

It will be a long time before we know how to act or speak again from the deep affective centres, without self-conscious perversion. And therefore, in the interim, whilst we learn, let us abolish all pretence at naïveté and childish self-expression. Let us have a bit of solid, hard, tidy work. And for the rest, *leave the children alone*. Pitch them out into the street or the playgrounds, and take no notice of them. Drive them savagely away from their posturings.

There must be an end to the self-conscious attitudinizing of our children. The self-consciousness and all the damned high-flownness must be taken out of them, and their little personalities must be nipped in the bud. Children shall be regarded as young *creatures*, not as young affected persons. Creatures, not persons.

7

As a matter of fact, our private hope is that by a sane system of education we may release the coming generation from our own nasty disease of self-consciousness: a disease quite as rampant among the working classes as among the well-to-do classes; and perhaps even more malignant there, because, having fewer forms of expression, it tends to pivot in certain ideas, which fix themselves in the psyche and become little less than manias. The wage is the mania of the moment: the working-man's consciousness of himself as a working man, which has now become an *idée fixe*, excluding any possibility of his remaining a lively human being.

What do we mean by self-consciousness? If we will realize that all spontaneous life, desire, impulse and first-hand individual consciousness arises and is effective at the great nerve-centres of the body, and *not* in the brain, we shall begin to understand. The great nerve-centres are in pairs, sympathetic and volitional. Again, they are polarized in upper and lower duality, above and below the diaphragm. Thus the solar plexus of the abdomen is the first great affective centre, sympathetic, and the lumbar ganglion, volitional, is its partner. At these two great centres arises our first consciousness, our primary impulses, desires, motives. These are our primal minds, here located in the dual great affective centres below the diaphragm. But immediately above the diaphragm we have the cardiac plexus and the thoracic ganglion, another great pair of conjugal affective centres, acting in immediate correspondence with the two lower centres. And these four great nerve-centres establish the first field of our consciousness, the first plane of our vital being. They are the four corner-stones of our psyche, the four powerful vital poles which, flashing darkly in polarized interaction one with another, form the four-fold issue of our individual life. At these great centres, primarily, we live and move and have our being. Thought and idea do not enter in. The motion arises spontaneous, we know not how, and is emitted in dark vibrations. The vibration goes forth, seeks its object, returns, establishing a life-circuit. And this life-circuit established internally between the four first poles, and established also externally between the primal affective centres in two different beings or creatures, this complex life-circuit or system of circuits constitutes in itself our profound primal consciousness, and contains all our radical knowledge, knowledge non-ideal, non-mental, yet still knowledge, primary cognition, individual and potent.

The mental cognition or consciousness is, as it were, distilled or telegraphed from the primal consciousness into a sort of written, final script, in the brain. If we imagine the infinite currents and meaningful vibrations in the world's atmosphere, and if we realize how some of these, at the great wireless stations, are ticked off and written down in fixed script, we shall form some sort of inkling of how the primary consciousness centralized in the great affective centres, and circulating in vital circuits of primary cognition, is captured by the supremely delicate registering apparatus in the brain and registered there like some strange code, the newly rising mental consciousness. The brain itself, no doubt, is a very tissue of memory, every smallest cell is a vast material memory which only needs to be roused, quickened by the vibration coming from the primary centres, only needs the new fertilization of a new quiver of experience, to blossom out as a mental conception, an idea. This power for the transfer of the pure affective experience, the primary consciousness, into final mental experience, ideal consciousness, varies extremely according to individuals. It would seem as if, in Negroes for example, the primary affective experience, the affective consciousness, is profound and intense, but the transfer into mental consciousness is comparatively small. In ourselves, in modern educated Europeans, on the other hand, the primal experience, the vital consciousness, grows weaker and weaker, the mind fixes the control and limits the life-activity. For, let us realize once and for all that the whole mental consciousness and the whole sum of the mental content of mankind is never, and can never be, more than a mere tithe of all the vast surging primal consciousness, the affective consciousness of mankind.

Yet we presume to limit the potent spontaneous consciousness to the poor limits of the mental consciousness. In us, instead of our life issuing spontaneously at the great affective centres, the mind, the mental consciousness, grown unwieldy, turns round upon the primary affective centres, seizes control, and proceeds to evoke our primal motions and emotions, didactically. The mind subtly, without knowing, provokes and dictates our own feelings and impulses. That is to say, a man helplessly and unconsciously *causes* from his mind every one of his own important reactions at the great affective centres. He can't help himself. It isn't his own fault. The old polarity has broken down. The primal centres have collapsed from their original spontaneity, they have become subordinate, neuter, negative, waiting for the mind's provocation, waiting to be worked according to some secondary idea. Thus arises our pseudo-spontaneous modern living.

We are in the toils of helpless self-consciousness. We can't help ourselves. It is like being in a boat with no oars. What can we do but drift? We know we are drifting, but we don't know how or where. Because there is no primary *resistance* in us, nothing that resists the helpless but fatal flux of ideas which streams us away. The resistant spontaneous centres have broken down in us.

Why does this happen? Because we have become too conscious? Not at all. Merely because we have become too fixedly conscious. We have limited our consciousness, tethered it to a few great ideas, like a goat to a post. We insist over and over again on what we know from one mere centre of ourselves, the mental centre. We insist that we are essentially spirit, that we are ideal beings, conscious personalities, mental creatures. As far as ever possible we have resisted the independence of the great affective centres. We have struggled for some thousands of years, not only to get our passions under control, but absolutely to eliminate certain passions, and to give all passion an ideal nature.

And so, at last, we succeed. We do actually give all our passions an ideal nature. Our passions at last are nothing more or less than ideas auto-suggested into practice. We try to persuade ourselves that it is all fine and grand and flowing. And for quite a long time we manage to take ourselves in. But we can't continue, *ad infinitum*, this life of self-satisfied auto-suggestion.

Because, if you think of it, everything which is provoked or originated *by an idea* works automatically or mechanically. It works by principle. So that even our wickedness today, being ideal in its origin, a sort of deliberate reaction to the *accepted* ideal, amounts to the same mechanism. It is an ideal working of the affective centres in the *opposite direction* from the accepted direction: opposite and opposite and opposite, till murder itself becomes an ideal at last. But it is all auto-affective. No matter which way you *work* the affective centres, once you work them from the mental consciousness you automatize them. And the human being craves for change in his automatism. Sometimes it seems to him horrible that he must, in a fixed routine, get up in the morning and put his clothes on, day in, day out. He can't bear his automatism. He is beside himself in his self-consciousness. But he is a damned little Oliver Twist: nothing but twist, and always wanting 'more'. He doesn't want to drop his self-consciousness. He wants more, always more. The damned little ideal being, he wants to work his own little psyche till the end of time, like a clever little god-in-the-machine that he is. And he despises any real spontaneity with all the street-arab insolence of depraved idealism. Man would rather be the ideal god inside his own automaton than anything else on earth. And woman is ten times worse. Woman as the goddess in the machine of the human psyche is a heroine who will drive us, like a female chauffeur, through all the avenues of hell, till she pitches us eventually down the bottomless pit. And even then she'll save herself, she'll kilt her skirts and look round for new passengers. She has a million more dodges for automatic self-stimulation than man has. When man has finished, woman can still cadge a million more sensational reactions out of herself and her co-respondent.

Man is accursed once he falls into the trick of ideal self-automatism. But he is infinitely conceited about it. He really works his own psyche! He really *is* the god of his own creation! Isn't this enough to puff him out? Here he is, tricky god and creator of himself at last! And he's not going to be ousted from his at-last-acquired godhead. Not he! The triumphant little god sits in the machine of his own psyche and turns on the petrol. It is like a story by H. G. Wells – too true to life, alas. There sits every man ensconced upon the engine of his own psyche, turning on the ideal taps and opening the ideal valves of his own nature, and so proud of himself, it's a wonder he hasn't set off to fly to the sun in one of his aeroplanes, like a new Icarus. But he lacks the fine boldness for such a flight. He wants to sit tight in his little hobby machine, near enough to his little hearth and home, this tubby, domestic little mechanical godhead.

A curse on idealism! A million curses on self-conscious automatic humanity, men and women both. Curses on their auto-suggestive self-reactions, from which they derive such inordinate self-gratification. Most curses of all upon the women, the self-conscious provokers of infinite sensations, of which man is the instrument. Let there be a fierce new Athanasian creed, to damn and blast all idealists. But let spiritual, ideal self-conscious woman be the most damned of all. Men, after all, don't get much more than aeroplane thrills and political thrills out of their god-in-the machine reactions. But women get soul-thrills and sexual thrills, they float and squirm on clouds of self-glorification, with a lot of knock-kneed would-be saints and apostles of the male sort goggling sanctified eyes upwards at them, as in some sickening Raphael picture.

It is enough to send a sane person mad, to see this goggling, squirming, self-glorifying idealized humanity carrying on its self-conscious little games. And how it loves its little games. Just heaven, how it wallows in them, ideally!

What is to be done? We talk about new systems of education, and here we have a civilized mankind sucking its fingers avidly, as if its own fingers were so many sticks of juicy barley-sugar. It loves itself so much, this ideal self-conscious humanity, that it could verily eat itself. And so it nibbles gluttishly at itself.

Is it the slightest good doing anything but joining in with the sucking and self-nibbling? Probably not. We'll throw stones at them none the less, even if every stone boomerangs back in our own teeth. Perhaps once we shall catch humanity one in the eye.

The question is, don't our children get this self-conscious, self-nibbling habit, in the very womb of their travesty mothers, before they are even born? We are afraid it is so. Our miserable offspring, churned in the abdomen of insatiable self-conscious woman, woman self-consciously every moment seeking and watching her own reactions, her own pregnancy and her own everything, grinding all her sensations from her head and reflecting them all back into her head, all her physical churnings ground exceeding small in the hateful self-conscious mills of her female mind, ideal and unremitting; do not our miserable offspring issue from the ovens of such a womb writhing and crisping with self-conscious morbid hunger of self? Alas and alack, to all appearance they do. The self-conscious devil is in them, either smirking and smarming, or preening and prancing, or irritably self-nibbling, and sentimentalizing, or stolidly *sufficient*, or hostile. But there it is, the hateful devil of self-conscious self-importance born with them, simmered into them in the acid-seething, irritable womb.

What's to be done? Why, of course, keep the game up. Tickle the poor little wretches into ecstasies of self-consciousness. Gather round them and stare at them and mouth over them and sentimentalize and rhapsodize over them. Get the doctor to paw them, the nurse to expose them naked to a horde of ideal prurient females, get the parson to preach over them and roll his eyes to heaven over their sanctity. Then send them to school to 'express themselves', in the hopes that they'll turn out infant prodigies. For, oh, dear me! *what* a feather in the cap of a mortal mother is an infant prodigy!

If *one* healthy sensitive mother in these days bore one healthy-souled, simple child she'd pick him up and bolt for her life from the mobs of our ghoulish 'charming' women, and the mobs of goggling adoring men. She'd run, poor Hagar, to some desert with her Ishmael. And there she'd give him to a she-wolf, or a she-bear, or a she-lion to suckle. She'd never trust herself. Verily, she'd have more faith in a rattlesnake, as far as motherhood is concerned.

Would God a she-wolf had suckled me, and stood over me with her paps, and kicked me back into a rocky corner when she'd had enough of me. It might have made a man of me.

But it's no use sighing. Romulus and Remus had all the luck. We see now why they bred a great, great race: because they had no mother: a race of men. Christians have no fathers: only these ogling woman-worshipping saints, and the self-conscious friction of exalted mothers.

Let us rail—why shouldn't we? It is subject enough for railing. But what about these infants? Alas, there isn't a wild she-wolf in the length and breadth of Britain. There isn't a crevice in the British Isles where you could suckle a brat undisturbed by the village constable. And therefore, no hope with us of heroic twins.

What are we going to do? Presumably, nothing: except carry on the pretty process of smirking and goggling which we call education. The sense of futility overwhelms us. The thought of all the exalted mothers of England, and of all the knock-kneed smug God-besprinkled fathers, is too much for us: all the hosts of the sentimental, self-conscious ones, the sensational self-conscious ones, the free-and-easy self-conscious ones, the downright no-nonsense-about-me self-conscious ones, the elegant self-conscious ones, the would-be dissolute self-conscious ones, the very-very-naughty self-conscious ones, the *chic* self-conscious ones, and spiritual self-conscious ones, and the *nuancy* self-conscious ones (those full of *nuances*), and the self-sacrificial self-conscious ones, and the do-all-you-can-for-others self-conscious ones, the do-your-bit self-conscious ones, the yearning, the aspiring, the sighing, the leering, the tip-the-winking self-conscious ones, females and so-called men: all the lot of them: *ad nauseam* and *ad nauseissimam* : they are too much for me. All of them like so many little barrel-organs grinding their own sensations, nay, their own very natures, out of their own little heads: and become so automatic at it they don't even know they're doing it. They think they are fine spontaneous angels, these little automata. And they are automata, self-turning little barrel-organs, all of them, from the millionaire down to the dustman. The dustman grinds himself off according to his own dustman-ideal prescription.

8

We've got to get on to a different tack: snap! off the old tack and veer on to a new one. No more seeing ourselves as others see us. No more seeing ourselves at all. A fig for such sights.

The primary conscious centres, the very first and deepest, are in the lower body. A button for your brain, whoever you are. If you are not darkly potent below the belt, you are nothing.

Let go the upper consciousness. Switch it off for a time. Release the cramped and tortured lower consciousness. Drop this loving and merging business. Fall back into your own isolation and the insuperable pride thereof. Break off the old polarity, the merging into oneness with others, with everything. Snap the old connections, Break clean away from the old yearning navel-string of love, which unites us to the body of everything. Break it, and be born. Fall apart into your own isolation; set apart single and potent in singularity for ever. One is one and all alone and ever more shall be so. Exult in it. Exult in the fact that you are yourself, and alone for ever. Exult in your own dark being. Across the gulf are strangers, myriad-faced dancing strangers like midges and like Pleiades. One draws near; there is a thrill and a fiery contact. But never a merging. A withdrawal, a bond of knowledge, but no identification. Recognition across space; across a dark and bottomless space; two beings who recognize each other across the chasm, who occasionally cross and meet in a fiery contact, but who find themselves invariably withdrawn afterwards, with dark, dusky-glowing faces glancing across the insuperable chasm which intervenes between two beings.

Have done; let go the old connections. Fall apart, fall asunder, each into his own unfathomable dark bath of isolation. Break up the old incorporation. Finish for ever the old unison with homogeneity. Let every man fall apart into a fathomless, single isolation of being, exultant at his own core, and apart. Then, dancing magnificent in our own space, as the spheres dance in space, we can set up the extra-individual communication. Across the space comes the thrill of communication. There is an approach, a flash and blaze of contact, and then the sheer fiery purity of a purer isolation, a more exultant singleness. Not a mass of homogeneity, like sunlight, but a fathomless multiplicity, like the stars at night, each one isolate in the darkly singing space. This symbol of Light, the homogeneous and universal Day, the daylight, symbolizes our universal mental consciousness, which we have in common. But our *being* we have in integral separateness, as the stars at night. To think of lumping the stars together into one mass is hideous. Each one separate, each one his own peculiar ray. So the universe is made up.

And the sun only hides all this. Imagine, if the sun shone all the time, we should never know there was anything but ourselves in the universe. Everything would be limited to the plane superficies of ourself and our own mundane nature. Everything would be as we see it and as we think it.

Which is what ails us. Living as we do entirely in the light of the mental consciousness, we think everything is as we see it and as we think it. Which is a vast illusion. Imagine a man who all his life has been shut up in a hermetically dark room, between sundown and sunrise, and let out only when light was full in the heavens. He would imagine that everything, all the time, was light, that the firmament was a vast blue space screened from us sometimes by our own vapours, but otherwise a blue, unblemished void occupied by ourselves and the sun, one blue unchanging blaze of eternal light, with ourselves for the only inhabitants, under the sun.

Which, in spite of Galileo, that star-master, is what we actually do think. If we proceed to imagine other worlds, we cook up a few distortions of our own world and scatter them into space. A Martian may have long ears and horns on his forehead, but he is only ourselves dressed up, busy making super-zeppelins. We are convinced, as a matter of fact, that the stars and ourselves are all seed of one sort.

And what holds true cosmologically holds much more true psychologically. The man sealed up during twilight and night-time would have a rare shock the first time he was taken out under the stars. To see all the blue heavens crumpled and shrivelled away! To see the pulsation of myriad orbs proudly moving in the endless darkness, insouciant, sunless, taking a stately path we know not whither or how. Ha, the day-time man would feel his heart and brain burst to a thousand shivers, he would feel himself falling like a seed into space. All that he counted *himself* would be suddenly dispelled. All that he counted eternal, infinite, *Everything*, suddenly shrivelled like a vast, burnt roof of paper, or a vast paper lantern: the eternal light gone out: and behold, multiplicity, twinkling, proud multiplicity, utterly indifferent of oneness, proud far-off orbs taking their lonely way beyond the bounds of knowledge, emitting their own unique and untransmutable rays, pulsing with their own isolate pulsation.

This is what must happen to us. We have kept up a false daylight all through our nights. Our sophistry has intervened like a lamp between us and the slow-stepping stars, we have turned our cheap lanterns on the dark and wizard face of Galileo, till lo and behold, his words are as harmless as butterflies. Of course the orbs are manifold: we admit it easily. But *light* is one and universal and infinite.

Put it in human terms: men are manifold, but Wisdom and Understanding are one and universal. Men are manifold, but the Spirit, the consciousness, is one, as sunlight is one. And therefore, because the consciousness of mankind is really one and universal, mankind is one and universal. Therefore each individual is a term of the Infinite.

A pretty bit of sophistry. Because the sunlight covers all the stars, therefore the stars are one, each is a homogeneous bit of light. Behold, how oneness achieves its ridiculous triumph, by self-deception. It is a famous dodge, this of self-deception. The Popes couldn't squash Galileo. But clever mankind has succeeded in smearing out his star-shine, by a trick of the psyche.

Mankind is an ostrich with its head in the bush of the Infinite. This doesn't prevent the stars all trooping past with a superb smile at the rump of the bird.

We don't find fault with the mental consciousness, the daylight consciousness of mankind. Not at all. We only find fault with the One-and-Allness which is attributed to it. It isn't One-and-All, any more than the sun is one and all. Has it never occurred to us that the sun serves no more than as a great lantern and bonfire to the ambulating intermediary world? Has it never occurred to us that the sun is not *superior* to our little earth, and to the other little stars, but just instrumental, a bonfire and a lamp and an axle-tree? After all, it is the little spheres which *live*, and the great sun is instrumental to their living, even as the powerful arc-lamps high over Piccadilly only serve to illuminate the little feet of foot-passengers.

So there we are. All our Oneness and our infinite, which does but mount up to the sum-total of human mentality or consciousness, is merely instrumental to the small individual consciousness of individual beings. Bigness as a rule means departure from life. Things which are vividly living are never so very big. Vastness is a term which applies to the non-vital universe. The moment we consider the vital universe, vastness and extensiveness cease to be terms of merit, and become terms of demerit. Whatever is vast and extensive in the *living* world is less quick, less alive than that which creates no impression of superlative size. In the *living* world, appreciation is intensive, not extensive. A small fowl like a lark or a kestrel is more to us than a flock of rooks or an ostrich or a condor. One is one and all alone and ever more shall be so.

Hence the little stellar orbs, living as we feel they must be, are more than the great sun they hover round: just as the shadowy human men are more than the great fire round which they squat and move in the dark camp. So, the universe is a great living camp squatted round the sun. We warm ourselves and prepare our food at the fire. But, after all, the fire is only the means to our living. So the sun. It is but the means to the living of the little mid-way spheres, the great fire camped in the middle of the sky, at which they warm themselves and prepare their meat.

And so with human beings. One is one, and as such, always more than an aggregation. Vitally, intensively, one human being is always more than six collective human beings. Because, in the collectivity, what is gained in bulk or number is lost in intrinsic being. The *quick* of any collective group is some consciousness they have in common. But the quick of the individual is the integral soul, for ever indescribable and unstateable. That which is *in common* is never any more than some mere property of the vital, individual soul.

Away then with the old system of valuation, that many is more than one. In the static material world it is so. But in the living world, the opposite is true. One is more than many. The Japanese know that one flower is lovelier than many flowers. Alone, one flower lives and has its own integral wonder. Massed with other flowers, it has a being-in-common, and this being-in-common is always inferior to the single aloneness of one creature. Being-in-common means the summing-up of one element held in common by many individuals. But this one common element, however many times multiplied, is never more than one mere part in any individual, and therefore much *less* than any individual.

The more common the element, the smaller is its part in the individual, and hence the greater its vital insignificance. So with humanity, or mankind, or the Infinite, as compared with one individual.

All of which is not mere verbal metaphysic, but an attempt to get in human beings a new attitude to life. Instead of finding our highest reality in an ever-extending aggregation with the rest of men, we shall realize at last that the highest reality for every living creature is in its purity of singleness and its perfect solitary integrity, and that everything else should be but a means to this end. All communion, all love and all communication, which is all consciousness, are but a means to the perfected singleness of the individual being.

Which doesn't mean anarchy and disorder. On the contrary, it means the most delicately and inscrutably established order, delicate, intricate, complicated as the stars in heaven, when seen in their strange groups and goings. Neither does it mean what is nowadays called individualism. The so-called individualism is no more than a cheap egotism, every self-conscious little ego assuming unbounded rights to display his self-consciousness. We mean none of this. We mean, in the first place, the recognition of the exquisite arresting *manifoldness* of being, multiplicity, plurality, as the stars are plural in their starry singularity. Lump the green flashing Sirius with red Mars, and what will you get? A muddy orb. Aggregate them, and what then? A mere smudgy cloudy nebula. One is one and all alone and ever more shall be so. Enveloped each one in its fathomless abyss of isolation. Magically, vitally alone, flashing with singleness.

Towards *this*, then, we are to educate our children and ourselves. Not towards any infinitely extended consciousness. Not towards any vastness or unlimitedness of any sort. Not towards any inordinate range of understanding or consciousness. Not towards any merging in any whole whatsoever. But delicately, through all the processes of communion and communication, love and consciousness, to the perfect singleness of a full and flashing, orb-like maturity.

And if this is the goal of all our striving and effort, then let us take the first stride by *leaving the child alone*, in his own soul. Take all due care of him, materially; give him all love and tenderness and wrath which the spontaneous soul emits: but always, always, at the very quick, leave him alone. Leave him alone. He is not you and you are not he. He is never to be merged into you nor you into him. Though you love him and he love you, this is but a communion in unfathomable difference, not an identification into oneness. There is *no* living oneness for two people: only a deadly oneness, of merged human beings.

Leave the child *alone*. Alone! That is the great word and world. Suppose the moon went through the sky, loving all the stars, hugging them to her breast, and crushing them into one beam with her. O vile thought! Like a swollen leper the dead moon would roll out of a void and corpse-like sky. Supposing she even caught the star Sirius as he passes low, and embraced him into oneness with herself, so that he merged amorphous into her. Immediately Orion would fall to pieces in the ruined heavens, the planets would drop from their orbits, a vast cataclysm and a rain of ruin in the cosmos.

Sirius must move and flash in his own circumambient space, single. Who knows what strange relation and intercommunion he has with Aldebaran, with the Pole Star, even with ourselves? But whatever his intercommunion, he is never raped from his own singleness, he never falls from his own isolate self.

The same for the child. After the navel-string breaks, he is alone in the aura of his own exquisite and mystic solitariness, and there must be no trespass into this solitariness. He is alone. *Leave* him alone. Never forget. Never forget to leave him alone, within his own soul's inviolability.

Do not be afraid, either, to *drive* him into his own soul's inviolable singleness. A child will trespass. It is born nowadays with an irritable craving to trespass into the nature of its mother. Nay, the parent–child relationship in these nervous days resolves itself into one series of trespasses across the confines of the two natures, till there is some unholy arrest.

Now the *seeking* centres of the human system are the great sympathetic centres. It is from these, and primarily from the solar plexus, that the individual goes forth seeking communion with another being or creature or thing. At the solar plexus the child yearns avidly for the mother, for contact, for unison, for absorption even. A nervous child yearns and frets ceaselessly for complete identification. It wants to merge, to merge back into the mother, with the ceaseless craving of morbid love.

What are we to do when a child a few weeks old is so smitten, nervously craving for the mother and for re-identification with her? What on earth are we to do?

It is quite simple. *Break* the spell. Set up the activity of the volitional centres. For at the volitional centres a creature keeps itself apart, integral, centred in its own isolation. Living as we have done in one mode only, the mode of love, praising as we have done the single mode of unification and identification through love with the beloved, and with all the rest of the universe, we have used all the strength of the upper, mentally directed *will* to break the power of these dark, proud, integral volitional centres of the lower body. And we have almost succeeded. So that human life is born now creeping, parasitic in its tendency. The proud volitional centres of the lower body, those which maintain a human being integral and distinct, these have collapsed, so that the whole individual crawls helplessly and parasitically from the sympathetic centres, to establish himself in a permanent life-oneness with another being, usually the mother. And the mother, too, rejoices in this horrible parasitism of her child, she feels exalted, like God, now she is the host of the parasite.

Break the horrible circle of this lust. Break it. Seize babies away from their mothers, with hard, fierce, terrible hands. Send the volts of fierce anger and severing force violently into the child. Volts of hard, violent anger, that shock the feeble volitional centres into life again. Smack the whimpering child. Smack it sharp and fierce on its small buttocks. With all the ferocity of a living, healthy anger, spank the little tail, till at last the powerful dynamic centres of the spinal system vibrate into life, out of their atrophied torture. It is not too late. Quick, quick, mothers of England, spank your wistful babies. Good God, spank their little bottoms; with sharp, red anger spank them and make men of them. Drive them back. Drive them back from their yearning, loving parasitism; startle them for ever out of their pseudo-angelic wistfulness; cure them with a quick wild yell of all their wonder-child spirituality. Sharp, sharp, before it is too late. Be *fierce* with the little darling, and put hell's temper into its soft little soul. Quick, before we are lost.

Let us get this wide, wistful look out of our children's eyes – this oh-so-spiritual look, varied by an oh-so-spiteful look. Let us cure them of their inordinate sensitiveness and consciousness. Kick the cat out of the room when the cat is a nuisance, and let the baby see you do it. And if the baby whimpers, kick the baby after the cat. In just mercy, do it. And then maybe you'll have a slim-muscled, independent cat that can walk with a bit of moon-devilish defiance, instead of the ravel of knitting-silk with a full belly and a sordid *meeau* which is 'Pussy' of our dear domestic hearth. More important than the cat, you'll get a healthily reacting human infant, animal and fierce and not-to-be-coddled, the first signs of a proud man whose neck won't droop like a weak lily, nor reach forward for ever like a puppy reaching to suck, and whose knees won't be aching all his life with a luscious, loose desire to slip into some woman's lap, dear darling, and feel her caress his brow.

This instant moment we've got to start to put some fire into the backbones of our children. Do you know what the backbone is? It is the long sword of the vivid, proud, *dark* volition of man, something primal and creative. Not that miserable mental obstinacy which goes in the name of *will* nowadays. Not a will-to-power or a will-to-goodness or a will-to-love or a will-*to* anything else. All these wills to this, that and the other are only so many obstinate mechanical directions given to some chosen mental idea. You may choose the idea of power, and fix your mechanical little will on that, as the Germans did; or the idea of love, and fix your equally mechanical and still more obstinate little will on *that*, as we do, privately. And all you'll get is some neurotic automaton or parasite, materialistic as hell. You must be automatic and materialistic once you substitute an ideal pivot for the spontaneous centres.

But at the centres of the primal will, situate in the spinal system, the great volitional centres, here a man arises in his own dark pride and singleness, his own sensual magnificence in single being. Here the flashing indomitable man himself takes rise. It is not any tuppenny mechanical instrumental thing, a will-to-this or a will-to-that.

And these, these great centres of primal proud volition, these, especially in the lower body, are the life-centres that have gone soft and rotten in us. Here we need sharp, fierce reaction; sharp discipline, rigour; fierce, fierce severity. We, who are willing to operate surgically on our physical sick, my God, we must be quick and operate psychically on our psychic sick, or they are done for.

Whipping, beating, yes, these alone will thunder into the moribund centres and bring them to life. Sharp, stinging whipping, keen, fierce smacks, and all the roused fury of reaction in the child, these alone will restore us to psychic health. Away with all mental punishments and reprobation. You *must* rouse the powerful physical reaction of anger, dark flushing anger in the child. You must. You *must* fight him, tooth and nail, if you're going to keep him healthy and alive. And if you're going to be able to love him with warm, rich bowels of love, my heaven, how you must fight him, how openly and fiercely and with no nonsense about it.

Rouse the powerful volitional centres at the base of the spine, and those between the shoulders. Even with stinging rods, rouse them.

9

In the early years a child's education should be entirely non-mental. Instead of trying to attract an infant's attention, trying to arouse its *notice*, to make it *perceive*, the mother or nurse should mindlessly put it into contact with the physical universe. What is the first business of the baby? To ascertain the physical reality of its own context, even of its own very self. It has to learn to wave its little hands and feet. To a baby it is for a long time a startling thing, to find its own hand waving. It does not know what is moving, nor how it moves. It is quite unconscious of having inaugurated the motion, as a cat is unconscious of what makes the shadow after which it darts, or in what its own elusive tail-tip consists. So a baby marvels over the transit of this strange *something* which moves again and again across its own little vision. Behold, it is only the small fist. So it watches and watches. What is it doing?

When a baby absorbedly, almost painfully, watches its own vagrant and spasmodic fist, is it trying to form a concept of that fist? Is it trying to formulate a little idea? 'That is *my* fist: it is *I* who move it: I wave it *so*, and *so*!' – Not at all. The concept of *I* is quite late in forming. Some children do not realize that they are themselves until they are four or five years old. They are something objective to themselves: 'Jackie wants it' – 'Baby wants it' – and not '*I* want it.' In the same way with the hand or the foot. A child for some years has no *conception* of its own foot as part of itself. It is '*the* foot'. In most languages it is always 'the foot, the hand', and not 'my foot, my hand'. But in English the ego is very insistent. We put it self-consciously in possession as soon as possible.

None the less, it is some time before a child is possessed of its own ego. A baby watches its little fist waving through the air, perilously near its nose. What is it doing, thinking about the fist? NO! It is establishing the *rapport* or connection between the primary affective centres which controls the fist. From the deep sympathetic plexus leaps out an impulse. The fist waves, wildly, to the peril of the little nose. It waves, does it! It leaps, it moves! And from the fountain of impulse deep in the little breast, it moves. But there is also a quiver of fear because of this spasmodic, convulsive motion. Fear! And the first volitional centre of the upper body struggles awake, between the shoulders. It moves, the arm moves, ah, convulsively, wildly, wildly! Ah, look, beyond control it moves, spurting from the wild source of impulse. Fear and ecstasy! Fear and ecstasy! But the other dawning power obtrudes. Shall it move, the wildly waving little arm? Then look, it shall move smoothly, it shall not flutter abroad. So! And so! Such a swing means such a balance, such an explosion of force means a leap in such and such a direction.

The volitional centre in the shoulders establishes itself bit by bit in relation to the sympathetic plexus in the breast, and forms a circuit of spontaneous-voluntary intelligence. The volitional centres are those which put us primarily into line with the earth's gravity. The wildly waving infant fist does not know how to swing attuned to the earth's gravity, the omnipresent force of gravity. Life flutters broadcast in the baby's arm. But at the thoracic ganglion acts a new vital power, which gradually seizes the motor energy that comes explosive from the sympathetic centre, and ranges it in line with all kinetic force, in line with the mysterious, omnipresent centre-pull of the earth's gravity. There is a true circuit now between the earth's centre and the centre of ebullient energy in the child. Everything depends on these true, polarized or orbital circuits. There is no disarray, no haphazard.

Once the flux of life from the spontaneous centres is put into its true kinetic relation with the earth's centre, adjusted to the force of gravity; once the gravitation of the baby's hand is spontaneously accepted and realized in the primary affective centres of the baby's psyche, then that little hand can take true and voluntary direction. The volitional centre is the pole that relates us, kinetically, to the earth's centre. The sympathetic plexus is the source whence the movement-impulse leaps out. Connect the two centres into a perfect circuit, and then, the moment the baby's fist leaps out for the tassel on its cradle, the volitional ganglion swings the leaping fist truly to its goal.

But this requires practice, for a baby. And in the course of the practice the infant bangs its own nose and swings its arm too far so that it hurts, and brings a fair amount of trouble upon itself. But in the end, the fluttering, palpitating movement of the first days becomes a true and perfect flight, a gesture, a motion.

Has the mind got anything to do with all this? Does there enter any *idea* of movement into the baby's head, does the child form any conception of what it is doing? NONE. This whole range of activity and consciousness is non-mental, effective at the primary centres. It is not mere automatism. Far from it. It is *spontaneous consciousness*, effective and perfect in itself.

And it is in this spontaneous consciousness that education arises. One of the reasons why uneducated peasant nurses are on the whole so much better for infants than over-conscious mothers is that an uneducated nurse does not introduce any *idea* into her attitude towards the child. When she claps her hands before the child, again and again, nods, smiles, coos, and claps again, she is stimulating the infant to motion, pure, mindless motion. She wants the child to clap too. She wants its one little hand to find the other little hand, she wants to start the quick touch-and-go in the little shoulders. When you see her, time after time, making a fierce, wild gesture with her arm, before the eyes of the baby, and the baby laughing and chuckling, she is rousing the infant to the same fierce, free, reckless *geste*. Fierce, free, wild reckless *geste*! How it excites the child to a quaint reckless chuckle! How it wakes in him the desire, the impulse for free, sheer motion! It starts the proud *geste* of independence.

This is the clue to early education: movement, physical motion, the attuning of the kinetic energy of the motor centres to the vast sway of the earth's centre. Without this we are nothing: clumsy, mechanical clowns, or pinched little automata.

But if you are going to make use of this form of education you must find teachers full of physical life and zest, of fine, physical, motor intelligence, and mentally rather stupid, or at least quiescent. Above all things, the *idea*, like a strangling worm, must not creep into the motor centres. It must be excluded. If we move, we must move primarily like a bird in the sky, which swings in supreme adjustment to the multiple forces of the winds of heaven and the pull of earth, mindless, idea-less, a speck of perfect physical animation. That is the whole point of real physical life: its joy in spontaneous mindless animation, in motion sheer and superb, like a leaping fish or a hovering hawk or a deer which bounds away, creatures which have never known the pride and the blight of the idea. The idea is a glorious thing in its place. But interposed in all our living, interpolated into our every gesture, it is like some fatal mildew crept in, some vile blight.

Let children be taught the pride of clear, clean movement. If it only be putting a cup on the table, or a book on a shelf, let it be a fine pure motion, not a slovenly shove. Parents and teachers should be keen as hawks, watching their young in motion. Do we imagine that a young hawk learns to fly and stoop, does a young swallow learn to skim, or a hare to dash uphill, or a hound to turn and seize him in full course, without long, keen pain of learning? Where there is no pain of effort there is a wretched, drossy degeneration, like the hateful cluttered sheep of our lush pastures. Look at the lambs, how they explode with new life, and skip up into the air. Already a *little* bit gawky! And then look at their mothers. Whereas a wild sheep is a fleet, fierce thing, leaping and swift like the sun.

So with our children. We, parents and teachers, must prevent their degenerating into physical cloddishness or mechanical affectation or fluttered nervousness. We must be after them, fiercely, sharpen and chasten their movements, their bearing, their walk. If a boy slouches out of a door, throw a book at him, like lightning. That will make him jump into keen and handsome alertness. And if a girl comes creeping, whining in, seize her by her pigtail and run her out again, full speed. That will bring the fire to her eyes and the poise to her head: if she's got any fire in her; and if she hasn't, why, give her a good knock to see if you can drive some in.

Anything, anything rather than the nervous, twisting, wistful, pathetic, centreless children we are cursed with; or the fat and self-satisfied, sheep-in-the-pasture children who are becoming more common; or the impudent, I'm-as-good-as-anybody smirking children who are far too numerous. But it's all our own fault. We're afraid to *fight* with our children, and so we let them degenerate. Poor loving parents *we* are!

There must be a fight. There must be an element of danger, always. How do the wild animals get their grace, their beauty, their allure? Through being on the *qui vive*, always on the *qui vive*. A lark on a sand-dune springs up to heaven in song. She leaps up in a pure, fine strength. She trills out in triumph, she is beside herself in mid-heaven. But let her mind her p's and q's. In the first place, if she doesn't flick her wings finely and rapidly, with exquisite skilful energy, she'll come a cropper to earth. Let her mind the winds of heaven, in the first place. And in the second, let her mind the shadow of Monsieur the kestrel. And in the third place, let her be wary how she drops. And in the fourth place, let her be wary of who sees her dropping. For, the moment she alights on this bristling earth she's got to dart to cover, and cut some secret track to her nest, or she's likely to be in trouble. It's all very well climbing a ladder of song to heaven. But you've got to have your wits about you all the time, even while you're cock-a-lorying on your ladder: and *inevitably* you've got to climb down. Mind you don't give your enemies too good a chance, that's all. And watch it that you don't indicate where your nest is, or your ladder of song will have been a sore business. On the *qui vive*, bright lark!

So with our children. On the *qui vive*. The old-fashioned parents were right, when they made their children watch what they were about. But old-fashioned parents were a bore, dragging in moral and religious justification. If we are to chase our children, and chasten them too, it must be because they make our blood boil, not because some ethical or religious code sanctifies us.

'Miss, if you eat in that piggish, mincing fashion, you shall go without a meal or two.'

'*Why?*'

'Because you're an objectionable sight.'

'Well, you needn't look at me.'

Here Miss should get a box on the ear.

'Take that! And know that I *need* look at you, since I'm responsible for you. And since I'm responsible for you, I'll watch it you don't behave like a mincing little pig.'

Observe, no morals, no 'What will people think of you?' or 'What would your Daddy say?' or 'What if Aunt Lucy saw you now!' or 'It's wrong for little girls to be mincing and ugly!' or 'You'll be sorry for it when you grow up!' or 'I thought you were a good little girl!' or '*Now*, what did teacher say to you in Sunday-school?' – None of all these old dodges for shifting responsibility somewhere else. The plain fact is that parents and teachers *are* responsible for the bearing and developing of their children, so they may as well accept the responsibility flatly, and without dodges.

'I am responsible for the way you grow up, milady, and I'll fulfil my responsibility. So stop pushing your food about on your plate and look-ing like a self-conscious cockatoo, or leave the table and walk well out of my sight.'

This is the tone that any honourable parent would take, seeing his little girl mincing and showing off at dinner. Let us keep the bowels of our compassion alive, and also the bowels of our wrath. No priggish brow-beating and mechanical authority, nor any disapproving superior-ity, but a plain, open anger when anger is aroused, and pleasure when this is waked.

The parent who sits at table in pained but disapproving silence while the child makes a nuisance of itself, and says: 'Dear, I should be *so* glad if you would try to like your pudding: or if you don't like it, have a little bread-and-butter,' and who goes on letting the brat be a nuisance, this ideal parent is several times at fault. First she is assuming a pained ideal aloofness which is the worst form of moral bullying, a sort of *Of course I won't interfere, but I am in the right* attitude which is insuffer-able. If a parent is in the right, then she *must* interfere, otherwise why does she bring up her child at all? If she doesn't interfere, what right has she to assume any virtue of superiority? Then, when she is angry with the child, what right has she to say 'Dear', which term implies a state of affectionate communion? This prefixing of the ideal rebuke with the term 'Dear' or 'Darling' is a hateful travesty of all good feeling. It is using love or affection as a bullying weapon: which vile, sordid act the idealist is never afraid to commit. It is assuming authority of love, when love, as an emotional relationship, can have no authority. Authority must rest on responsible wisdom, and love must be a spontaneous thing, or nothing: an emotional *rapport*. Love and authority have nothing to do with one another. 'Whom the Lord loveth, He chasteneth.' True! But the Lord's love is not supposed to be an emotional business, but a sort of divine responsibility and purpose. And so is parental love, a respon-sibility and a living purpose, not an emotion. To make the *emotion* responsible for the purpose is a fine falsification. One says 'Dear' or

'Darling' when the heart opens with spontaneous cherishment, not when the brow draws with anger or irritation. But the deep purpose and responsibility of parenthood remains unchanged no matter how the emotions flow. The emotions should flow unfalsified, in the very strength of that purpose.

Therefore parents should *never* seek justification outside themselves. They should never say, 'I do this for your good.' You *don't* do it for the child's good. Parental responsibility is much deeper than an ideal responsibility. It is a vital connection. Parent and child are polarized together still, somewhat as before birth. When the child in the womb kicks, it may almost hurt the parent. And the reaction is just as direct during all the course of childhood and parenthood. When a child is loose or ugly it is a direct *hurt* to the parent. The parent reacts and retaliates spontaneously. There is no justification, save the bond of parenthood, and certainly there is no ideal intervention.

We must accept the bond of parenthood primarily as a vital, mindless conjunction, non-ideal, passional. A parent *owes* the child all the natural passional reactions provoked. If a child provokes anger, then to deny it this anger, the open, passional anger, is as bad as to deny it food or love. It causes an atrophy in the child, at the volitional centres, and a perversion of the true life-flow.

Why are we so afraid of anger, of wrath, and clean, fierce rage? What cowardice possesses us? Why would we reduce a child to a nervous, irritable wreck, rather than spank it wholesomely? Why do we make such a fuss about a row? A row, a fierce storm in a family is a natural and healthy thing, which we ought even to have the courage to enjoy and exult in, as we can enjoy and exult in a storm of the elements. What makes us so namby-pamby? We ought all to fight: husbands and wives, parents and children, sisters and brothers and friends, all ought to fight, fiercely, freely, openly; and they ought to enjoy it. It stiffens the backbone and makes the eyes flash. Love without a fight is nothing but degeneracy. But the fight must be spontaneous and natural, without fixities and perversions.

The same with parenthood: spontaneous and natural, without any ideal taint.

And this is the beginning of true education: first, the stimulus to physical motion, physical trueness and *élan*, which is given to the infant. And this is continued during the years of early childhood *not by deliberate instruction*, but by the keen, fierce unremitting swiftness of the parent, whose warm love opens the valves of glad motion in the child, so that the child plays in delicious security and freedom, and whose fierce, vigilant anger sharpens the child to a trueness and boldness of motion and bearing such as are impossible save in children of strong-hearted parents.

Open the valves of warm love so that your child can play in serene joy by itself, or with others, like young weasels safe in a sunny nook of a wood, or young tiger-cubs whose great parents lie grave and apart, on guard. And open also the sharp valves of wrath, that your child may be alert, keen, proud and fierce in his turn. Let parenthood and child-hood be a spontaneous, animal relationship, non-ideal, swift, a con-tinuous interplay of shadow and light, ever-changing relationship and mood. And, parents, keep in your heart, like tigers, the grave and vivid responsibility of parenthood, remote and natural in you, not fanciful and self-conscious.

10

From earliest childhood, let us have independence, independence, self-dependence. Every child to do all it can for itself, wash and dress itself, clean its own boots, brush and fold its own clothes, fetch and carry for itself, mend its own stockings, boy or girl alike, patch its own garments, and as soon as possible make as well as mend for itself. Man and woman are happy when they are busy, and children the same. But there must be the right motive behind the work. It must not always, for a child, be 'Help mother' or 'Help father' or 'Help somebody'. This altruism be-comes tiresome, and causes disagreeable reaction. Neither must the motive be the ideal of work. 'Work is service, hence work is noble. *Laborare est orare.*' Never was a more grovelling motto than this, that work is prayer. Work is not a prayer at all: not in the same category. Work is a practical business, prayer is the soul's yearning and desire. Work is not an ideal, save for slaves. But work is quite a pleasant occu-pation for a human creature, a natural activity.

And the aim of work is neither the emotional helping of mother and father, nor the ethical-religious service of mankind. Nor is it the greedy piling-up of stupid possessions. An individual works for his own pleasure and independence: but chiefly in the happy pride of personal indepen-dence, personal liberty. No man is free who depends on servants. Man can never be quite free. Indeed he doesn't want to be. But in his *personal* immediate life he can be vastly freer than he is.

How? By doing things for himself. Once we wake the quick of per-sonal pride, there is a pleasure in performing our own personal service, every man sweeping his own room, making his own bed, washing his own dishes – or in proportion: just as a soldier does. We have got a mistaken notion of ourselves. We conceive of ourselves as ideal beings, nothing but consciousness, and therefore actual work has become degrading, menial to us. But let us change our notion of ourselves. We are only in part ideal beings. For the rest we are lively physical creatures whose life consists in motion and action. We have two feet which need tending, and which need socks and shoes. This is our own personal affair, and it behoves us to see to it. Let me look after my own socks and shoes, since these are private to me. Let me tend to my own apparel and my own personal service. Every bird builds its own nest and preens its own feathers: save perhaps a cuckoo or a filthy little sparrow which likes to oust a swallow, or a crazy ostrich which squats in the sand. Proud personal privacy, personal liberty, gay individual self-dependence. Awake in a child the gay, proud sense of its own aloof individuality, and it will busy itself about its own affairs happily. It all depends what centre you try to drive from, what motive is at the back of all your movement. It is just as irksome to *have* a servant as to *be* a servant: particularly a personal servant. A servant moving about me, or even anybody moving about me, doing things for me, is a horrible drag on my freedom. I feel it as a sort of prostitution. *Noli me tangere.* It is our motto as it is the motto of a wild wolf or deer. I want about me a clear, cool space across which nobody trespasses. I want to remain intact within my own natural isolation, save at those moments when I am drawn to a rare and significant intimacy. The horrible personal promiscuity of our life is extremely ugly and distasteful. As far as possible, let *nobody* do anything for me, personally, save those who are near and dear to me: and even then as little as possible. Let me be by myself, and leave me my native distance. *Sono io* – and not a thing of public convenience.

Self-dependence is independence. To be free one must be self-sufficient, particularly in small, material, personal matters. In the great business of love, or friendship, or living human intercourse one meets and communes with another free individual; there is no service. Service is degrading, both to the servant and the one served: a promiscuity, a sort of prostitution. No one should do for me that which I can reasonably do for myself. Two individuals may be intimately interdependent on one another, as man and wife, for example. But even in this relation each should be as self-dependent, as self-supporting as ever possible. We should be each as single in our independence as the wild animals are. That is the only true pride. To have a dozen servants is to be twelve times prostituted in human relationship, sold and bought and automatized, divested of individual singleness and privacy.

The actual doing things is in itself a joy. If I wash the dishes I learn a quick, light touch of china and earthenware, the feel of it, the weight and roll and poise of it, the peculiar hotness, the quickness or slowness of its surface. I am at the middle of an infinite complexity of motions and adjustments and quick, apprehensive contacts. Nimble faculties hover and play along my nerves, the primal consciousness is alert in me. Apart from all the moral or practical satisfaction derived from a thing well done, I have the *mindless* motor activity and reaction in primal consciousness, which is a pure satisfaction. If I am to be well and satisfied, as a human being, a large part of my life must pass in mindless motion, quick, busy activity in which I am neither bought nor sold, but acting alone and free from the centre of my own active isolation. Not self-consciously, however. Not watching my own reactions. If I wash dishes, I wash them to get them clean. Nothing else.

Every man must learn to be proud and single and alone, and after that, he will be worth knowing. Mankind has degenerated into a conglomerate mass, where everybody strives to look and to be as much as possible an impersonal, non-individual, abstracted unit, a standard. A high *standard* of perfection: that's what we talk about. As if there could be any *standard* among living people, all of whom are separate and single, each one natively distinguished from every other one. Yet we all wear boots made from the abstract 'perfect' or standard foot, and coats made as near as possible for the abstract shoulders of Mr Everyman.

I object to the abstract Mr Everyman being clapped over me like an extinguisher. I object to wearing his coat and his boots and his hat. Me, in a pair of 'Lotus' boots, and a 'Burberry', and 'Oxonian' hat, why, I might just as well be anybody else. And I strenuously object. I am myself, and I don't want to be rigged out as a poor specimen of Mr Everyman. I don't want to be standardized, or even idealized.

If I could, I would make my own boots and my own trousers and coats. I suppose even now I could if I would. But in Rome one must do as Rome does: the bourgeois is not worth my while, I can't demean myself to *épater* him, and I am much too sensitive to my own isolation to want to draw his attention.

Although in Rome one must do as Rome does; and although all the world is Rome today, yet even Rome falls. Rome fell, and Rome will fall again. That is the point.

And it is to prepare for this fall of Rome that we conjure up a new system of education. When I say that every boy shall be taught cobbling and boot-making, it is in the hopes that before long a man will make his own boots to his own fancy. If he likes to have Maltese sandals, why, he'll have Maltese sandals; and if he likes better high-laced buskins, why, he can stalk like an Athenian tragedian. Anyhow he'll sit happily devising his own covering for his own feet, and machine-made boots be hanged. They even hurt him, and give him callosities. And yet, so far, he thinks their machine-made standardized nullity is perfection. But wait till we have dealt with him. He'll be gay-shod to the happiness and vanity of his own toes and to the satisfaction of his own desire. And the same with his trousers. If he fancies his legs, and likes to flutter on his own elegant stem, like an Elizabethan, here's to him. And if he has a hankering after scarlet trunk-hose, I say hurray. *Chacun à son goût*: or ought to have. Unfortunately nowadays nobody has his own taste; everybody is trying to turn himself into a eunuch Mr Everyman, standardized to his collar-stud. A woman is a little different. She wants to look ultra-smart and *chic* beyond words. And so she knows that if she can set all women bitterly asking 'Isn't her dress Paquin?' or 'Surely it's Poiret', or Lucile, or Chéruit, or somebody *very* Parisian, why, she's done it. She wants to create an *effect*: not the effect of being just *herself*, her one and only self, as a flower in all its spots and frills is its own candid self. Not at all. A modern woman wants to hit you in the eye with her get-up. She wants to be a picture. She wants to derive her own nature from her accoutrements. Put her in a khaki uniform and she's a man shrilly whistling K-K-K-Katie. Let her wear no bodice at all, but just a row of emeralds and an aigrette, and she's a *cocotte* before she's eaten her hors-d'oeuvre, even though she was a Bible worker all her life. She lays it all on from the outside, powders her very soul.

But of course, when the little girls from *our* schools grow up they will really consider the lily, and put forth their flowers from their own roots. See them, the darlings, the women of the future, silent and rapt, spinning their own fabric out of their own instinctive souls – and cotton and linen and silk and wool into the bargain, of course – and delicately unfolding the skirts and bodices, or the loose Turkish trousers and little vests, or whatever else they like to wear, evolving and unfurling them in sensitive form, according to their own instinctive desire. She puts on her clothes as a flower unfolds its petals, as an utterance from her own nature, instinctive and individual.

Oh, if only people can learn to do as they like and to have what they like, instead of madly aspiring to do what everybody likes and to look as everybody would like to look. Fancy everybody looking as everybody else likes, and nobody looking like anybody. It sounds like Alice in Wonderland. A well-dressed woman before her mirror says to herself, if she is satisfied: 'Every woman would like to look as I look now. Every woman will envy me.'

Which is absurd. Fancy a petunia leaning over to a geranium and saying: 'Ah, miss, *wouldn't* you just love to be in mauve and white, like me, instead of that common turkey-red!' To which the geranium: 'You! In your cheap material! You don't look more than one-and-a-ha'penny a yard. You'd thank your lucky stars if you had an inch of *chiffon velvet* to your name.'

Of course, a petunia is a petunia, and a geranium is a geranium. And I'll bet Solomon in all his glory was not arrayed like one of these. Why? Because he was trying to cut a dash and look like something beyond nature, overloading himself. Without doubt Solomon in all his nakedness was a lovely thing. But one has a terrible misgiving about Solomon in all his glory. David probably unfolded his nakedness into clothes that came naturally from him. But that Jewish glory of Solomon's suggests diamonds in lumps. Though we may be wrong, and Solomon in all his glory may have moved in fabrics that rippled naturally from him as his own hair, and his jewels may have glowed as his soul glowed, intrinsic. Let us hope so, in the name of wisdom.

All of which may seem a long way from the education of the people. But it isn't really. It only means to say, don't set up standards and regulation patterns for people. Don't have criteria. Let every individual be single and self-expressive: not self-expressive in the self-conscious, smirking fashion, but busy making something he *needs* and wants to have just so, according to his own soul's desire. Everyone individually and spontaneously busy, like a bird that builds its own nest and preens its own feathers, busy about its own business, alone and unaware.

The fingers must almost live and think by themselves. It is no good working from the idea, from the fancy: the creation must evolve itself from the vital activity of the fingers. Here's the difference between living evolving work and that ideal mental business we call 'handicraft instruction' or 'handwork' in school today.

Dozens of high-souled idealists sit today at hand-looms and spiritually weave coarse fabrics. It is a high-brow performance. As a rule it comes to an end. But sometimes it achieves another effect. Sometimes actually the mind is lulled, by the steady repetition of mechanical, productive labour, into a kind of swoon. Gradually the idealism moults away, the high-brow resolves into a busy, unconscious worker, perhaps even a night-and-day slogger, absorbed in the process of work.

One should go to the extremity of any experience. But that one should stay there, and make a habit of the extreme, is another matter. A great part of the life of every human creature should pass in mindless, active occupation. But not all the days. There is a time to work, and a time to be still, a time to think, and a time to forget. And they are all different times.

The point about any handwork is that it should not be mindwork. Supposing we are to learn to solder a kettle. The theory is told in a dozen words. But it is not a question of applying a theory. It is a question of *knowing*, by direct physical contact, your kettle-substance, your kettle-curves, your solder, your soldering-iron, your fire, your resin, and all the fusing, slipping interaction of all these. A question of direct knowing by contact, not a question of understanding. The mental understanding of what is happening is quite unimportant to the job. If you are of an inquiring turn of mind, you can inquire afterwards. But while you are at the job, *know* what you're doing, and don't bother about understanding. Know by immediate sensual contact. Know by the tension and reaction of the muscles, know, know profoundly but for ever untellably, at the spontaneous primary centres. Give yourself in an intense, mindless attention, almost as deep as sleep, but not charged with random dreams, charged with potent effectiveness. Busy, intent, absorbed work, forgetfulness, this is one of the joys of life. Thoughts may be straying through the mind all the time. But there is no attention to them. They stream on like dreams, irrelevant. The soul is attending with joy and active purpose to the kettle and the soldering-iron; the mindless psyche concentrates intent on the unwilling little rivulet of solder which runs grudgingly under the nose of the hot tool. To be or not to be. Being isn't a conscious effort, anyhow.

So we realize that there must be a deep gulf, an oblivion, between pedagogy and handwork. Don't let a pedagogue come fussing about in a workshop. He will only muddle up the instincts.

Not that a schoolmaster is necessarily a pedagogue. Poor devil, he starts by being a man, and it isn't always easy to turn a man into that thing. And therefore many a schoolmaster is a thousand times happier turning a lathe or soldering a kettle than expounding long division. But the two activities are incompatible. Not incompatible in the same individual, but incompatible with each other. So, separate the two activities. Let the pedagogue of the morning disappear in the afternoon. If he appears in a workshop, let it be before children who have not known him as a school-teacher.

And in the workshop, let real jobs be done. Workshops may be mere tin sheds, or wooden sheds. Let the parents send the household kettles, broken chairs, boots and shoes, simple tailoring and sewing and darning and even cooking, to the workshop. Let the family business of this sort be given to the children, who will set off to the work-shed and get the job done, under supervision, in the hours of occupation. A good deal can be done that way, instead of the silly theoretic fussing making fancy knick-knacks or specimen parts, such as goes on at present.

What we want is for every child to be *handy*: physically adaptable, and handy. If a boy shows any desire to go forward in any craft, he will have his opportunity. He can go on till he becomes an expert. But he must start by being, like Jack at sea, just a handy man. The same with a girl.

Let the handwork be a part of the family and communal life, an extension of family life. Don't muddle it up with the mindwork. Mindwork at its best is theoretic. Our present attempts to make mindwork 'objective' and physical, and to instil theoretic mathematics through carpentry and joinery, is silly. If we are teaching arithmetic, let us teach pure arithmetic, without bothering with piles of sham pennies and shillings and pounds of sham sugar. In actual life, when we do our shopping, every one of our calculations is made quickly in abstraction: a pure mental act, everything abstracted. And let our mental acts be pure mental acts, not adulterated with 'objects'. What ails modern education is that it is trying to cram primal physical experience into mental activity – with the result of mere muddledness. Pure physical experience takes place at the great affective centres, and is *de facto* pre-mental, non-mental. Mental experience on the other hand is pure and different, a process of abstraction, and therefore *de facto* not physical.

If our consciousness is dual, and active in duality; if our human activity is of two incompatible sorts, why try to make a mushy oneness of it? The *rapport* between the mental consciousness and the affective or physical consciousness is always a polarity of contradistinction. The two are never one save in their incomprehensible duality. Leave the two modes of activity separate. What connection is necessary will be effected spontaneously.

11

The essence of most games, let us not forget, lies in the element of *contest*: contest in force, contest in skill, contest in wit. The essence of work, on the other hand, lies in single, absorbed, mindless productivity. Now here again we have done our best to muck up the natural order of things. All along the line we have tried to introduce the mean and impoverishing factor of *emulation* into work-activities, and we have tried to make games as little as possible contests, and as much as possible fanciful self-conscious processes.

Work is an absorbed and absorbing process of productivity. Introduce this mean motive of emulation, and you cause a flaw at once in the absorption. You introduce a worm-like *arrière-pensée*; you corrupt the true state. Pah, it makes us sick to think of the glib spuriousness which is doled out to young school-teachers, purporting to be 'theory of education'. The whole system seems to be a conspiracy to falsify and corrupt human nature, introduce an element of meanness, duplicity and self-consciousness. Emulation is a dirty spirit, introduced into work, a petty, fostered jealousy and affectation. And this is true whether the work be mental or physical.

On the other hand, rivalry is a natural factor in all sport and in practically all games, simple, natural rivalry, the spirit of contest.

Again let us draw attention to a duality in the human psychic activity. There is the original duality between the physical and the mental psyche. And now there is another duality, a duality of mode and direction chiefly: the natural distinction between productive and contestive activities. The state of soul of a man engaged in productive activity is, when pure, quite distinct from that of the same man engaged in some competitive activity.

Let us note here another fatal defect in our modern system. Having attempted, according to ideals, to convert all life and all living into one mode only, the productive mode, we have been forced to introduce into our productive activities the spirit of contest which is original and in-eradicable in us. This spirit of contest takes the form of competition: commercial, industrial, spiritual, educational, and even religious competition.

Was ever anything more humiliating than this spectacle of a mankind active in nothing but productive competition, all idea of pure, single-hearted production lost entirely, and all honest fiery contest condemned and tabooed? Here is the clue to the bourgeois. He will have no honest fiery contest. He will have only the mean, Jewish competition in productivity, in money-making. He won't have any single, absorbed production. All work must be a scramble of contest against some other worker.

Is anything more despicable to be conceived? How make an end of it? By separating the two modes. By realizing that man is in at least one-half of his nature a pure fighter – not a competitor competing for some hideous silver mug, or some pot of money – but a fighter, a contester, a warrior.

We must wake again the flashing centres of volition in the fierce, proud backbone, there where we should be superb and indomitable, where we are actually so soft. We can move in herds of self-sacrificing heroism. But laughing defiance has gone out of our shop-keeping world.

And so for the third part of education, games and physical instruction and drill. We are all on the wrong tack again. In the elementary schools physical instruction is a pitiful business, this Swedish drill business. It is a mere pettifogging attempt to turn the body into a mental instrument, and seems warranted to produce nothing but a certain sulky hatred of physical command, and a certain amount of physical self-consciousness.

Physical training and Sandowism altogether is a ridiculous and puerile business. A man sweating and grunting to get his muscles up is one of the maddest and most comical sights. And the modern athlete parading the self-conscious mechanism of his body, reeking with a degraded physical, muscular self-consciousness and nothing but self-consciousness, is one of the most stupid phenomena mankind has ever witnessed. The physique is all right in itself. But to have your physique in your head, like having sex in the head, is unspeakably repulsive. To have your own physique on your mind all the time: why, it is a semi-pathological state, the exact counterpoise to the querulous, peevish invalid.

To have one's mind full of one's own physical self, and to have one's own physical self pranking and bulging under one's own mental direction, is a good old perversion. The athlete is perhaps, of all the self-conscious objects of our day, the most self-consciously objectionable.

It is all wrong to mix up the two modes of consciousness. To the physique belongs the mindless, spontaneous consciousness of the great plexuses and ganglia. To the mind belongs pure abstraction, the *idea*. To drag down the idea into the bulging athletic physique; and to drag the body up into the head, till it becomes an obsession: horror.

Let the two modes of consciousness act in their duality, reciprocal, but polarized in difference, not to be muddled and transfused. If you are going to be physically active, physically strenuous and conscious, then *put off your mental attention*, put off all idea, and become a mindless physical spontaneous Consciousness.

Away with all physical culture. Banish it to the limbo of human prostitutions: self-prostitution as it is: the prostitution of the primary self to the secondary idea.

If you will have the gymnasium; and certainly let us have the gymnasium: let it be to get us ready for the great *contests* and games of skill. Never, never let the motive be self-produced, the act self-induced. It is as bad as masturbation. Let there be the profound motive of *battle*. Battle, battle; let that be the word that rouses us to pure physical efforts.

Not Mons or Ypres, of course. Ah, the horror of machine explosions! But living, naked battle, flesh-to-flesh contest. Fierce, tense struggle of man with man, struggle to the death. That is the spirit of the gymnasium. Fierce, unrelenting, honourable contest.

Let all physical culture be pure *training*: training for the contest, and training for the expressive dance. Let us have a gymnasium as the Greeks had it, and for the same purpose: the purpose of pure, perilous delight in contest, and profound, mystic delight in unified motion. Drop morality. But don't drop morality until you've dropped the ideal self-consciousness.

Set the boys one against the other like young bantam cocks. Let them fight. Let them hurt one another. Teach them again to fight with gloves and fists, egg them on, spur them on. Let it be fine balanced contest in skill and fierce pride. Egg them on, and look on the black eye and the bloody nose as insignia of honour, like the Germans of old.

Bring out the foils and teach fencing. Teach fencing, teach wrestling, teach ju-jutsu, every form of fierce hand-to-hand contest. And praise the wounds. And praise the valour that will be killed rather than yield. Better fierce and unyielding death than our degraded creeping life.

We are all fighters. Let us fight. Has it come down to chasing a poor fox and kicking a leather ball? Heaven, what a spectacle we should be to the Lacedaemonian. Rouse the old male spirit again. The male is always a fighter. The human male is a superb and god-like fighter, unless he is contravened in his own nature. In fighting to the death he has one great crisis of his being.

What, are we going to revoke our own being? Are we going to soften and soften in self-sacrificial ardour till we are white worms? Are we going to get our battle out of some wretched competition in trade or profession?

We will have a new education, where a black eye is a sign of honour, and where men strip stark for the fierce business of the fight.

What is the fight? It is a primary physical thing. It is not a horrible obscene ideal process, like our last war. It is not a ghastly and blasphemous translation of ideas into engines, and men into cannon-fodder. Away with such war. A million times away with such obscenity. Let the desire of it die out of mankind.

But let us keep the real war, the real fight. And what is the fight? It is a sheer immediate conflict of physical men: that, and that best of all. What does death matter, if a man die in a flame of passionate conflict? He goes to heaven, as the ancients said: somehow, somewhere his soul is at rest, for death is to him a passional consummation.

But to be blown to smithereens while you are eating a sardine: horrible and monstrous abnormality. The soul should leap fiery into death, a consummation. Then nothing is lost. But our horrible cannon-fodder! – let us go the right way about making an end of it.

And the right way, and the only way, is to rouse new, living, passionate desires and activities in the soul of man. Your universal brotherhood, league-of-nations smoshiness and pappiness is no good. It will end in foul hypocrisy, and nothing can ever prevent its so ending.

It is a sort of idiocy to talk about putting an end to all fighting, and turning all energy into some commercial or trades-union competition. What is a fight? It's not an ideal business. It is a physical business. Perhaps up to now, in our ideal world, war was necessarily a terrific conflict of ideas, engines and explosives derived out of man's cunning ideas. But now we know we are not ideal beings only: now we know that it is hopeless and wretched to confuse the ideal conscious activity with the primal physical conscious activity: and now we know that true contest belongs to the primal physical self, that ideas, *per se*, are static; why, perhaps we shall have sense enough to fight once more hand-to-hand as fierce, naked men. Perhaps we shall be able to abstain from the unthinkable baseness of pitting one ideal engine against another ideal engine, and supplying human life as the fodder for these ideal machines.

Death is glorious. But to be blown to bits by a machine is mere horror. Death, if it be violent death, should come as a grand passional climax and consummation, and then all is well with the soul of the dead.

The human soul is really capable of honour, once it has a true choice. But when it has a choice only of war with explosive engines and poison-gases, and a universal peace which consists in the most sordid commercial and industrial competition, why, believe me, the human soul will choose war, in the long run, inevitably it will; if only with a remote hope of at last destroying utterly this stinking industrial-competitive humanity.

Man *must* have the choice of war. But, raving, insane idealist as he is, he must no longer have the choice of bombs and poison-gases and Big Berthas. That must not be. Let us beat our soldering-irons into swords, if we will. But let us blow all guns and explosives and poison-gases sky-high. Let us shoot every man who makes one more grain of gunpowder, with his own powder.

After all, we are masters of our own inventions. Are we really so feeble and inane that we cannot get rid of the monsters we have brought forth? Why not? Because we are afraid of somebody else's preserving them? Believe me, there's nothing which every man – except insane criminals, and these we ought to hang right off – there's nothing which every man would be so glad to think had vanished out of the world as guns, explosives and poison-gases. I don't care when my share in them goes sky-high. I'll take every risk of the Japanese or the Germans having a secret store.

Pah, men are all human, till you drive them mad. And for centuries we have been driving each other mad with our idealism and universal love. Pretty weapons they have spawned, pretty fruits of our madness. But the British people tomorrow could destroy all guns, all explosives, all poison-gases and all apparatus for the making of these things. Perhaps you might leave one-barrelled pistols: but not another thing. And the world would get on its sane legs the very next day. And we should run no danger at all: danger, perhaps, of the loss of some small property. But nothing at all compared with the great sigh of relief.

It's the only way to do it. Melt down *all* your guns of all sorts. Destroy all your explosives, save what bit you want for quarries and mines. Keep no explosive weapon in England bigger than a one-barrelled pistol, which may live for one year longer. At the end of one year no explosive weapon shall exist.

The world at once starts afresh. – Well, do it. Your confabs and your meetings, your discussions and your international agreements will serve you nothing. League of Nations is all bilberry jam: bilge: and you know it. Put your guns in the fire and drown your explosives, and you've done your share of the League of Nations.

But don't pretend you've abolished war. Send your soldiers to Ireland, if you must send them, armed with swords and shields, but with no *engines* of war. Trust the Irish to come out with swords and shields as well: they'll do it. And then have a rare old lively scrap, such as the heart can rejoice in. But in the name of human sanity, never point another cannon: never. And it lies with Britain to take the lead. Nobody else will.

Then, when all your explosive weapons are destroyed – which may be before Christmas – then introduce a proper system of martial training in the schools. Let every boy and every citizen be a soldier, a fighter. Let him have sword and spear and shield, and know how to use them. Let him be determined to use them, too.

For, what does life consist in? Not in being some ideal little monster, a superman. It consists in remaining inside your own skin, and living inside your own skin, and not pretending you're any bigger than you are. And so, if you've got to go in for a scrap, go in your own skin. Don't turn into some ideal-obscene monster, and invent explosive engines which will blow up an ideal enemy whom you've never set eyes on and probably never will set eyes on. Loathsome and hateful insanity that.

If you have an enemy, even a national enemy, go for him in your own skin. Meet him, see him, come into contact and fierce struggle with him. What good is an enemy if he's only abstract and invisible? That's merely ideal. If he is an enemy he is a flesh-and-blood fellow whom I meet and fight with, to the death. I don't blow bombs into the vast air, hoping to scatter a million bits of indiscriminate flesh. God save us, no more of that.

Let us get back inside our own skins, sensibly and sanely. Let us fight when our dander is up: but hand-to-hand, hand-to-hand, always hand-to-hand. Let us meet a man like a man, not like some horrific idea-born machine.

Let us melt our guns. Let us just simply do it as an act of reckless, defiant sanity. Why be afraid? It is such fear that has caused all the bother. Spit on such fear. After all, it can't do anything so vile as it has done already. Let us have a national holiday, melting the guns and drowning the powder. Let us make a spree of it. Let's have it on the Fifth of November: bushels of squibs and rockets. If we're quick we can have them ready. And as a squib fizzes away, we say, 'There goes the guts out of a half-ton bomb.'

And then let us be soldiers, hand-to-hand soldiers. Lord, but it is a bitter thing to be born at the end of a rotten, idealistic machine-civilization. Think what we've missed: the glorious bright passion of anger and pride, recklessness and dauntless cock-a-lory.

12

Our life today is a sort of sliding-scale of shifted responsibility. The man, who is supposed to be the responsible party, as a matter of fact flings himself either at the feet of a woman, and makes her his conscience-keeper; or at the feet of the public. The woman, burdened with the lofty importance of a man's conscience and decision, turns to her infant and says: 'It is all for you, my sacred child. For *you* are the future!' And the precious baby, saddled with the immediate responsibility of all the years, puckers his poor face and howls: as well he may.

Or the public, meaning the ordinary working man, being told for the fifty-millionth time that everything is for him, every effort and every move is made for his sake, naturally inquires at length: 'Then why doesn't everything come my way?' To which, under the circumstances, there is no satisfactory answer.

So here we are, grovelling before two gods, the baby-in-arms and the people. In the sliding-scale of shirked responsibility, man puts the golden crown of present importance on the head of the woman, and the nimbus of sanctity round the head of the infant, and then grovels in an ecstasy of worship and self-exoneration before the double idol. A disgusting and shameful sight. After which he gets up and slinks off to his money-making and his commercial competition, and feels holy-holy-holy about it. 'It is all for sacred woman and her divine child.' The most disillusioning part about woman is that she sits on the Brummagem throne and laps up this worship. The baby, poor wretch, gets a stomachache. The other god, poor Demogorgon, the gorgon of the People, is even in a worse state. He sees the idealist kneeling before him, crying: 'You are Demos, you are the People, you are the All in All. You have ten million heads and ten million voices and twenty million hands. Ah, how wonderful you are! Hail to you! Hail to you! Hail to you!'

Poor Demogorgon Briareus scratches his ten million heads with ten million of his hands, and feels a bit bothered-like. Because every one of the ten million heads is slow and flustered.

'Do you mean it, though?' he says.

'Ah!' shrieks the idealist. 'Listen to the divine voice. Ten million throats, and one message! Divine, divine!'

Unfortunately, each of the ten million throats is a little hoarse, each voice a little clumsy and mistrustful.

'All right, then,' mumbles Demogorgon Briareus; 'fob out, then.'

'Certainly! Certainly! Ah, the bliss with which we sacrifice our all to thee!' And he flings a million farthings at the feet of the many-headed.

Briareus picks up a farthing with one million out of his twenty million hands, turns over the coin, spits on it for luck, and puts it in his pocket. Feels, however, that this isn't everything.

'Now work a little harder for us, Great One, Supreme One,' cajoles the idealist.

And Demogorgon, not knowing any better, but with some misgiving rumbling inside him, sets to for a short spell, whilst the idealist shrills out:

'Behold him, the worker, the producer, the provider! Our Providence, our Great One, our God of gods. Demos! Demogorgon!'

All of which flatters Briareus for a long time, till he realizes once more that if he's as divine as all that he ought to see a few more bradburys fluttering his way. So he strikes, and says: 'Look here, what do you mean by it?'

'You're quite right, O Great One,' replies the idealist. 'You are *always* right, Almighty Demos. Only don't stop working, otherwise the whole universe, which is *yours*, mind you, will stop working too. And *then* where will you be?'

Demos thinks there's something in it, so he slogs at it again. But always with a bee buzzing in his bonnet. Which bee stings him from time to time, and then he jumps, and the world jumps with him.

It's time to get the bee out of the bonnet of Briareus, or he'll be jumping right on top of us, he'll become a real Demogorgon.

'Keep still, Demos, my dear. You've got a nasty wasp in your bowler. Keep still; it's dangerous if it stings you. Let me get it out for you.'

And so we begin to remove the lie which the idealist has slipped us.

'You're big, Briareus, my dear fellow. You've got ten million heads. But every one of your ten million heads works rather slowly, and not one of your twenty million eyes sees much further than the end of your nose: which is only about an inch and a half, and not ten-million times an inch and a half. And your great ten-million-times voice, rather rough and indistinct, though of course *very* loud, doesn't really tell me anything, Briareus, Demos, O Democracy. Your wonderful cross which you make with your ten-million hands when you vote, it's a stupid and meaningless little mark. You don't know what you're doing: and anyhow it's only a choice of evils, on whose side you put your little cross. A thing repeated ten million times isn't any more important for the repetition: it's a weary, stupid little thing. Go now; be still, Briareus, and let a better man than yourself think for you, with his one clear head. For you must admit that ten million muddled heads are not better than one muddled head, and have no more right to authority. So just be quiet, Briareus, and listen with your twenty million ears to one clear voice, and one bit of sense, and one word of truth. No, don't ramp and gnash your ten million sets of teeth. You won't come it over us with any of your Demogorgon turns. We shan't turn to stone. We shall think what a fool you are.'

The same with the infant.

'My poor, helpless child, let's get this nimbus off, so that you can sleep in comfort. There now, play with your toes and digest your pap in peace; the future isn't yours for many a day. We'll look after the present. And that's all *you* will be able to do. Take care of the present, and the past and future can take care of themselves.'

After which, to the woman enthroned:

'I'm sorry to trouble you, my dear, but do you mind coming down? We want that throne for a pigeon-place. And do you mind if I put a bottom in your crown? It'll make a good cake-tin. You can bake a nice dethronement-cake in it. You and I, my dear, we've had enough of this worship farce. You're nothing but a woman, a human female creature, and I'm nothing but a man, a human male creature, and there's absolutely no call for worship on either hand. The fact that you're female doesn't mean that I ought to set about worshipping you, and the fact that I'm male doesn't intend to start you worshipping me. It's all bunkum and lies, this worshipping process, anyhow. We're none of us gods: just two-legged human creatures. You're just yourself, and I'm just myself; we're different, and we'll agree to differ. No more of this puffing-up business. It makes us sick.

'You are yourself, a woman, and I'm myself, a man: and that makes a breach between us. So let's leave the breach, and walk across occasionally on some suspension bridge. But you live on one side, and I live on the other. Don't let us interfere with each other's side. We can meet and have a chat and swing our legs mid-stream on the bridge. But you live on that side and I on this. You're not a man and I'm not a woman. Don't let's pretend we are. Let us stick to our own side, and meet like the magic foreigners we are. There's much more fun in it. Don't bully me, and I won't bully you.

'I've got most of the thinking, abstracting business to do, and most of the mechanical business, so let me do it. I hate to see a woman trying to be abstract, and being abstract, just as I hate and loathe to see a woman doing mechanical work. You hate me when I'm feminine. So I'll let you be womanly; you let me be manly. You look after the immediate personal life, and I'll look after the further, abstracted and mechanical life. You remain at the centre, I scout ahead. Let us agree to it, without conceit on either side. We're neither better nor worse than each other; we're an equipoise in difference – but in difference, mind, not in sameness.'

And then, beyond this, let the men scout ahead. Let them go always ahead of their women, in the endless trek across life. Central, with the wagons, travels the woman, with the children and the whole responsibility of immediate, personal living. And on ahead, scouting, fighting, gathering provision, running on the brink of death and at the tip of the life advance, all the time hovering at the tip of life and on the verge of death, the men, the leaders, the outriders.

And between men let there be a new, spontaneous relationship, a new fidelity. Let men realize that their life lies ahead, in the dangerous wilds of advance and increase. Let them realize that they must go beyond their women, projected into a region of greater abstraction, more inhuman activity.

There, in these womanless regions of fight, and pure thought and abstracted instrumentality, let men have a new attitude to one another. Let them have a new reverence for their heroes, a new regard for their comrades: deep, deep as life and death.

Let there be again the old passion of deathless friendship between man and man. Humanity can never advance into the new regions of unexplored futurity otherwise. Men who can only hark back to woman become automatic, static. In the great move ahead, in the wild hope which rides on the brink of death, men go side by side, and faith in each other alone stays them. They go side by side. And the extreme bond of deathless friendship supports them over the edge of the known and into the unknown.

Friendship should be a rare, choice, immortal thing, sacred and inviolable as marriage. Marriage and deathless friendship, both should be inviolable and sacred: two great creative passions, separate, apart, but complementary: the one pivotal, the other adventurous: the one, marriage, the centre of human life; and the other, the leap ahead.

Which is the last word in the education of a people.

Education and Sex in Man, Woman and Child

The one thing we have to avoid, then, even while we carry on our own old process of education, is this development of the powers of so-called self-expression in a child. Let us beware of artificially stimulating his self-consciousness and his so-called imagination. All that we do is to pervert the child into a ghastly state of self-consciousness, making him affectedly try to show off as we wish him to show off. The moment the least little trace of self-consciousness enters into a child, good-bye to everything except falsity.

Much better just pound away at the ABC and simple arithmetic, and so on. The modern methods do make children sharp, give them a sort of slick finesse, but it is the beginning of the mischief. It ends in the great 'unrest' of a nervous, hysterical proletariat. Begin to teach a child of five to 'understand'. To understand the sun and moon and daisy and the secrets of procreation, bless your soul. Understanding all the way. And when the child is twenty he'll have a hysterical understanding of his own invented grievance, and there's an end of him. Understanding is the devil.

A child mustn't understand things. He must have them his own way. His vision isn't ours. When a boy of eight sees a horse, he doesn't see the correct biological object we intend him to see. He sees a big living presence of no particular shape with hair dangling from its neck and four legs. If he puts two eyes in the profile, he is quite right. Because he does *not* see with optical, photographic vision. The image on his retina is *not* the image of his consciousness. The image on his retina just does not go into him. His unconsciousness is filled with a strong, dark, vague prescience of a powerful presence, a two-eyed, four-legged, long-maned presence looming imminent.

And to *force* the boy to see a correct one-eyed horse-profile is just like pasting a placard in front of his vision. It simply kills his inward seeing. We don't *want* him to see a proper horse. The child is *not* a little camera. He is a small vital organism which has direct dynamic *rapport* with the objects of the outer universe. He perceives from his breast and his abdomen, with deep-sunken realism, the elemental nature of the creature. So that to this day a Noah's Ark tree is more real than a Corot tree or a Constable tree: and a flat Noah's Ark cow has a deeper vital reality than even a Cuyp cow.

The mode of vision is not one and final. The mode of vision is manifold. And the optical image is a mere vibrating blur to a child – and, indeed, to a passionate adult. In this vibrating blur the soul sees its own true correspondent. It sees, in a cow, horns and squareness, and a long tail. It sees, for a horse, a mane, and a long face, round nose and four legs. And in each case a darkly vital presence. Now horns and squareness and a long thin ox-tail, these are the fearful and wonderful elements of the cow-form, which the dynamic soul perfectly perceives. The ideal-image is just outside nature, for a child – something false. In a picture, a child wants elemental recognition, and not correctness or expression, or least of all, what we call understanding. The child distorts inevitably and dynamically. But the dynamic abstraction is more than mental. If a huge eye sits in the middle of the cheek, in a child's drawing, this shows that the deep dynamic consciousness of the eye, its relative exaggeration, is the life-truth, even if it is a scientific falsehood.

On the other hand, what on earth is the good of saying to a child, 'The word is a flattened sphere, like an orange.' It is simply pernicious. You had much better say the world is a poached egg in a frying-pan. *That* might have some dynamic meaning. The only thing about the flattened orange is that the child just sees this orange disporting itself in blue air, and never bothers to associate it with the earth he treads on. And yet it would be so much better for the mass of mankind if they never heard of the flattened sphere. They should never be told that the earth is round. It only makes everything unreal to them. They are baulked in their impression of the flat good earth, they can't get over this sphere business, they live in a fog of abstraction, and nothing is anything. Save for purposes of abstraction, the earth is a great plain, with hills and valleys. Why force abstractions and kill the reality, when there's no need?

As for children, will we never realize that their abstractions are never based on observations, but on subjective exaggerations? If there is an eye in the face, the face is all eye. It is the child-soul which cannot get over the mystery of the eye. If there is a tree in a landscape, the landscape is all tree. Always this partial focus. The attempt to make a child focus for a whole view – which is really a generalization and an adult abstraction – is simply wicked. Yet the first thing we do is to set a child making relief maps in clay, for example, of his own district. Imbecility! He has not even the faintest impression of the total hill on which his home stands. A steepness going up to a door – and front garden railings – and perhaps windows. That's the lot.

The top and bottom of it is, that it is a crime to teach a child anything at all, school-wise. It is just evil to collect children together and teach them through the head. It causes absolute starvation in the dynamic centres, and sterile substitute of brain knowledge is all the gain. The children of the middle classes are so vitally impoverished, that the miracle is they continue to exist at all. The children of the lower classes do better, because they escape into the streets. But even the children of the proletariat are now infected.

And, of course, as my critics point out, under all the school-smarm and newspaper-cant, man is today as savage as a cannibal, and more dangerous. The living dynamic self is denaturalized instead of being educated.

We talk about education – leading forth the natural intelligence of a child. But ours is just the opposite of leading forth. It is a ramming in of brain facts through the head, and a consequent distortion, suffocation and starvation of the primary centres of consciousness. A nice day of reckoning we've got in front of us.

Let us lead forth, by all means. But let us not have mental knowledge before us as the goal of the leading. Much less let us make of it a vicious circle in which we lead the unhappy child-mind, like a cow in a ring at a fair. We don't want to educate children so that they may understand. Understanding is a fallacy and a vice in most people. I don't even want my child to know, much less to understand. *I* don't want my child to know that five fives are twenty-five, any more than I want my child to wear my hat or my boots. I *don't* want my child to *know*. If he wants five fives let him count them on his fingers. As for his little mind, give it a rest, and let his dynamic self be alert. He will ask 'why' often enough. But he more often asks why the sun shines, or why men have moustaches, or why grass is green, than anything sensible. Most of a child's questions are, and should be, unanswerable. They are not questions at all. They are exclamations of wonder, they are *remarks* half-sceptically addressed. When a child says, 'Why is grass green?' he half implies, 'Is it really green, or is it just taking me in?' And we solemnly begin to prate about chlorophyll. Oh, imbeciles, idiots, inexcusable owls!

The whole of a child's development goes on from the great dynamic centres, and is basically non-mental. To introduce mental activity is to arrest the dynamic activity and stultify true dynamic development. By the age of twenty-one our young people are helpless, hopeless, selfless, floundering mental entities, with nothing in front of them, because they have been starved from the roots, systematically, for twenty-one years, and fed through the head. They have had all their mental excitements, sex and everything, all through the head, and when it comes to the actual thing, why, there's nothing in it. *Blasé*. The affective centres have been exhausted from the head.

Before the age of fourteen children should be taught only to move, to act, to *do*. And they should be taught as little as possible even of this. Adults simply cannot and do not know any more what the mode of childish intelligence is. Adults *always* interfere. They *always* force the adult mental mode. Therefore children must be preserved from adult instructions.

Make a child work – yes. Make it do little jobs. Keep a fine and delicate and fierce discipline, so that the little jobs are performed as perfectly as is consistent with the child's nature. Make the child alert, proud and becoming in its movements. Make it know very definitely that it shall not and must not trespass on other people's privacy or patience. Teach it songs, tell it tales. But *never* instruct it school-wise. And mostly, leave it alone, send it away to be with other children and to get in and out of mischief, and in and out of danger. Forget your child altogether as much as possible.

All this is the active and strenuous business of parents, and must not be shelved off on to strangers. It is the business of parents *mentally* to forget but dynamically never to forsake their children.

It is no use expecting parents to know *why* schools are closed, and *why* they, the parents, must be quite responsible for their own children during the first ten years. If it is quite useless to expect parents to understand a theory of relativity, much less will they understand the development of the dynamic consciousness. But why should they understand?

It is the business of very few to understand, and for the mass, it is their business to believe and not to bother, but to be honourable and humanly to fulfil their human responsibilities. To give active obedience to their leaders, and to possess their own souls in natural pride.

Some must understand why a child is not to be mentally educated. Some must have a faint inkling of the processes of consciousness during the first fourteen years. Some must know what a child beholds, when it looks at a horse, and what it means when it says, 'Why is grass green?' The answer to this question, by the way, is 'Because it is.'

The interplay of the four dynamic centres follows no one conceivable law. Mental activity continues according to a law of correlation. But there is no logical or rational correlation in the dynamic consciousness. It pulses on inconsequential, and it would be impossible to determine any sequence. Out of the very lack of sequence in dynamic consciousness does the individual himself develop. The dynamic abstraction of a child's precepts follows no mental law, and even no law which can ever be mentally propounded. And this is why it is utterly pernicious to set a child making a clay relief-map of its own district, or to ask a child to draw conclusions from given observations. Dynamically, a child draws no conclusions. All things still remain dynamically possible. A conclusion drawn is a nail in the coffin of a child's developing being. Let a child make a clay landscape if it likes. But entirely according to its own fancy, and without conclusions drawn. Only, let the landscape be vividly made – always the discipline of the soul's full attention. 'Oh, but where are the factory chimneys?' – or else – 'Why have you left out the gas-works?' or 'Do you call that sloppy thing a church?' The particular focus should be vivid and the record in some way true. The soul must give earnest attention, that is all.

And so actively disciplined, the child develops for the first ten years. We need not be afraid of letting children see the passions and reactions of adult life. Only we must not strain the *sympathies* of a child, in *any* direction, particularly the direction of love and pity. Nor must we introduce the fallacy of right and wrong. Spontaneous distaste should take the place of right and wrong. And least of all must there be a cry: 'You see, dear, you don't understand. When you are older –' A child's sagacity is better than an adult understanding anyhow.

Of course it is ten times criminal to tell young children facts about sex or to implicate them in adult relationships. A child has a strong evanescent sex consciousness. It instinctively writes impossible words on back walls. But this is not a fully conscious mental act. It is a kind of dream act – quite natural. The child's curious, shadowy, indecent sex-

knowledge is quite in the course of nature, and does nobody any harm
at all. Adults had far better not notice it. But if a child sees a cockerel
tread a hen, or two dogs coupling, well and good. It *should* see these
things. Only, without comment. Let nothing be exaggeratedly hidden. By
instinct, let us preserve the decent privacies. But if a child occasionally
sees its parent nude, taking a bath, all the better. Exaggerated secrecy is
bad. But indecent exposure is also very bad. But worst of all is dragging
in the *mental* consciousness of these shadowy dynamic realities.

In the same way, to talk to a child about an adult is vile. Let adults
keep their adult feelings and communications for people of their own
age. But if a child sees its parents violently quarrel, all the better. There
must be storms. And a child's dynamic understanding is far deeper and
more penetrating than our sophisticated interpretation. But *never* make
a child a party to adult affairs. Never drag the child in. Refuse its sympathy on such occasions. Always treat it as if it had *no* business to hear,
even if it is present and *must* hear. Truly, it has no business mentally to
hear. And the dynamic soul will always weigh things up and dispose of
them properly, if there be no interference of adult comment or adult
desire for sympathy. It is despicable for any one parent to accept a
child's sympathy against the other parent. And the one who *received*
the sympathy is always more contemptible than the one who is hated.

Of course so many children are born today unnaturally mentally
awake and alive to adult affairs, that there is nothing left but to tell them
everything, crudely; or else, much better, to say: 'Ah, get out, you know
too much, you make me sick.'

To return to the question of sex. A child is born sexed. A child is either
male or female; in the whole of its psyche and physique is either male
or female. Every single living cell is either male or female, and will
remain either male or female as long as life lasts. And every single cell
in every male child is male, and every cell in every female child is
female. The talk about a third sex, or about the indeterminate sex, is
just to pervert the issue.

Biologically, it is true, the rudimentary formation of both sexes is
found in every individual. That doesn't mean that every individual is a
bit of both, or either, *ad lib.* After a sufficient period of idealism, men
become hopelessly self-conscious. That is, the great affective centres no
longer act spontaneously, but always wait for control from the head.
This always breeds a great fluster in the psyche, and the poor self-
conscious individual cannot help posing and posturing. Our ideal has
taught us to be gentle and wistful: rather girlish and yielding, and *very*
yielding in our sympathies. In fact, many young men feel so very like

what they imagine a girl must feel, that hence they draw the conclusion that they must have a large share of female sex inside them. False conclusion.

These girlish men have often, today, the finest maleness, once it is put to the test. How is it then that they feel, and look, so girlish? It is largely a question of the direction of the polarized flow. Our ideal has taught us to be *so* loving and *so* submissive and *so* yielding in our sympathy, that the mode has become automatic in many men. Now in what we will call the 'natural' mode, man has his positivity in the volitional centres, and women in the sympathetic. In fulfilling the Christian love ideal, however, men have reversed this. Man has assumed the gentle, all-sympathetic role, and woman has become the energetic party, with the authority in her hands. The male is the sensitive, sympathetic nature, the woman the active, effective, authoritative. So that the male acts as the passive, or recipient pole of attraction, the female as the active, positive, exertive pole, in human relations. Which is a reversal of the old flow. The woman is now the initiator, man the responder. They seem to play each other's parts. But man is purely male, playing woman's part, and woman is purely female, however manly. The gulf between Heliogabalus, or the most womanly man on earth, and the most manly woman, is just the same as ever; just the same old gulf between the sexes. The man is male, the woman is female. Only they are playing one another's parts, as they must at certain periods. The dynamic polarity has swung around.

If we look a little closer, we can define this positive and negative business better. As a matter of fact, positive and negative, passive and active cuts both ways. If the man, as thinker and doer, is active, or positive, and the woman negative, then, on the other hand, as the initiator of emotion, of feeling and of sympathetic understanding the woman is positive, the man negative. The man may be the initiator in action, but the woman is initiator in emotion. The man has the initiative as far as voluntary activity goes and the woman the initiative as far as sympathetic activity goes. In love, it is the woman naturally who loves, the man who is loved. In love, woman is the positive, man the negative. It is woman who asks, in love, and man who answers. In life, the reverse is the case. In knowing and in doing, man is positive and woman negative: man initiates, and woman lives up to it.

Naturally this nicely arranged order of things may be reversed. Action and utterance, which are male, are polarized against feeling, emotion, which are female. And which is positive, which negative? Was man, the eternal protagonist, born of woman, from her womb of fathomless emotion? Or was woman, with her deep womb of emotion, born from the rib of active man, the first created? Man, the doer, the knower, the original *being*, is he lord of life? Or is woman, the great Mother, who bore us from the womb of love, is she the supreme Goddess?

This is the question of all time. And as long as man and woman endure, so will the answer be given, first one way, then the other. Man, as the utterer, usually claims that Eve was created out of his spare rib: from the field of the creative, upper dynamic consciousness, that is. But woman, as soon as she gets a word in, points to the fact that man inevitably, poor darling, is the issue of his mother's womb. So the battle rages.

But some men always agree with the woman. Some men always yield to woman the creative positivity. And in certain periods, such as the present, the majority of men concur in regarding woman as the source of life, the first term in creation: woman, the mother, the prime being.

And then, the whole polarity shifts over. Man still remains the doer and thinker. But he is so only in the service of emotional and procreative woman. His highest moment is now the emotional moment when he gives himself up to the woman, when he forms the perfect answer for her great emotional and procreative asking. All his thinking, all his activity in the world only contributes to this great moment, when he is fulfilled in the emotional passion of the woman, the birth of rebirth, as Whitman calls it. In his consummation in the emotional passion of a woman, man is reborn, which is quite true.

And there is the point at which we all now stick. Life, thought and activity, all are devoted truly to the great end of Woman, wife and mother.

Man has now entered on to his negative mode. Now, his consummation is in feeling, not in action. Now, his activity is all of the domestic order, and all his thought goes to proving that nothing matters except that birth shall continue and woman shall rock in the nest of this globe like a bird who covers her eggs in some tall tree. Man is the fetcher, the carrier, the sacrifice, the crucified, and the reborn of woman.

This being so, the whole tendency of his nature changes. Instead of being assertive and rather insentient, he becomes wavering and sensitive. He begins to have as many feelings – nay, more than a woman. His heroism is all in altruistic endurance. He worships pity and tenderness and weakness, even in himself. In short, he takes on very largely the original role of woman. Woman meanwhile becomes the fearless, inwardly relentless, determined positive party. She grips the responsibility. The hand that rocks the cradle rules the world. Nay, she makes man discover that cradles should not be rocked, in order that her hands may be left free. She is now a queen of the earth, and inwardly a fearsome tyrant. She keeps pity and tenderness emblazoned on her banners. But God help the man whom she pities. Ultimately she tears him to bits.

Therefore we see the reversal of the old poles. Man becomes the emotional party, woman the positive and active. Man begins to show strong signs of the peculiarly strong passive sex desire, the desire to be taken, which is considered characteristic of woman. Man begins to have all the feelings of woman – or all the feelings which he attributed to woman. He becomes more feminine than woman ever was, and worships his own femininity, calling it the highest. In short, he begins to exhibit all signs of sexual complexity. He begins to imagine he really is half female. And certainly woman seems very male. So the hermaphrodite fallacy revives again.

But it is all a fallacy. Man, in the midst of all his effeminacy, is still male and nothing but male. And woman, though she harangue in Parliament or patrol the streets with a helmet on her head, is still completely female. They are only playing each other's roles, because the poles have swung into reversion. The compass is reversed. But that doesn't mean that the north pole has become the south pole, or that each is a bit of both.

Of course a woman should stick to her own natural emotional positivity. But then man must stick to his own positivity of *being*, of action, *disinterested*, *non-domestic*, *male* action, which is not devoted to the increase of the female. Once man vacates his camp of sincere, passionate positivity in disinterested being, his supreme responsibility to fulfil his own profoundest impulses, with reference to none but God or his own soul, not taking woman into count at all, in this primary responsibility to his own deepest soul; once man vacates this strong citadel of his own genuine, not spurious, divinity, then in comes woman, picks up the sceptre and begins to conduct a rag-time band.

Man remains man, however he may put on wistfulness and tenderness like petticoats, and sensibilities like pearl ornaments. Your sensitive little big-eyed boy, so much more gentle and loving than his harder sister, is male for all that, believe me. Perhaps evilly male, so mothers may learn to their cost: and wives still more.

Of course there should be a great balance between the sexes. Man, in the daytime, must follow his own soul's greatest impulse, and give himself to life-work and risk himself to death. It is not woman who claims the highest in man. It is a man's own religious soul that drives him on beyond woman, to his supreme activity. For his highest, man is responsible to God alone. He may not pause to remember that he has a life to lose, or a wife and children to leave. He must carry forward the banner of life, though seven worlds perish, with all the wives and mothers and children in them. Hence Jesus, 'Woman, what have I to do with thee?' Every man that lives has to say it again to his wife or mother, once he has any work or mission in hand, that comes from his soul.

But again, no man is a blooming marvel for twenty-four hours a day. Jesus or Napoleon or any other of them ought to have been man enough to be able to come home at tea-time and put his slippers on and sit under the spell of his wife. For there you are, the woman has her world, her positivity: the world of love, of emotion, of sympathy. And it behoves every man in his hour to take off his shoes and relax and give himself up to his woman and her world. Not to give up his purpose. But to give up himself for a time to her who is his mate. And so it is one detests the clockwork Kant, and the petit-bourgeois Napoleon divorcing his Josephine for a Hapsburg – or even Jesus, with his 'Woman, what have I to do with thee?' He might have added 'just now'. They were all failures.

Letter to Lady Cynthia Asquith

My dear Lady Cynthia: I am not in a mood to write you about John, because I feel churlish. When we talked in Brighton, lying on the cliff, I did not take much notice of what I said, because my subconsciousness was occupied with the idea of how pleasant it would be to walk over the edge of the cliff. There seemed another, brighter sort of world away below, and this world on top is all torture and a flounder of stupidity.

I don't know much about John, and probably anything I say is pure bosh, a tangle of theory of my own. And you will be treating me as a sort of professional, directly, a mixture between a professor of psychology and a clairvoyant, a charlatan expert in psychiatry. You won't be able to prevent yourself. I rather resent this demand for a letter. Why can't you leave our relationship commonly human, and not set me writing out prescriptions. You should listen to what I say, which comes spontaneously, and not set me deliberately dictating. I must tell you I resent it. Why do you want a letter, in what spirit do you ask?

But I will write to you because I feel a sort of love for your hard, stoical spirit – not for anything else.

I don't think John is very extraordinary, I think, if we could consider it intrinsically, he has a sensitive, happy soul. But every soul is born into an existing world. The world is not made fresh for every new soul, as the shell for every egg. And long before John was ever born or conceived, your soul knew that, within the hard form of existing conditions, of the existing 'world', it was like a thing born to remain forever in prison. Your own soul knew, before ever John was possible, that it was itself bound in like a tree that grows under a low roof and can never break through, and which must be deformed, unfulfilled. Herbert Asquith must have known the same thing, in his soul.

Now a soul that knows it is bound in by existing conditions, bound in and formed or deformed by the world wherein it comes to being, this soul is a living-dead soul. Every living soul believes that the conditions will be modified to its own growth or expression. Every living soul believes that all things real are within the scope of a Great Will which is working itself out in all things, but also and most vitally in the soul itself. This I call a belief in God, or belief in Love – what you like. Now if a soul believes that the Great Will is working in all things, even though itself be thwarted and deformed and frustrated, that is what I call a *dead* belief: not a living belief. Because every *living* soul believes that, whatever the conditions, there will be that conjunction between the conditions and the soul itself which shall fulfil the Great Will. The soul which believes that the Great Will, or God, will make all things right and that the agency of the particular soul is insignificant, this soul is an unbeliever affirming belief. Because every living soul says, 'I am of God.' Then, if I am insignificant, God in me is insignificant. Which is unbelief – *much more insidious* than atheism.

Now the soul which was born into John was born in the womb of your unbelief and from the loins of its father's unbelief – the unbelief affirming belief. It is born of unbelief, but into an affirmation of belief. Which is why the soul of John acts from your soul, even from the start: because he knows that you are Unbelief, and he reacts from your affirmation of belief always with hostility.

The nurse, being a smaller soul, has plenty of room to grow within the existing condition, as a fern in a room, where a tree would be worse than dead. So she is a believer – her soul fulfills itself, because it is a good small soul and has room. John knows her, and has some inkling of belief. You are his great doubt. He knows your unbelief. He fights your affirmation of belief, when he throws down the crust.

Don't try to make him love you, or obey you – don't do it. The love that he would have for you would be a much greater love than he would ever have for his nurse, or anybody else, because it would be a love born of trust and confirmation of joy and belief. But you can never fight for this love. That you fight is only a sign that you are wanting in yourself. The child knows that. Your own soul is deficient, so it fights for the love of the child. And the child's soul, born in the womb of your unbelief, laughs at you and defies you, almost jeers at you, almost hates you.

The great thing is, *not* to exert authority unnecessarily over the child – no prerogative, only the prerogative of pure justice. That he is not to throw down crusts is a pure autocratic command. That he is not to throw down crusts because it is a trouble to the nurse to pick them up, is an appeal to a sense of justice and love, which is an appeal to the believing soul of the child.

Put yourself aside with regard to him. You have no right to his love. Care only for his good and well-being: make *no* demands on him.

But for yourself, you must learn to believe in God. Believe me, in the end, we will unite in our knowledge of God. Believe me, this England, we very English people, will at length join together and say, 'We will not do these things, because in our knowledge of God we know them wrong.' We shall put away our greatness and our living for material things only, because we shall agree we don't want these things. We know they are inferior, base, we shall have courage to put them away. We shall unite in our knowledge of God – not perhaps in our expression of God – but in our *knowledge* of God: and we shall agree that we don't want to live only to write and make riches, that England does not care only to have the greatest Empire or the greatest commerce, but that she does care supremely for the pure truth of God, which she will try to fulfil.

This isn't ranting, it is pure reasoning from the knowledge of God and the truth. It is not our wickedness that kills us, but our unbelief. You learn to believe in your very self, that we in England shall unite in our knowledge of God to live according to the best of our knowledge, Prime Ministers and capitalists and artisans all working in pure effort towards God – here, tomorrow, in this England – and you will save your own soul and the soul of your son. *Then* there will be love enough.

You see, this change must come to pass. But nobody will believe it, however obvious it is. So it almost sends me mad, I am almost a lunatic.

Please write to me and ask me anything you like – but please do believe that the thing *shall* be.

[P.S.] Remember, if you are inclined to take this half as a joke, it was an impertinence on your part to ask me for it in any but a non-flippant spirit.

Benjamin Franklin

The Perfectibility of Man! Ah heaven, what a dreary theme! The perfectibility of the Ford car! The perfectibility of which man? I am many men. Which of them are you going to perfect? I am not a mechanical contrivance.

Education! Which of the various me's do you propose to educate, and which do you propose to suppress?

Anyhow, I defy you. I defy you, oh society, to educate me or to suppress me, according to your dummy standards.

The ideal man! And which is he, if you please? Benjamin Franklin or Abraham Lincoln? The ideal man! Roosevelt or Porfirio Diaz?

There are other men in me, besides this patient ass who sits here in a tweed jacket. What am I doing, playing the patient ass in a tweed jacket? Who am I talking to? Who are you, at the other end of this patience?

Who are you? How many selves have you? And which of these selves do you want to be?

Is Yale College going to educate the self that is in the dark of you, or Harvard College?

The ideal self! Oh, but I have a strange and fugitive self shut out and howling like a wolf or a coyote under the ideal windows. See his red eyes in the dark? This is the self who is coming into his own.

The perfectibility of man, dear God! When every man as long as he remains alive is in himself a multitude of conflicting men. Which of these do you choose to perfect, at the expense of every other?

Old Daddy Franklin will tell you. He'll rig him up for you, the pattern American. Oh, Franklin was the first downright American. He knew what he was about, the sharp little man. He set up the first dummy American.

At the beginning of his career this cunning little Benjamin drew up for himself a creed that should 'satisfy the professors of every religion, but shock none'.

Now wasn't that a real American thing to do?

'*That there is One God who made all things.*'

(But Benjamin made Him.)

'*That He governs the world by His Providence.*'

(Benjamin knowing all about Providence.)

'*That He ought to be worshipped with adoration, prayer and thanks-giving.*'

(Which costs nothing.)

'*But –*' But me no buts, Benjamin, saith the Lord.

'*But that the most acceptable service of God is doing good to men.*'

(God having no choice in the matter.)

'*That the soul is immortal.*'

(You'll see why, in the next clause.)

'*And that God will certainly reward virtue and punish vice, either here or hereafter.*'

Now if Mr Andrew Carnegie, or any other millionaire, had wished to invent a God to suit his ends, he could not have done better. Benjamin did it for him in the eighteenth century. God is the supreme servant of men who want to get on, to *produce*. Providence. The provider. The heavenly storekeeper. The everlasting Wanamaker.

And this is all the God the grandsons of the Pilgrim Fathers had left. Aloft on a pillar of dollars.

'*That the soul is immortal.*'

The trite way Benjamin says it!

But man has a soul, though you can't locate it either in his purse or his pocket-book or his heart or his stomach or his head. The *wholeness* of a man is his soul. Not merely that nice little comfortable bit which Benjamin marks out.

It's a queer thing is a man's soul. It is the whole of him. Which means it is the unknown him, as well as the known. It seems to me just funny, professors and Benjamins fixing the functions of the soul. Why, the soul of man is a vast forest, and all Benjamin intended was a neat back garden. And we've all got to fit into his kitchen garden scheme of things. Hail Columbia!

The soul of man is a dark forest. The Hercynian Wood that scared the Romans so, and out of which came the white-skinned hordes of the next civilization.

Who knows what will come out of the soul of man? The soul of man is a dark vast forest, with wild life in it. Think of Benjamin fencing it off!

Oh, but Benjamin fenced a little tract that he called the soul of man, and proceeded to get it into cultivation. Providence forsooth! And they think that bit of barbed wire is going to keep us in pound for ever? More fools they.

This is Benjamin's barbed-wire fence. He made himself a list of virtues, which he trotted inside like a grey nag in a paddock.

1 *Temperance*

Eat not to fullness; drink not to elevation.

2 *Silence*

Speak not but what may benefit others or yourself; avoid trifling conversation.

3 *Order*

Let all your things have their places; let each part of your business have its time.

4 *Resolution*

Resolve to perform what you ought; perform without fail what you resolve.

5 *Frugality*

Make no expense but to do good to others or yourself – i.e., waste nothing.

6 *Industry*

Lose no time, be always employed in something useful; cut off all unnecessary action.

7 *Sincerity*

Use no hurtful deceit; think innocently and justly, and, if you speak, speak accordingly.

8 *Justice*

Wrong none by doing injuries, or omitting the benefits that are your duty.

9 *Moderation*

Avoid extremes, forbear resenting injuries as much as you think they deserve.

10 *Cleanliness*

Tolerate no uncleanliness in body, clothes or habitation.

11 *Tranquillity*

Be not disturbed at trifles, or at accidents common or unavoidable.

12 *Chastity*

Rarely use venery but for health and offspring, never to dullness, weakness, or the injury of your own or another's peace or reputation.

13 *Humility*

Imitate Jesus and Socrates.

A Quaker friend told Franklin that he, Benjamin, was generally considered proud, so Benjamin put in the Humility touch as an afterthought. The amusing part is the sort of humility it displays. 'Imitate Jesus and Socrates', and mind you don't outshine either of these two. One can just imagine Socrates and Alcibiades roaring in their cups over Philadelphian Benjamin, and Jesus looking at him a little puzzled, and murmuring, 'Aren't you wise in your own conceit, Ben?'

'Henceforth be masterless,' retorts Ben. 'Be ye each one his own master unto himself, and don't let even the Lord put His spoke in.' 'Each man his own master' is but a puffing up of masterlessness.

Well, the first of Americans practised this enticing list with assiduity, setting a national example. He had the virtues in columns, and gave himself good and bad marks according as he thought his behaviour deserved. Pity these conduct charts are lost to us. He only remarks that Order was his stumbling block. He could not learn to be neat and tidy.

Isn't it nice to have nothing worse to confess?

He was a little model, was Benjamin. Doctor Franklin. Snuff-coloured little man! Immortal soul and all!

The immortal soul part was a sort of cheap insurance policy.

Benjamin had no concern, really, with the immortal soul. He was too busy with social man.

1 He swept and lighted the streets of young Philadelphia.

2 He invented electrical appliances.

3 He was the centre of a moralizing club in Philadelphia, and he wrote the moral humourisms of Poor Richard.

4 He was a member of all the important councils of Philadelphia, and then of the American colonies.

5 He won the cause of American Independence at the French Court, and was the economic father of the United States.

Now what more can you want of a man? And yet he is *infra dig*, even in Philadelphia.

I admire him. I admire his sturdy courage first of all, then his sagacity, then his glimpsing into the thunders of electricity, then his common-sense humour. All the qualities of a great man, and never more than a great citizen. Middle-sized, sturdy, snuff-coloured Doctor Franklin, one of the soundest citizens that ever trod or 'used venery'.

I do not like him.

And, by the way, I always thought books of Venery were about hunting deer.

There is a certain earnest naïveté about him. Like a child. And like a little old man. He has again become as a little child, always as wise as his grandfather, or wiser.

Perhaps, as I say, the most complete citizen that ever 'used venery'.

Printer, philosopher, scientist, author and patriot, impeccable husband and citizen, why isn't he an archetype?

Pioneers, Oh Pioneers! Benjamin was one of the greatest pioneers of the United States. Yet we just can't do with him.

What's wrong with him then? Or what's wrong with us?

I can remember, when I was a little boy, my father used to buy a scrubby yearly almanac with the sun and moon and stars on the cover. And it used to prophesy bloodshed and famine. But also crammed in corners it had little anecdotes and humorisms, with a moral tag. And I used to have my little priggish laugh at the woman who counted her chickens before they were hatched and so forth, and I was convinced that honesty was the best policy, also a little priggishly. The author of these bits was Poor Richard, and Poor Richard was Benjamin Franklin, writing in Philadelphia well over a hundred years before.

And probably I haven't got over those Poor Richard tags yet. I rankle still with them. They are thorns in young flesh.

Because, although I still believe that honesty is the best policy, I dislike policy altogether; though it is just as well not to count your chickens before they are hatched, it's still more hateful to count them with gloating when they *are* hatched. It has taken me many years and countless smarts to get out of that barbed-wire moral enclosure that Poor Richard rigged up. Here am I now in tatters and scratched to ribbons, sitting in the middle of Benjamin's America looking at the barbed wire, and the fat sheep crawling under the fence to get fat outside, and the watchdogs yelling at the gate lest by chance anyone should get out by the proper exit. Oh America! Oh Benjamin! And I just utter a long loud curse against Benjamin and the American corral.

Moral America! Most moral Benjamin. Sound, satisfied Ben!

He had to go to the frontiers of his State to settle some disturbance among the Indians. On this occasion he writes:

We found that they had made a great bonfire in the middle of the square; they were all drunk, men and women quarrelling and fighting. Their dark-coloured bodies, half-naked, seen only by the gloomy light of the bonfire, running after and beating one another with fire-brands, accompanied by their horrid yellings, formed a scene the most resembling our ideas of hell that could well be imagined. There was no appeasing the tumult, and we retired to our lodging.

At midnight a number of them came thundering at our door, demanding more rum, of which we took no notice.

The next day, sensible they had misbehaved in giving us that disturbance, they sent three of their counsellors to make their apology. The orator acknowledged the fault, but laid it upon the rum, and then endeavoured to excuse the rum by saying: 'The Great Spirit, who made all things, made everything for some use; and whatever he designed anything for, that use it should always be put to. Now, when he had made the rum, he said: "Let this be for the Indians to get drunk with." And it must be so.'

And, indeed, if it be the design of Providence to extirpate these savages in order to make room for the cultivators of the earth, it seems not improbable that rum may be the appointed means. It has already annihilated all the tribes who formerly inhabited all the seacoast. . . .

This, from the good doctor with such suave complacency, is a little disenchanting. Almost too good to be true.

But there you are! The barbed-wire fence. 'Extirpate these savages in order to make room for the cultivators of the earth.' Oh, Benjamin Franklin! He even 'used venery' as a cultivator of seed.

Cultivate the earth, ye gods! The Indians did that, as much as they needed. And they left off there. Who built Chicago? Who cultivated the earth until it spawned Pittsburgh, Pa.?

The moral issue! Just look at it! Cultivation included. If it's a mere choice of Kultur or cultivation, I give it up.

Which brings us right back to our question, what's wrong with Benjamin, that we can't stand him? Or else, what's wrong with us, that we find fault with such a paragon?

Man is a moral animal. All right. I am a moral animal. And I'm going to remain such. I'm not going to be turned into a virtuous little automaton as Benjamin would have me. 'This is good, that is bad. Turn the little handle and let the good tap flow,' said Benjamin, and all America with him. 'But first of all extirpate those savages who are always turning on the bad tap.'

I am a moral animal. But I am not a moral machine. I don't work with a little set of handles or levers. The Temperance-silence-order-resolution-frugality-industry-sincerity-justice-moderation-cleanliness-tranquillity-chastity-humility keyboard is not going to get me going. I'm really not just an automatic piano with a moral Benjamin getting tunes out of me.

Here's my creed, against Benjamin's. This is what I believe:

'*That I am I*.'

'*That my soul is a dark forest*.'

'*That my known self will never be more than a little clearing in the forest.*'

'*That gods, strange gods, come forth from the forest into the clearing of my known self, and then go back.*'

'*That I must have the courage to let them come and go.*'

'*That I will never let mankind put anything over me, but that I will try always to recognize and submit to the gods in me and the gods in other men and women.*'

There is my creed. He who runs may read. He who prefers to crawl, or to go by gasoline, can call it rot.

Then for a 'list'. It is rather fun to play at Benjamin.

1 *Temperance*
Eat and carouse with Bacchus, or munch dry bread with Jesus, but don't sit down without one of the gods.

2 *Silence*
Be still when you have nothing to say; when genuine passion moves you, say what you've got to say, and say it hot.

3 *Order*
Know that you are responsible to the gods inside you and to the men in whom the gods are manifest. Recognize your superiors and your inferiors, according to the gods. This is the root of all order.

4 *Resolution*
Resolve to abide by your own deepest promptings, and to sacrifice the smaller thing to the greater. Kill when you must, and be killed the same: the *must* coming from the gods inside you, or from the men in whom you recognize the Holy Ghost.

5 *Frugality*
Demand nothing; accept what you see fit. Don't waste your pride or squander your emotion.

6 *Industry*
Lose no time with ideals; serve the Holy Ghost; never serve mankind.

7 *Sincerity*
To be sincere is to remember that I am I, and that the other man is not me.

8 *Justice*
The only justice is to follow the sincere intuition of the soul, angry or
gentle. Anger is just, and pity is just, but judgement is never just.

9 *Moderation*
Beware of absolutes. There are many gods.

10 *Cleanliness*
Don't be too clean. It impoverishes the blood.

11 *Tranquillity*
The soul has many motions, many gods come and go. Try and find your
deepest issue, in every confusion, and abide by that. Obey the man in
whom you recognize the Holy Ghost; command when your honour
comes to command.

12 *Chastity*
Never 'use' venery at all. Follow your passional impulse, if it be
answered in the other being; but never have any motive in mind, neither
offspring nor health nor even pleasure, nor even service. Only know that
'venery' is of the great gods, an offering-up of yourself to the very great
gods, the dark ones, and nothing else.

13 *Humility*
See all men and women according to the Holy Ghost that is within
them. Never yield before the barren.

There's my list. I have been trying dimly to realize it for a long time,
and only America and old Benjamin have at last goaded me into trying
to formulate it.

And now I, at least, know why I can't stand Benjamin. He tries to take
away my wholeness and my dark forest, my freedom. For how can any
man be free, without an illimitable background? And Benjamin tries to
shove me into a barbed-wired paddock and make me grow potatoes or
Chicagoes.

And how can I be free, without gods that come and go? But Benjamin
won't let anything exist except my useful fellow-men, and I'm sick of
them; as for his Godhead, his Providence, He is Head of nothing except
a vast heavenly store that keeps every imaginable line of goods, from
victrolas to cat-o'-nine-tails.

And how can any man be free without a soul of his own, that he believes in and won't sell at any price? But Benjamin doesn't let me have a
soul of my own. He says I am nothing but a servant of mankind – galley-

slave I call it – and if I don't get my wages here below – that is, if Mr Pierpont Morgan or Mr Nosey Hebrew or the grand United States Government, the great US, US or SOMEOFUS, manages to scoop in my bit along with their lump – why, never mind, I shall get my wages HEREAFTER.

Oh, Benjamin! Oh Binjum! You do NOT suck me in any longer.

And why, oh why should the snuff-coloured little trap have wanted to take us all in? Why did he do it?

Out of sheer cussedness, in the first place. We do all like to get things inside a barbed-wire corral. Especially our fellow-men. We love to round them up inside the barbed-wire enclosure of FREEDOM, and make 'em work. '*Work, you free jewel, WORK!*' shouts the liberator, cracking his whip. Benjamin, I will not work. I do not choose to be a free democrat. I am absolutely a servant of my own Holy Ghost.

Sheer cussedness! But there was as well the salt of a subtler purpose. Benjamin was just in his eyeholes – to use an English vulgarism, meaning he was just delighted – when he was at Paris judiciously milking money out of the French monarchy for the overthrow of all monarchy. If you want to ride your horse to somewhere you must put a bit in his mouth. And Benjamin wanted to ride his horse so that it would upset the whole apple-cart of the old masters. He wanted the whole European apple-cart upset. So he had to put a strong bit in the mouth of his ass.

'Henceforth be masterless.'

That is, he had to break-in the human ass completely, so that much more might be broken, in the long run. For the moment it was the British Government that had to have a hole knocked in it. The first real hole it ever had: the breach of the American rebellion.

Benjamin, in his sagacity, knew that the breaking of the old world was a long process. In the depths of his own under-consciousness he hated England, he hated Europe, he hated the whole corpus of the European being. He wanted to be American. But you can't change your nature and mode of consciousness like changing your shoes. It is a gradual shedding. Years must go by, and centuries must elapse before you have finished. Like a son escaping from the domination of his parents. The escape is not just one rupture. It is a long and half-secret process.

So with the American. He was a European when he first went over the Atlantic. He is in the main a recreant European still. From Benjamin Franklin to Woodrow Wilson may be a long stride, but it is a stride along the same road. There is no new road. The same old road, become dreary and futile. Theoretic and materialistic.

Why then did Benjamin set up this dummy of a perfect citizen as a pattern to America? Of course, he did it in perfect good faith, as far as he knew. He thought it simply was the true ideal. But what we *think* we do is not very important. We never really know what we are doing. Either we are materialistic instruments, like Benjamin, or we move in the gesture of creation, from our deepest self, usually unconscious. We are only the actors, we are never wholly the authors of our own deeds or works. I T is the author, the unknown inside us or outside us. The best we can do is to try to hold ourselves in unison with the deeps which are inside us. And the worst we can do is to try to have things our own way, when we run counter to I T, and in the long run get our knuckles rapped for our presumption.

So Benjamin contriving money out of the Court of France. He was contriving the first steps of the overthrow of all Europe, France included. You can never have a new thing without breaking an old. Europe happens to be the old thing. America, unless the people in America assert themselves too much in opposition to the inner gods, should be the new thing. The new thing is the death of the old. But you can't cut the throat of an epoch. You've got to steal the life from it through several centuries.

And Benjamin worked for this both directly and indirectly. Directly, at the Court of France, making a small but very dangerous hole in the side of England, through which hole Europe has by now almost bled to death. And indirectly in Philadelphia, setting up this unlovely, snuff-coloured little ideal, or automaton, of a pattern American. The pattern American, this dry, moral, utilitarian little democrat, has done more to ruin the old Europe than any Russian nihilist. He has done it by slow attrition, like a son who has stayed at home and obeyed his parents, all the while silently hating their authority, and silently, in his soul, destroying not only their authority but their whole existence. For the American spiritually stayed at home in Europe. The spiritual home of America was, and still is, Europe. This is the galling bondage, in spite of several billions of heaped-up gold. Your heaps of gold are only so many muck-heaps, America, and will remain so till you become a reality to yourselves.

All this Americanizing and mechanizing has been for the purpose of overthrowing the past. And now look at America, tangled in her own barbed wire, and mastered by her own machines. Absolutely got down by her own barbed wire of shalt-nots, and shut up fast in her own 'productive' machines like millions of squirrels running in millions of cages. It is just a farce.

Now is your chance, Europe. Now let Hell loose and get your own back, and paddle your own canoe on a new sea, while clever America lies on her muck-heaps of gold, strangled in her own barbed wire of shalt-not ideals and shalt-not moralisms. While she goes out to work like millions of squirrels in millions of cages. Production!

Let Hell loose, and get your own back, Europe!

On Human Destiny

Man is a domesticated animal that must think. His thinking makes him a little lower than the angels. And his domestication makes him, at times, a little lower than the monkey.

It is no use retorting that most men *don't* think. It is quite true, most men don't have any original thoughts. Most men, perhaps, are incapable of original thought, or original thinking. This doesn't alter the fact that they are all the time, all men, all the time, thinking. Man cannot even sleep with a blank mind. The mind refuses to be blank. The millstones of the brain grind on while the stream of life runs. And they grind on the grist of whatever ideas the mind contains.

The ideas may be old and ground to powder already. No matter. The mill of the mind grinds on, grinds the old grist over and over and over again. The blackest savage in Africa is the same, in this respect, as the whitest Member of Parliament in Westminster. His risk of death, his woman, his hunger, his chieftain, his lust, his immeasurable fear, all these are fixed ideas in the mind of the black African savage. They are ideas based on certain sensual reactions in the black breast and bowels, that is true. They are nonetheless ideas, however 'primitive'. And the difference between a primitive idea and a civilized one is not very great. It is remarkable how little change there is in man's rudimentary ideas.

Nowadays we like to talk about spontaneity, spontaneous feeling, spontaneous passion, spontaneous emotion. But our very spontaneity is just an idea. All out modern spontaneity is fathered in the mind, gestated in self-consciousness.

Since man became a domesticated, thinking animal, long, long ago, a little lower than the angels, he long, long ago left off being a wild instinctive animal. If he ever was such, which I don't believe. In my opinion, the most prognathous cave-man was an ideal beast. He ground on his crude, obstinate ideas. He was no more like the wild deer or the jaguar among the mountains than we are. He ground his ideas in the slow ponderous mill of his heavy cranium.

Man is never spontaneous, as we imagine the thrushes or the sparrow-hawk, for example, to be spontaneous. No matter how wild, how savage, how apparently untamed the savage may be, Dyak or Hottentot, you may be sure he is grinding upon his own fixed, peculiar ideas, and he's no more spontaneous than a London bus conductor: probably not as much.

The simple innocent child of nature does not exist. If there be an occasional violet by a mossy stone in the human sense, a Wordsworthian Lucy, it is because her vitality is rather low, and her simple nature is very near a simpleton's. You may, like Yeats, admire the simpleton, and call him God's Fool. But for me the village idiot is a cold egg.

No, no, let man be as primitive as primitive can be, he still has a mind. Give him at the same time a certain passion in his nature, and between his passion and his mind he'll beget himself ideas, ideas more or less good, more or less monstrous, but whether good or monstrous, absolute.

The savage grinds on his fetish or totem or taboo ideas even more fixedly and fatally than we on our love and salvation and making-good ideas.

Let us dismiss the innocent child of nature. He does not exist, never did, never will, and never could. No matter at what level man may be, he still has a mind, he has also passions. And the mind and the passions between them beget the scorpion brood of ideas. Or, if you like, call it the angelic hosts of the ideal.

Let us accept our own destiny. Man *can't* live by instinct, because he's got a mind. The serpent, with a crushed head, learned to brood along his spine, and take poison in his mouth. He has a strange sapience. But even he doesn't have ideas. Man has a mind and ideas, so it is just puerile to sigh for innocence and naïve spontaneity. Man is never spontaneous. Even children aren't spontaneous, not at all. It is only that their few and very dominant young ideas don't make logical associations. A child's ideas are ideas hard enough, but they hang together in a comical way, and the emotion that rises jumbles them ludicrously.

Ideas are born from a marriage between mind and emotion. But surely, you will say, it is possible for emotions to run free, without the dead hand of the ideal mind upon them.

It is impossible. Because, since man ate the apple and became endowed with mind, or mental consciousness, the human emotions are like a wedded wife; lacking a husband she is only a partial thing. The emotions cannot be 'free'. You can let your emotions run loose, if you like. You can let them run absolutely 'wild'. But their wildness and their looseness are a very shoddy affair. They leave nothing but boredom afterwards.

Emotions by themselves become just a nuisance. The mind by itself becomes just a sterile thing, making everything sterile. So what's to be done?

You've got to marry the pair of them. Apart, they are no good. The emotions that have not the approval and inspiration of the mind are just hysterics. The mind without the approval and inspiration of the emotions is just a dry stick, a dead tree, no good for anything unless to make a rod to beat and bully somebody with.

So, taking the human psyche, we have this simple trinity: the emotions, the mind, and then the children of this venerable pair, ideas. Man is controlled by his own ideas: there's no doubt about that.

Let us argue it once more. A pair of emancipated lovers are going to get away from the abhorred old ideal suasion. They're just going to fulfil their lives. That's all there is to it. They're just going to live their lives.

And then look at them! They do all the things that they know people do, when they are 'living their own lives'. They play up to their own ideas of being naughty instead of their ideas of good. And then what? It's the same old treadmill. They are just enacting the same set of ideas, only in the widdishins direction, being naughty instead of being good, treading the old circle in the opposite direction, and going round in the same old mill, even if in a reversed direction.

A man goes to a *cocotte*. And what of it? He does the same thing he does with his wife, but in the reverse direction. He just does everything naughtily instead of from his good self. It's a terrible relief perhaps, at first, to get away from his good self. But after a little while he realizes, rather drearily, that he's only going round in the same old treadmill, in the reversed direction. The Prince Consort turned us giddy with goodness, plodding round and round in the earnest mill. King Edward drove us giddy with naughtiness, trotting round and round in the same mill, in the opposite direction. So that the Georgian era finds us flummoxed, because we know the whole cycle back and forth.

At the centre is the same emotional idea. You fall in love with a woman, you marry her, you have bliss, you have children, you devote yourself to your family and to the service of mankind, and you live a happy life. Or, same idea but in the widdishins direction, you fall in love with a woman, you don't marry her, you live with her under the rose and enjoy yourself in spite of society; you leave your wife to swallow

her tears or spleen, as the case may be; you spend the dowry of your
daughters, you waste your substance, and you squander as much of
mankind's heaped-up corn as you can.

The ass goes one way, and threshes out the corn from the chaff. The
ass goes the other way and kicks the corn into the mud. At the centre is
the same idea: love, service, self-sacrifice, productivity. It just depends
upon which way round you run.

So there you are, poor man! All you can do is to run round like an
ass, either in one direction or another, round the fixed pole of a certain
central idea, in the track of a number of smaller, peripheral ideas. This
idea of love, these peripheral ideals of service, marriage, increase, etc.

Even the vulgarist self-seeker trots in the same tracks and gets the
same reactions, minus the thrill of the centralized passion.

What's to be done? What is being done?

The ring is being tightened. Russia was a complication of mixed ideas,
old barbaric ideas of divine kingship, of irresponsible power, of sacred
servility, conflicting with modern ideas of equality, serviceableness, productivity, etc. This complication had to be cleaned up. Russia was a great
and bewildering but at the same time fascinating circus, with her splen-
dours and miseries and brutalities and mystery. *Il faut changer tout cela.*
So modern men have changed it. And the bewildering, fascinating circus
of human anomalies is to be turned into a productive threshing-floor, an
ideal treadmill. The treadmill of the one accomplished idea.

What's to be done? Man is an ideal animal: an idea-making animal.
In spite of all his ideas, he remains an animal, often a little lower than
the monkey. And in spite of all his animal nature, he can only act in
fulfillment of disembodied ideas. What's to be done?

That too is quite simple. Man is not pot-bound in his ideas. Then let
him burst the pot that contains him. Ideally he is pot-bound. His roots
are choked, squeezed, and the life is leaving him, like a plant that is
pot-bound and is gradually going sapless.

Break the pot, then.

But it's no good waiting for the slow accumulation of circumstance to
break the pot. That's what men are doing today. They know the pot's
got to break. They know our civilization has got to smash, sooner or
later. So they say: 'Let it! But let me live my life first!'

Which is all very well, but it's a coward's attitude. They say glibly:
'Oh, well, every civilization must fall at last. Look at Rome!' Very
good, look at Rome. And what do you see? A mass of 'civilized' so-
called Romans, airing their *laissez-faire* and *laissez-aller* sentiments.

And a number of barbarians, Huns, etc. coming down to wipe them out, and expending themselves in the effort.

What of it, the Dark Ages? What about the Dark Ages, when the fields of Italy ran wild as the wild wastes of the undiscovered world, and wolves and bears roamed in the streets of the grey city of Lyons?

Very nice! But what else? Look at the other tiny bit of a truth. Rome was pot-bound, the pot was smashed to atoms, and the highly developed Roman tree of life lay on its side and died. But not before a new young seed had germinated. There in the spilt soil, small, humble, almost indiscernible, was the little tree of Christianity. In the howling wilderness of slaughter and *débâcle,* tiny monasteries of monks, too obscure and poor to plunder, kept the eternal light of man's undying effort at consciousness alive. A few poor bishops wandering through the chaos, linking up the courage of these men of thought and prayer. A scattered, tiny minority of men who had found a new way to God, to the life-source, glad to get again into touch with the Great God, glad to know the way and to keep the knowledge burningly alive.

That is the essential history of the Dark Ages, when Rome fell. We talk as if the flame of human courage and perspicacity had, in this time, gone out entirely, and that it miraculously popped into life again, out of nowhere, later on. Fusion of races, new barbaric blood, etc. Blarney! The fact of the matter is, the exquisite courage of brave men goes on in an unbroken continuity, even if sometimes the thread of flame becomes very thin. The exquisite delicate light of ever-renewed human consciousness is never blown out. The lights of great cities go out, and there is howling darkness to all appearance. But always, since men began, the light of the pure, God-knowing human consciousness has kept alight; sometimes, as in the Dark Ages, tiny but perfect flames of purest God-knowledge here and there; sometimes, as in our precious Victorian era, a huge and rather ghastly glare of human 'understanding'. But the light never goes out.

And that's the human destiny. The light shall never go out till the last day. The light of the human adventure into consciousness, which is, essentially, the light of human God-knowledge.

And human God-knowledge waxes and wanes, fed, as it were, from different oil. Man is a strange vessel. He has a thousand different essential oils in him, to keep the light of consciousness fed. Yet, apparently, he can only draw on one source at a time. And when the source he has been drawing on dries up, he has a bad time sinking a new well of oil, or guttering to extinction.

So it was in Roman times. The great old pagan fire of knowledge gradually died, its sources dried up. Then Jesus started a new, strange little flicker.

Today, the long light of Christianity is guttering to go out and we have to get at new resources in ourselves.

It is no use waiting for the *débâcle*. It's no use saying: 'Well, I didn't make the world, so it isn't up to me to mend it. Time and the event must do the business.' – Time and the event will do nothing. Men are worse after a great *débâcle* than before. The Russians who have 'escaped' from the horrors of the revolution are most of them extinguished as human beings. The real manly dignity has gone, all that remains is a collapsed human creature saying to himself: 'Look at me! I am alive. I can actually eat more sausage.'

Débâcles don't save men. In nearly every case, during the horrors of a catastrophe the light of integrity and human pride is extinguished in the soul of the man or the woman involved, and there is left a painful, unmanned creature, a thing of shame, incapable any more. It is the a great danger of *débâcles*, especially in times of unbelief like these. Men lack the faith and courage to keep their souls alert, kindled and unbroken. Afterwards there is a great smouldering of shamed life.

Man, poor, conscious, forever-animal man, has a very stern destiny, from which he is never allowed to escape. It is his destiny that he must move on and on, in the thought-adventure. He is a thought-adventurer, and adventure he must. The moment he builds himself a house and begins to think he can sit still in his knowledge, his soul becomes deranged, and he begins to pull down the house over his own head.

Man is now house-bound. Human consciousness today is too small, too tight to let us live and act naturally. Our dominant idea, instead of being a pole-star, is a millstone round our necks, strangling us. Old tablets of stone.

That is part of our destiny. As a thinking being, man is destined to seek God and to form some conception of Life. And since the invisible God *cannot* be conceived, and since Life is always more than any idea, behold, from the human conception of God and of Life, a great deal of necessity is left out. And this God whom we have left out and his Life that we have shut out from our living, must in the end turn against us and rend us. It is our destiny.

Nothing will alter it. When the Unknown God whom we ignore turns savagely to rend us, from the darkness of oblivion, and when the Life that we exclude from our living turns to poison and madness in our veins, then there is only one thing left to do. We have to struggle down to the heart of things, where the everlasting flame is, and kindle ourselves another beam of light. In short, we have to make another bitter adventure in pulsating thought, far, far to the one central pole of energy. We have to germinate inside us, between our undaunted mind and our reckless, genuine passions, a new germ. The germ of a new idea. A new germ of God-knowledge, or Life-knowledge. But a new germ.

And this germ will expand and grow, and flourish to a great tree, maybe. And in the end die again. Die like all the other human trees of knowledge.

But what does that matter? We walk in strides, we live by days and nights. A tree slowly rises to a great height, and quickly falls to dust. There is a long life-day for the individual. Then a very dark, spacious death-room –

I live and I die. I ask no other. Whatever proceeds from me lives and dies. I am glad, too. God is eternal, but my idea of Him is my own, and perishable. Everything human, human knowledge, human faith, human emotions, all perishes. And that is very good; if it were not so, everything would turn to cast-iron. There is too much of this cast-iron of permanence today.

Because I know the tree will ultimately die, shall I therefore refrain from planting a seed? Bah! it would be conceited cowardice on my part. I love the little sprout and the weak little seedling. I love the thin sapling, and the first fruit, and the falling of the first fruit. I love the great tree in its splendour. And I am glad that at last, at the very last, the great tree will go hollow, and fall on its side with a crash, and the little ants will run through it, and it will disappear like a ghost back into the humus.

It is the cycle of all things created, thank God. Because, given courage, it saves even eternity from staleness.

Man fights for a new conception of life and God, and he fights to plant seeds in the spring: because he knows that is the only way to harvest. If after harvest there is winter again, what does it matter? It is just seasonable.

But you have to fight even to plant seed. To plant seed you've got to kill a great deal of weeds and break much ground.

Reflections

Hymns in a Man's Life

Nothing is more difficult than to determine what a child takes in, and does not take in, of its environment and its teaching. This fact is brought home to me by the hymns which I learned as a child, and never forgot. They mean to me almost more than the finest poetry, and they have for me a more permanent value, somehow or other.

It is almost shameful to confess that the poems which have meant most to me, like Wordsworth's 'Ode to Immortality' and Keats's Odes, and pieces of *Macbeth* or *As You Like It* or *Midsummer Night's Dream*, and Goethe's lyrics, such as 'Über allen Gipfeln ist Ruh', and Verlaine's 'Ayant poussé la porte qui chancelle' – all these lovely poems which after all give the ultimate shape to one's life; all these lovely poems woven deep into a man's consciousness, are still not woven so deep in me as the rather banal Nonconformist hymns that penetrated through and through my childhood.

Each gentle dove
And sighing bough
That makes the eve
So fair to me
Has something far
Diviner now
To draw me back
To Galilee.
O Galilee, sweet Galilee
Where Jesus loved so much to be,
O Galilee, sweet Galilee,
Come sing thy songs again to me!

To me the word Galilee has a wonderful sound. The Lake of Galilee! I don't want to know where it is. I never want to go to Palestine. Galilee is one of those lovely, glamorous worlds, not places, that exist in the golden haze of a child's half-formed imagination. And in my man's imagination it is just the same. It has been left untouched. With regard to the hymns which had such a profound influence on my childish consciousness, there has been no crystallizing out, no dwindling into actuality, no hardening into the commonplace. They are the same to my man's experience as they were to me nearly forty years ago.

The moon, perhaps, has shrunken a little. One has been forced to learn about orbits, eclipses, relative distances, dead worlds, craters of the moon, and so on. The crescent at evening still startles the soul with its delicate flashing. But the mind works automatically and says: 'Ah, she is in her first quarter. She is all there, in spite of the fact that we see only this slim blade. The earth's shadow is over her.' And, willy-nilly, the intrusion of the mental processes dims the brilliance, the magic of the first apperception.

It is the same with all things. The sheer delight of a child's apperception is based on *wonder*; and deny it as we may, knowledge and wonder counteract one another. So that as knowledge increases wonder decreases. We say again: familiarity breeds contempt. So that as we grow older, and become more familiar with phenomena, we become more contemptuous of them. But that is only partly true. It has taken some races of men thousands of years to become contemptuous of the moon, and to the Hindu the cow is still wondrous. It is not familiarity that breeds contempt: it is the assumption of knowledge. Anybody who looks at the moon and says, 'I know all about that poor orb,' is, of course, bored by the moon.

Now the great and fatal fruit of our civilization, which is a civilization based on knowledge, and hostile to experience, is boredom. All our wonderful education and learning is producing a grand sum-total of boredom. Modern people are inwardly thoroughly bored. Do as they may, they are bored.

They are bored because they experience nothing. And they experience nothing because the wonder has gone out of them. And when the wonder has gone out of a man he is dead. He is henceforth only an insect.

When all comes to all, the most precious element in life is wonder. Love is a great emotion, and power is power. But both love and power are based on wonder. Love without wonder is a sensational affair, and power without wonder is mere force and compulsion. The one universal element in consciousness which is fundamental to life is the element of wonder. You cannot help feeling it in a bean as it starts to grow and pulls itself out of its jacket. You cannot help feeling it in the glisten of the nucleus of the amoeba. You recognize it, willy-nilly, in an ant busily tugging at a straw; in a rook, as it walks the frosty grass.

They all have their own obstinate will. But also they all live with a sense of wonder. Plant consciousness, insect consciousness, fish consciousness, all are related by one permanent element, which we may call the religious element inherent in all life, even in a flea: the sense of wonder. That is our sixth sense. And it is the *natural* religious sense.

Somebody says that mystery is nothing, because mystery is something you don't know, and what you don't know is nothing to you. But there is more than one way of knowing.

Even the real scientist works in the sense of wonder. The pity is, when he comes out of his laboratory he puts aside his wonder along with his apparatus, and tries to make it all perfectly didactic. Science in its true condition of wonder is as religious as any religion. But didactic science is as dead and boring as dogmatic religion. Both are wonderless and productive of boredom, endless boredom.

Now we come back to the hymns. They live and glisten in the depths of the man's consciousness in undimmed wonder, because they have not been subjected to any criticism or analysis. By the time I was sixteen I had criticized and got over the Christian dogma.

It was quite easy for me; my immediate forebears had already done it for me. Salvation, heaven, Virgin birth, miracles, even the Christian dogmas of right and wrong – one soon got them adjusted. I never could really worry about them. Heaven is one of the instinctive dreams. Right and wrong is something you can't dogmatize about; it's not so easy. As for my soul, I simply don't and never did understand how I could 'save' it. One can save one's pennies. But how can one save one's soul? One can only *live* one's soul. The business is to live, really alive. And this needs wonder.

So that the miracle of the loaves and fishes is just as good to me now as when I was a child. I don't care whether it is historically a fact or not. What does it matter? It is part of the genuine wonder. The same with all the religious teaching I had as a child, *apart* from the didacticism and sentimentalism. I am eternally grateful for the wonder with which it filled my childhood.

Sun of my soul, thou Saviour dear,
It is not night if Thou be near –

That was the last hymn at the board-school. It did not mean to me any Christian dogma or any salvation. Just the words, 'Sun of my soul, thou Saviour dear,' penetrated me with wonder and the mystery of twilight. At another time the last hymn was:

Fair waved the golden corn
In Canaan's pleasant land –

And again I loved 'Canaan's pleasant land'. The wonder of 'Canaan', which could never be localized.

I think it was good to be brought up a Protestant: and among Protestants, a Nonconformist, and among Nonconformists, a Congregationalist. Which sounds pharisaic. But I should have missed bitterly a direct knowledge of the Bible, and a direct relation to Galilee and Canaan, Moab and Kedron, those places that never existed on earth. And in the Church of England one would hardly have escaped those snobbish hierarchies of class, which spoil so much for a child. And the Primitive Methodists, when I was a boy, were always having 'revivals' and being 'saved', and I always had a horror of being saved.

So, altogether, I am grateful to my 'Congregational' upbringing. The Congregationalists are the oldest Nonconformists, descendants of the Oliver Cromwell Independents. They still had the Puritan tradition of no ritual. But they avoided the personal emotionalism which one found among the Methodists when I was a boy.

I liked our chapel, which was tall and full of light, and yet still; and colour-washed pale green and blue, with a bit of lotus pattern. And over the organ-loft, 'O worship the Lord, in the beauty of holiness', in big letters.

That was a favourite hymn, too:

O worship the Lord, in the beauty of holiness,
  Bow down before Him, His glory proclaim;
With gold of obedience and incense of lowliness
  Kneel and adore Him, the Lord is His name.

I don't know what the 'beauty of holiness' is exactly. It easily becomes cant, or nonsense. But if you don't think about it – and why should you? – it has a magic. The same with the whole verse. It is rather bad, really, 'gold of obedience' and 'incense of lowliness'. But in me, to the music, it still produces a sense of splendour.

I am always glad we had the Bristol hymn-book, not Moody and Sankey. And I am glad our Scotch minister on the whole avoided sentimental messes such as 'Lead, Kindly Light', or even 'Abide with Me'. He had a healthy preference for healthy hymns.

At even, ere the sun was set,
  The sick, O Lord, around Thee lay.
Oh, in what divers pains they met!
  Oh, in what joy they went away!

And often we had 'Fight the good fight with all thy might'.

In Sunday School I am eternally grateful to old Mr Remington, with his round white beard and his ferocity. He made us sing! And he loved the martial hymns:

Sound the battle-cry,
See, the foe is nigh.
Raise the standard high
For the Lord.

The ghastly sentimentalism that came like a leprosy over religion had not yet got hold of our colliery village. I remember when I was in Class Two in the Sunday School, when I was about seven, a woman teacher trying to harrow us about the Crucifixion. And she kept saying: 'And aren't you sorry for Jesus? Aren't you sorry?' And most of the children wept. I believe I shed a crocodile tear or two, but very vivid is my memory of saying to myself: 'I don't *really* care a bit.' And I could never go back on it. I never *cared* about the Crucifixion, one way or another. Yet the *wonder* of it penetrated very deep in me.

Thirty-six years ago men, even Sunday School teachers, still believed in the fight for life and the fun of it. 'Hold the fort, for I am coming.' It was far, far from any militarism or gun-fighting. But it was the battle-cry of a stout soul, and a fine thing too.

Stand up, stand up for Jesus,
Ye soldiers of the Lord.

Here is the clue to the ordinary Englishman – in the Nonconformist hymns.

Nottingham and the Mining Countryside

I was born nearly forty-four years ago, in Eastwood, a mining village of some three thousand souls, about eight miles from Nottingham, and one mile from the small stream, the Erewash, which divides Nottinghamshire from Derbyshire. It is hilly country, looking west to Crich and towards Matlock, sixteen miles away, and east and north-east towards Mansfield and the Sherwood Forest district. To me it seemed, and still seems, an extremely beautiful countryside, just between the red sandstone and the oak-trees of Nottingham, and the cold limestone, the ash-trees, the stone fences of Derbyshire. To me, as a child and a young man, it was still the old England of the forest and agricultural past; there were no motor-cars, the mines were, in a sense, an accident in the landscape, and Robin Hood and his merry men were not very far away.

The string of coal mines of B.W. & Co. had been opened some sixty years before I was born, and Eastwood had come into being as a consequence. It must have been a tiny village at the beginning of the nineteenth century, a small place of cottages and fragmentary rows of little four-roomed miners' dwellings, the homes of the old colliers of the eighteenth century, who worked in the bits of mines, foot-rill mines with an opening in the hillside into which the miners walked, or windlass mines, where the men were wound up one at a time, in a bucket, by a donkey. The windlass mines were still working when my father was a boy – and the shafts of some were still there, when I was a boy.

But somewhere about 1820 the company must have sunk the first big shaft – not very deep – and installed the first machinery of the real industrial colliery. Then came my grandfather, a young man trained to be a tailor, drifting from the south of England, and got the job of company tailor for the Brinsley mine. In those days the company supplied the men with the thick flannel vests, or singlets, and the moleskin trousers lined at the top with flannel, in which the colliers worked. I remember the great rolls of coarse flannel and pit-cloth which stood in the corner of my grandfather's shop when I was a small boy, and the big, strange old sewing-machine, like nothing else on earth, which sewed the massive pit-trousers. But when I was only a child the company discontinued supplying the men with pit-clothes.

My grandfather settled in an old cottage down in a quarry-bed, by the brook at Old Brinsley, near the pit. A mile away, up at Eastwood, the company built the first miners' dwellings – it must be nearly a hundred years ago. Now Eastwood occupies a lovely position on a hilltop, with the steep slope towards Derbyshire and the long slope towards Nottingham. They put up a new church, which stands fine and commanding, even if it has no real form, looking across the awful Erewash Valley at the church of Heanor, similarly commanding, away on a hill beyond. What opportunities, what opportunities! These mining villages *might* have been like the lovely hill-towns of Italy, shapely and fascinating. And what happened?

Most of the little rows of dwellings of the old-style miners were pulled down, and dull little shops began to rise along the Nottingham Road, while on the down-slope of the north side the company erected what is still known as the New Buildings, or the Square. These New Buildings consist of two great hollow squares of dwellings planked down on the rough slope of the hill, little four-room houses with the 'front' looking outward into the grim, blank street, and the 'back', with a tiny square brick yard, a low wall, and a WC and ash-pit, looking into the desert of the square, hard, uneven, jolting black earth tilting rather steeply down, with these little black yards all round, and openings at the corners. The squares were quite big, and absolutely desert, save for the posts for clothes lines, and people passing, children playing on the hard earth. And they were shut in like a barracks enclosure, very strange.

Even fifty years ago the squares were unpopular. It was 'common' to live in the Square. It was a little less common to live in the Breach, which consisted of six blocks of rather more pretentious dwellings erected by the company in the valley below, two rows of three blocks, with an alley between. And it was most 'common', most degraded of all, to live in Dakins Row, two rows of the old dwellings, very old, black, four-roomed little places, that stood on the hill again, not far from the Square.

So the place started. Down the steep street between the squares, Scargill Street, the Wesleyans' chapel was put up, and I was born in the little corner shop just above. Across the other side of the Square the miners themselves built the big, barn-like Primitive Methodist chapel. Along the hill-top ran the Nottingham Road, with its scrappy, ugly mid-Victorian shops. The little market-place, with a superb outlook, ended the village on the Derbyshire side, and was just left bare, with the Sun Inn on one side, the chemist across, with the gilt pestle-and-mortar, and a shop at the other corner, the corner of Alfreton Road and Nottingham Road.

In this queer jumble of the old England and the new, I came into consciousness. As I remember, little local speculators already began to straggle dwellings in rows, always in rows, across the fields : nasty red-brick, flat-faced dwellings with dark slate roofs. The bay-window period only began when I was a child. But most of the country was untouched.

There must be three or four hundred company houses in the squares and the streets that surround the squares, like a great barracks wall. There must be sixty or eighty company houses in the Breach. The old Dakins Row will have thirty or forty little holes. Then counting the old cottages and rows left with their old gardens down the lanes and along the twitchells, and even in the midst of Nottingham Road itself, there were houses enough for the population, there was no need for much building. And not much building went on when I was small.

We lived in the Breach, in a corner house. A field-path came down under a great hawthorn hedge. On the other side was the brook, with the old sheep-bridge going over into the meadows. The hawthorn hedge by the brook had grown tall as tall trees, and we used to bathe from there in the dipping-hole, where the sheep were dipped, just near the fall from the old mill-dam, where the water rushed. The mill only ceased grinding the local corn when I was a child. And my father, who always worked in Brinsley pit, and who always got up at five o'clock, if not at four, would set off in the dawn across the fields at Coney Grey, and hunt for mushrooms in the long grass, or perhaps pick up a skulking rabbit, which he would bring home at evening inside the lining of his pit-coat.

So that the life was a curious cross between industrialism and the old agricultural England of Shakespeare and Milton and Fielding and George Eliot. The dialect was broad Derbyshire, and always 'thee' and 'thou'. The people lived almost entirely by instinct, men of my father's age could not really read. And the pit did not mechanize men. On the contrary. Under the butty system, the miners worked underground as a sort of intimate community, they knew each other practically naked, and with curious close intimacy, and the darkness and the underground remoteness of the pit 'stall', and the continual presence of danger, made the physical, instinctive and intuitional contact between men very highly developed, a contact almost as close as touch, very real and very powerful. This physical awareness and intimate *togetherness* was at its strongest down pit. When the men came up into the light, they blinked. They had, in a measure, to change their flow. Nevertheless, they brought with them above ground the curious dark intimacy of the mine, the naked sort of contact, and if I think of my childhood, it is always as if there was a lustrous sort of inner darkness, like the gloss of coal, in which we moved and had our real being. My father loved the pit. He was hurt badly, more than once, but he would never stay away. He loved the contact, the intimacy, as men in the war loved the intense male comradeship of the dark days. They did not know what they had lost till they lost it. And I think it is the same with the young colliers of today.

Now the colliers had also an instinct of beauty. The colliers' wives had not. The colliers were deeply alive, instinctively. But they had no daytime ambition, and no daytime intellect. They avoided, really, the rational aspect of life. They preferred to take life instinctively and intuitively. They didn't even care very profoundly about wages. It was the women, naturally, who nagged on this score. There was a big discrepancy, when I was a boy, between the collier who saw, at the best, only a brief few hours of daylight – often no daylight at all during the winter weeks – and the collier's wife, who had all the day to herself when the man was down pit.

The great fallacy is, to pity the man. He didn't dream of pitying himself, till agitators and sentimentalists taught him to. He was happy: or more than happy, he was fulfilled. Or he was fulfilled on the receptive side, not on the expressive. The collier went to the pub and drank in order to continue his intimacy with his mates. They talked endlessly, but it was rather of wonders and marvels, even in politics, than of facts. It was hard facts, in the shape of wife, money and nagging home necessities, which they fled away from, out of the house to the pub, and out of the house to the pit.

The collier fled out of the house as soon as he could, away from the nagging materialism of the woman. With the woman it was always: 'This is broken, now you've got to mend it!' or else: 'We want this, that and the other, and where is the money coming from?' The collier didn't know and didn't care very deeply – his life was otherwise. So he escaped. He roved the countryside with his dog, prowling for a rabbit, for nests, for mushrooms, anything. He loved the countryside, just the indiscriminating feel of it. Or he loved just to sit on his heels and watch – anything or nothing. He was not intellectually interested. Life for him did not consist in facts, but in a flow. Very often, he loved his garden. And very often he had a genuine love of the beauty of flowers. I have known it often and often, in colliers.

Now the love of flowers is a very misleading thing. Most women love flowers as possessions, and as trimmings. They can't look at a flower, and wonder a moment, and pass on. If they see a flower that arrests their attention, they must at once pick it, pluck it. Possession! A possession! Something added on to *me*! And most of the so-called love of flowers today is merely this reaching out of possession and egoism: something I've *got*: something that embellishes *me*. Yet I've seen many a collier stand in his back garden looking down at a flower with that odd, remote sort of contemplation which shows a *real* awareness of the presence of beauty. It would not even be admiration, or joy, or delight, or any of those things which so often have a root in the possessive instinct. It would be a sort of contemplation: which shows the incipient artist.

The real tragedy of England, as I see it, is the tragedy of ugliness. The country is so lovely: the man-made England is so vile. I know that the ordinary collier, when I was a boy, had a peculiar sense of beauty, coming from his intuitive and instinctive consciousness, which was awakened down pit. And the fact that he met with just cold ugliness and raw materialism when he came up into daylight, and particularly when he came to the Square or the Breach, and to his own table, killed something in him, and in a sense spoiled him as a man. The woman almost invariably nagged about material things. She was taught to do it; she was encouraged to do it. It was a mother's business to see that her sons 'got on', and it was the man's business to provide the money. In my father's generation, with the old wild England behind them, and the lack of education, the man was not beaten down. But in my generation, the boys I went to school with, colliers now, have all been beaten down, what with the din-din-dinning of board-schools, books, cinemas, clergymen, the whole national and human consciousness hammering on the fact of material prosperity above all things.

The men are beaten down, there is prosperity for a time, in their defeat – and then disaster looms ahead. The root of all disaster is disheartenment. And men are disheartened. The men of England, the colliers in particular, are disheartened. They have been betrayed and beaten.

Now though perhaps nobody knew it, it was ugliness which really betrayed the spirit of man, in the nineteenth century. The great crime which the moneyed classes and promoters of industry committed in the palmy Victorian days was the condemning of the workers to ugliness, ugliness, ugliness: meanness and formless and ugly surroundings, ugly ideals, ugly religion, ugly hope, ugly love, ugly clothes, ugly furniture, ugly houses, ugly relationship between workers and employers. The human soul needs actual beauty even more than bread. The middle classes jeer at the colliers for buying pianos – but what is the piano, often as not, but a blind reaching out for beauty. To the woman it is a possession and a piece of furniture and something to feel superior about. But see the elderly colliers trying to learn to play, see them listening with queer alert faces to their daughter's execution of *The Maiden's Prayer*, and you will see a blind, unsatisfied craving for beauty. It is far more deep in the men than the women. The women want show. The men want beauty, and still want it.

If the company, instead of building those sordid and hideous Squares, then, when they had that lovely site to play with, there on the hilltop: if they had put a tall column in the middle of the small market-place, and run three parts of a circle of arcade round the pleasant space, where people could stroll or sit, and with handsome houses behind! If they had made big, substantial houses, in apartments of five or six rooms, and with handsome entrances. If above all, they had encouraged song and dancing – for the miners still sang and danced – and provided handsome space for these. If only they had encouraged some form of beauty in dress, some form of beauty in interior life – furniture, decoration. If they had given prizes for the handsomest chair or table, the loveliest scarf, the most charming room that the men or women could make! If only they had done this, there would never have been an industrial problem. The industrial problem arises from the base forcing of all human energy into a competition of mere acquisition.

You may say the working man would not have accepted such a form of life: the Englishman's home is his castle, etc., etc. – 'my own little home'. But if you can hear every word the next-door people say, there's not much castle. And if you can see everybody in the square if they go to the WC! And if your one desire is to get out of your 'castle' and your 'own little home'! – well, there's not much to be said for it. Anyhow, it's only the woman who idolizes 'her own little home' – and it's always the woman at her worst, her most greedy, most possessive, most mean. There's nothing to be said for the 'little home' any more: a great scrabble of ugly pettiness over the face of the land.

As a matter of fact, till 1800 the English people were strictly a rural people – very rural. England has had towns for centuries, but they have never been real towns, only clusters of village streets. Never the real *urbs*. The English character has failed to develop the real *urban* side of a man, the civic side. Siena is a bit of a place, but it is a real city, with citizens intimately connected with the city. Nottingham is a vast place sprawling towards a million, and it is nothing more than an amorphous agglomeration. There *is* no Nottingham, in the sense that there is Siena. The Englishman is stupidly undeveloped, as a citizen. And it is partly due to his 'little home' stunt, and partly to his acceptance of hopeless paltriness in his surroundings. The new cities of America are much more genuine cities, in the Roman sense, than is London or Manchester. Even Edinburgh used to be more of a true city than any town England ever produced.

That silly little individualism of 'the Englishman's home is his castle' and 'my own little home' is out of date. It would work almost up to 1800, when every Englishman was still a villager, and a cottager. But the industrial system has brought a great change. The Englishman still likes to think of himself as a 'cottager' – 'my home, my garden'. But it is puerile. Even the farm-labourer today is psychologically a town-bird. The English are town-birds through and through, today, as the inevitable result of their complete industrialization. Yet they don't know how to build a city, how to think of one, or how to live in one. They are all suburban, pseudo-cottagy, and not one of them knows how to be truly urban – the citizen as the Romans were citizens – or the Athenians – or even the Parisians, till the war came.

And this is because we have frustrated that instinct of community which would make us unite in pride and dignity in the bigger gesture of the citizen, not the cottager. The great city means beauty, dignity, and a certain splendour. This is the side of the Englishman that has been thwarted and shockingly betrayed. England is a mean and petty scrabble of paltry dwellings called 'homes'. I believe in their heart of hearts all Englishmen loathe their little homes – but not the women. What we want is a bigger gesture, a greater scope, a certain splendour, a certain grandeur, and beauty, big beauty. The American does far better than we, in this.

And the promoter of industry, a hundred years ago, dared to perpetrate the ugliness of my native village. And still more monstrous, promoters of industry today are scrabbling over the face of England with miles and square miles of red-brick 'homes', like horrible scabs. And the men inside these little red rat-traps get more and more helpless, being more and more humiliated, more and more dissatisfied, like trapped rats. Only the meaner sort of women go on loving the little home which is no more than a rat-trap to her man.

Do away with it all, then. At no matter what cost, start in to alter it. Never mind about wages and industrial squabbling. Turn the attention elsewhere. Pull down my native village to the last brick. Plan a nucleus. Fix the focus. Make a handsome gesture of radiation from the focus. And then put up big buildings, handsome, that sweep to a civic centre. And furnish them with beauty. And make an absolute clean start. Do it place by place. Make a new England. Away with little homes! Away with scrabbling pettiness and paltriness. Look at the contours of the land, and build up from these, with a sufficient nobility. The English may be mentally or spiritually developed. But as citizens of splendid cities they are more ignominious than rabbits. And they nag, nag, nag all the time about politics and wages and all that, like mean narrow housewives.

Return to Bestwood

The black-slate roofs beyond the wind-worn young trees at the end of the garden are the same thick layers of black roofs of blackened brick houses, as ever. There is the same smell of sulphur from the burning pit bank. Smuts fly on the white violas. There is a harsh sound of machinery. Persephone couldn't quite get out of hell, so she let Spring fall from her lap along the upper workings.

But no! There are no smuts, there is even no smell of the burning pit bank. They cut the bank, and the pits are not working. The strike has been going on for months. It is September, but there are lots of roses on the lawn beds.

'Where shall we go this afternoon. Shall we go to Hardwick?'

Let us go to Hardwick. I have not been for twenty years. Let us go to Hardwick:

Hardwick Hall
More window than wall.

Built in the days of good Queen Bess, by that other Bess, termagant and tartar, Countess of Shrewsbury.

Butterley, Alfreton, Tibshelf – what was once the Hardwick district is now the Notts-Derby coal area. The country is the same, but scarred and splashed all over with mines and mining settlements. Great houses loom from hill-brows, old villages are smothered in rows of miners' dwellings, Bolsover Castle rises from the mass of the colliery village of Bolsover. – Böwser, we called it, when I was a boy.

Hardwick is shut. On the gates, near the old inn, where the atmosphere of the old world lingers perfect, is a notice: 'This park is closed to the public and to all traffic until further notice. No admittance.'

Of course! The strike! They are afraid of vandalism.

Where shall we go? Back into Derbyshire, or to Sherwood Forest.

Turn the car. We'll go on through Chesterfield. If I can't ride in my own carriage, I can still ride in my sister's motor-car.

It is a still September afternoon. By the ponds in the old park, we see colliers slowly loafing, fishing, poaching in spite of all notices.

And at every lane end there is a bunch of three or four policemen, 'blue-bottles', big, big-faced, stranger policemen. Every field path, every stile seems to be guarded. There are great pits, coal mines, in the fields. And at the end of the paths coming out of the field from the colliery, along the high-road, the colliers are squatted on their heels, on the way-side grass, silent and watchful. Their faces are clean, white, and all the months of the strike have given them no colour and no tan. They are pit-bleached. They squat in silent remoteness, as if in the upper galleries of hell. And the policemen, alien, stand in a group near the stile. Each lot pretends not to be aware of the others.

It is past three. Down the path from the pit come straggling what my little nephew calls 'the dirty ones'. They are the men who have broken strike, and gone back to work. They are not many: their faces are black, they are in their pit-dirt. They linger till they have collected, a group of a dozen or so 'dirty ones', near the stile, then they trail off down the road, the policemen, the alien 'blue-bottles', escorting them. And the 'clean ones', the colliers still on strike, squat by the wayside and watch without looking. They say nothing. They neither laugh nor stare. But here they are, a picket, and with their bleached faces they see without looking, and they register with the silence of doom, squatted down in rows by the road-side.

The 'dirty ones' straggle off in the lurching, almost slinking walk of colliers, swinging their heavy feet and going as if the mine-roof were still over their heads. The big blue policemen follow at a little distance. No voice is raised: nobody seems aware of anybody else. But there is the silent, hellish registering in the consciousness of all three groups, clean ones, dirty ones and blue-bottles.

So it is now all the way into Chesterfield, whose crooked spire lies below. The men who have gone back to work – they seem few, indeed – are lurching and slinking in quiet groups, home down the high-road, the police at their heels. And the pickets, with bleached faces, squat and lean and stand, in silent groups, with a certain pale fatality, like Hell, upon them.

And I, who remember the homeward-trooping of the colliers when I was a boy, the ringing of the feet, the red mouths and the quick whites of the eyes, the swinging pit bottles, and the strange voices of men from the underworld calling back and forth, strong and, it seemed to me, gay with the queer, absolved gaiety of miners – I shiver, and feel I turn into a ghost myself. The colliers were noisy, lively, with strong underworld voices such as I have never heard in any other men, when I was a boy. And after all, it is not so long ago. I am only forty-one.

But after the war, the colliers went silent: after 1920. Till 1920 there was a strange power of life in them, something wild and urgent, that one could hear in their voices. They were always excited, in the afternoon, to come up above-ground: and excited, in the morning, at going down. And they called in the darkness with strong, strangely evocative voices. and at the little local football matches, on the damp, dusky Saturday afternoons of winter, great, full-throated cries came howling from the football field, in the zest and the wildness of life.

But now, the miners go by to the football match in silence like ghosts, and from the field comes a poor, ragged shouting. These are the men of my own generation, who went to the board-school with me. And they are almost voiceless. They go to the welfare clubs, and drink with a sort of hopelessness.

I feel I hardly know any more the people I come from, the colliers of the Erewash Valley district. They are changed, and I suppose I am changed. I find it so much easier to live in Italy. And they have got a

239 Return to Bestwood

new kind of shallow consciousness, all newspaper and cinema, which I am not in touch with. At the same time, they have, I think, an underneath ache and heaviness very much like my own. It must be so, because when I see them, I feel it so strongly.

They are the only people who move me strongly, and with whom I feel myself connected in deeper destiny. It is they who are, in some peculiar way, 'home' to me. I shrink away from them, and I have an acute nostalgia for them.

And now, this last time, I feel a doom over the country, and a shadow of despair over the hearts of the men, which leaves me no rest. Because the same doom is over me, wherever I go, and the same despair touches my heart.

Yet it is madness to despair, while we still have the course of destiny open to us.

One is driven back to search one's own soul, for a way out into a new destiny.

A few things I know, with inner knowledge.

I know that what I am struggling for is life, more life ahead, for myself and the men who will come after me: struggling against fixations and corruptions.

I know that the miners at home are men very much like me, and I am very much like them: ultimately, we want the same thing. I know they are, in the life sense of the word, good.

I know that there is ahead the mortal struggle for property.

I know that the ownership of property has become, now, a problem, a religious problem. But it is one we can solve.

I know I want to own a few things: my personal things. But I also know I want to own no more than those. I don't want to own a house, nor land, nor a motor-car, nor shares in anything. I don't want a fortune – not even an assured income.

At the same time, I don't want poverty and hardship. I know I need enough money to leave me free in my movements, and I want to be able to earn that money without humiliation.

I know that most decent people feel very much the same in this respect: and the indecent people must, in their indecency, be subordinated to the decent.

I know that we could, if we would, establish little by little a true democracy in England: we could nationalize the land and industries and means of transport, and make the whole thing work infinitely better than at present, *if we would*. It all depends on the spirit in which the thing is done.

I know we are on the brink of a class war.

I know we had all better hang ourselves at once, than enter on a struggle which shall be a fight for the ownership or non-ownership of property, pure and simple, and nothing beyond.

I know the ownership of property is a problem that may have to be fought out. But beyond the fight must lie a new hope, a new beginning.

I know our vision of life is all wrong. We must be prepared to have a new conception of what it means, *to live*. And everybody should try to help to build up this new conception, and everybody should be prepared to destroy, bit by bit, our old conception.

I know that man cannot live by his own will alone. With his soul, he must search for the sources of the power of life. It is life we want.

I know that where there is life, there is essential beauty. Genuine beauty, which fills the soul, is an indication of life, and genuine ugliness, which blasts the soul, is an indication of morbidity. – But prettiness is opposed to beauty.

I know that, first and foremost, we must be sensitive to life and to its movements. If there is power, it must be sensitive power.

I know that we must look after the quality of life, not the quantity. Hopeless life should be put to sleep, the idiots and the hopeless sick and the true criminal. And the birth-rate should be controlled.

I know we must take up the responsibility for the future, now. A great change is coming, and must come. What we need is some glimmer of a vision of a world that shall be, beyond the change. Otherwise we shall be in for a great *débâcle*.

What is alive, and open, and active, is good. All that makes for inertia, lifelessness, dreariness, is bad. This is the essence of morality.

What we should live for is life and the beauty of aliveness, imagination, awareness and contact. To be perfectly alive is to be immortal.

I know these things, along with other things. And it is nothing very new to know these things. The only new thing would be to act on them.

And what is the good of saying these things, to men whose whole education consists in the fact that twice two are four? – which, being interpreted, means that twice tuppence is fourpence. All our education, the whole of it, is formed upon this little speck of dust.

Source List
Titles bracketed are those given by the editors

Autobiographical Sketch
first published as 'Myself Revealed', *Sunday Dispatch*, 17 February 1929.
Reprinted in *Phoenix II*, 1968.

The Proper Study
first published in *Adelphi*, December 1923. Reprinted in *Phoenix I*, 1936.

The Novel and the Feelings
Phoenix I, 1936. Written *c.* 1923(?).

Why the Novel Matters
Phoenix I, 1936. Written *c.* 1925.

(Schoolgirl)
from chapter 12, *The Rainbow*, 1915.

(Assistant Teacher)
from chapters 13 and 14, *The Rainbow*, 1915.

(Training College)
from chapter 15, *The Rainbow*, 1915.

Class-Room
chapter 3, *Women in Love*, 1921; written 1915–16.

Lessford's Rabbits
Phoenix II, 1968. Written 1908–12.

A Lesson on a Tortoise
Phoenix II, 1968. Written 1908–12.

Men Must Work and Women as Well
first published as 'Men and Women', *Star Review*, November 1929.
Reprinted in *Phoenix II*, 1968.

Education of the People
Phoenix I, 1936. Written 1918.

Education and Sex in Man, Woman and Child
chapter 8, *Fantasia of the Unconscious*, 1923.

Letter to Lady Cynthia Asquith
Collected Letters, vol. 1, 1962. Written 1 May 1915.

Benjamin Franklin
from *Studies in American Literature*, 1923. Written 1917–18.

On Human Destiny
first published in *Adelphi*, March 1924. Reprinted in *Phoenix II*, 1968.

Hymns in a Man's Life
first published in *Evening News*, 13 October 1928. Reprinted in *Phoenix II*, 1968.

Nottingham and the Mining Countryside
first published in *Adelphi*, June–August 1930. Reprinted in *Phoenix I*, 1936.

Return to Bestwood
Phoenix II, 1968. Written September 1926.

Published simultaneously with *Lawrence on Education*

Arnold on Education
Edited by Gillian Sutherland

Matthew Arnold is best known for his literary and social criticism and his poetry. But for thirty-five years his main day-to-day concern was with state elementary schools as one of Her Majesty's Inspectors of Schools.

It was not a job he relished. As Gillian Sutherland makes clear in her introduction, although Arnold was professionally concerned with working-class education, this concern paradoxically engendered a preoccupation with the schools he was *not* allowed to inspect – the fee-charging schools for the middle classes. The view of education he developed was based on the feeling that the education of the middle classes was both more difficult and more important: here were the new leaders of society who could retrieve culture from the barbarism that engulfed it.

This selection of Arnold's educational writings includes selections from his school reports as well as some of his better-known articles like *A French Eton*. Overall it provides a fascinating case study, not only of a critical period in the history of education, but also of the ways in which educational theories of class structure, culture and elites can be developed and sustained with conviction and scrupulousness. If the world has passed Arnold by, his case is still worth pondering.

Gillian Sutherland is Director of Studies in History at Cambridge University.

Recent books from Penguin Education include:

Education for a Change
Colin and Mog Ball

This is a simple book. It is also an uncompromising one. It is the first Education Special written not merely for adults, but also directly for the consumers of education themselves. It is a book about youth taking matters into its own hands, on its own terms.

Colin and Mog Ball show how community service, once doomed as a worthy alternative for 'early leavers' on Thursday afternoons, can be transformed into a potent agent for radical change. They describe experiments which have taken activities out of the hands of the professionals and placed them with the young – for example, tutoring in schools. They show how community action can spread across the whole curriculum, through and beyond the school, bringing young people and adults together in genuine participation. The only skill required is willingness: the motto is 'helping one another' instead of the pervasive 'survival of the fittest'.

On behalf of the bored, the frustrated and the isolated, *Education for a Change* demands for the young the opportunity of becoming 'the investigators of the inadequacies of the system in which they are enmeshed, the callers for an education that will have some meaning in the life they are to lead'.

Tinker, tailor ...
Edited by Nell Keddie

... soldier, sailor, rich man, poor man, beggar man, thief. Nobody has
ever quite assumed that human development, achievement, status was ever
as arbitrary as the traditional rhyme suggests. But the assumption is
widespread and profound that there are inevitabilities which schools and
other social institutions combat with difficulty and even against an almost
crippling adversity.

Chief among these inevitabilities in the last decade or more has been the
concept of 'cultural deprivation'. It is possible that we should regard
'cultural deprivation' as a mythology developed to mask and support a
class system to which we are all, wittingly or not, committed. It may even
be – as Nell Keddie argues in her lucid and persuasive introduction – that
it is essential we do so.

This collection of papers has been designed to raise questions, and it
neither pretends nor expects to provide solutions. In raising these questions,
as Nell Keddie writes, 'we must inevitably raise wider issues about
education ... and ultimately about what we take to be the prevailing
values in the society in which we live.'

Nell Keddie is Lecturer in Sociology at Goldsmiths' College, University
of London.

The Forsaken Lover
Chris Searle

Before he moved to Stepney, Chris Searle spent a year teaching English in a secondary school in Tobago. In *The Forsaken Lover* (the title of a poem by a West Indian girl in his class), he uses the children's own writing to demonstrate the crisis of identity facing black people saddled with a language and culture that speak against them.

In a sensitive exploration of the children's use of poetry, prose and drama, Searle attacks the cultural imperialism which imposes an alien identity by means of the legacy of a dominant white language. He urges that 'ways have to be found so the black child, whether he lives in the Caribbean, or whether he lives in Britain, can speak for himself and his own life without having to adopt white forms and values. He must grow up with his identity intact, unbetrayed.' The rich and imaginative work which the children of Tobago produced with Searle shows clearly what can happen when such ways *are* found.

'*The Forsaken Lover* . . . should be published in paperback, distributed widely among educators involved with black children – and the children themselves – and regarded as useful, caring information from the front line' – Paddy Kitchen reviewing the original edition in the *New Statesman*